It's been twenty years since Arnold Palmer
and Joe Gibbs flipped the switch to beam
Golf Channel into the homes, lives,
and hearts of the world's players and
fans. Those two decades mark the most
compelling, controversial, inspiring,
transformative stretch the royal and
ancient game has ever known.

The story of golf over the past twenty years is in many ways the story of Tiger Woods, the most dominant player of all time and without doubt the most compelling.

Trends come and go, but the constant is the delicate art of joining earth and man in a struggle that maximizes both. The game itself is a blessing granted only by the fields on which it's played

The professional tours represent a sliver of the sport, that finite collection of plus-8 handicappers who play for pay. Yet the tours are the most exciting, enticing, and wonder-inducing expression of the game.

Not so long ago, the Ryder Cup was a forlorn appendage to the game. Now, it stands as the game's most epic format, with international pride, inhuman pressure, and humanizing emotion accompanying each swing.

Combine boundless passion for golf in Asia with the inclusion of the sport in the 2016 Olympic Games, and the next twenty years promise an exciting new era.

The Golf Book

CHRIS MILLARD | FOREWORD BY ARNOLD PALMER

20 YEARS OF THE PLAYERS, SHOTS, AND MOMENTS THAT CHANGED THE GAME

An Imprint of HarperCollinsPublishers

Contents

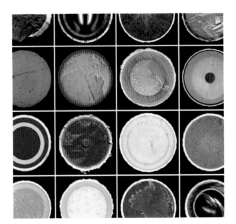

Foreword

I've been involved in the game of golf for the better part of the past century. I've seen a lot of change during that time, but the past twenty years have proven to be one of the most interesting eras in the game that I have ever seen.

As a boy, I would eagerly watch my father, Deacon, as he tended to the greens or gave lessons at Latrobe Country Club. I played competitive golf through high school and on into college at Wake Forest. Even during my three-year stint in the United States Coast Guard, I was able to find my way to a golf course now and then. Later, in 1954, after completing my Coast Guard service, a brief return to Wake Forest, and a stint selling paint supplies, I won the U.S. Amateur title. Feeling then that I had enough game to give the PGA Tour a try, I turned pro, married Winnie Walzer that December, and went on tour at the start of the 1955 season. As things subsequently occurred, that worked out pretty well.

On the surface, and particularly in retrospect it all seems easy, almost pre-ordained, but that couldn't be further from the truth. The odds that a boy from the blue-collar world would travel the globe, win major championships and befriend presidents and international royalty were incredibly slim. It only happened because of a lot of hard work and the generosity and support of others. Whether it was my parents, my friends, my business partners, or my competitors—on the course or off—each of them had a hand in my success.

There is no better example of that than my relationship with Joe Gibbs. I met Joe in 1990 and we quickly became friends. It was a few years later that he first approached me with a wild idea: a twenty-four-hour cable television network devoted solely to golf. I didn't know much about television, particularly cable television. Nor did many of my closest advisers, most of whom were skeptical at first. In fact, at least twice I told Joe that I was probably not his guy, but he insisted this would not work without me. Joe was so committed, so persuasive, so knowledgeable that I ultimately bought in. We launched Golf Channel in 1995 and it remains one of my proudest accomplishments, right up there with major championships and Ryder Cup wins.

I'm proud of Golf Channel because it embodies excellence and passion. Joe assembled a remarkable team of golf lovers—businesspeople and communicators—that has evolved over the past twenty years into a team that has served as the voice of the greatest game in the world, and I've been there to witness it all. Joe and I long ago sold our individual stakes in the network, and he retired as CEO over a decade ago, but we remain in touch. I stayed involved in the Golf Channel to this day as a consultant and watch almost every day.

What a blessing this all has been. At the age of sixty-five, when most people are slowing down, I was given a whole new way to share the game with billions

of people all around the world, and a way to expand my personal passion for golf.

With all the positives the game of golf is experiencing—the explosion of golf in Asia, its imminent return to the Olympic Games, the staggering rise in interest in the Ryder Cup—the game does face its share of challenges. The future of golf depends on a continual infusion of a youth following, and initiatives like The First Tee program need to be effective in drawing kids to the golf course. I remain involved with Golf Channel as a consultant, and I am convinced that we have demonstrated that we can expose the game in a very effective and appealing way. However, while maintaining its loyal viewership on its traditional platforms, Golf Channel can reach out to the next generation of potential golfers, many of whom can be targeted through the evolving technology of their own viewing devices. I know that the very talented team at Golf Channel can be sufficiently creative to meet these challenges. And I offer them my sincere best wishes in support of their endeavors.

Arnold Palmer

Arnold Palmer
August 2014

For a game that's nearly five hundred years old, twenty years seems an insignificant, unworthy speck. A comma in a centuries-old saga. On the surface, focusing on a twenty-year stretch in the grand old game would be akin to writing an epic poem about this morning's paper or drafting a coming-of-age novel about a child. The project would starve for material.

Yet when Golf Channel began to think about its two decades on the air, it quickly became clear that the years in question, from 1995 to 2014, were no ordinary twenty years. Since 1995 we've seen Jack Nicklaus retire, Greg Norman recede, Tiger Woods rule, rue, and relinquish. We've seen golf courses, bloated and stretched beyond practicality in the 1990s, embrace the new minimalism of 2014. There have been more meaningful improvements in equipment since 1995 than in the preceding fifty years. Golf balls last longer and fly farther. Clubs can be adjusted on the fly. Just as launch monitors have taken the guesswork out of clubfitting, Shotlink has taken the guesswork out of stats. With the USGA's blessing on rangefinders, we know how far our slices go. We've witnessed the emergence of Asia as a global golf power, the rise of Europe in the Ryder Cup, the re-entry of golf into the Olympic Games, and the virtual extinction of the metal spike. Majors are now routinely scheduled for public golf courses. The sport that used to be checkered with prohibitions that kept kids off golf courses now has several highly regarded charities, led by The First Tee, which pushes kids onto the course.

Since Golf Channel launched, Augusta National has welcomed women. Ben Hogan, Byron Nelson, and Sam Snead have died. Tiger Woods won the Masters. And thirteen other majors. All of it unfolded on the network. In the twenty short years since founders Arnold Palmer and Joe Gibbs launched it, Golf Channel has emerged as the authoritative voice of the game, the indomitable supplier of its television coverage, and the simpatico friend across the room who loves the game as much as you do. True, for a game measured in centuries, twenty years is a blip. But

The Channel

It went from a crazy idea in a bootstrap entrepreneur's head to the fastest-growing network in cable television. Replete with sport, celebrity, derring-do, and the ever-present specter of failure, launching Golf Channel was the ultimate reality show.

24 hours.
That's an awful lot of golf.

NICK FALDO

Golf Channel cofounders Arnold Palmer and Joe Gibbs.

For fans of the game, it's hard to imagine golf without Golf Channel. A string of fall tournaments that don't even get on TV? Often no televised golf on Thursday or Friday? Young fans probably don't remember the days when network broadcasts routinely reached their "allotted time" and simply signed off, regardless of the downhill five-footer remaining. No *Golf Central*? No *Live From...?*, which have become opiates for the major-championship aficionado. To get a sense of how much a fixture the channel has become, consider that some of today's PGA Tour players have never really known the game without it. Rory McIlroy wasn't quite four years old when Golf Channel launched.

"Despite my early skepticism, Golf Channel has had a tremendous and enduring impact on golf," says veteran golf journalist Pete McDaniel. "From the early years, when others in the media, including me, complained that it lacked golf news coverage, Golf Channel has responded with a host of golf writers who cut their teeth on newspaper reporting. It has also covered the international game well, familiarizing us with players we would otherwise only discover on a leader board at a major."

Beyond feeding the passion of fans and future stars, the channel has made an enormous mark on the golf business. Advertisers, those proffering indigenous equipment but also those seeking to reach the golf lifestyle demographic, now had a dedicated digital-age pipeline to their best customers. Just as significantly, Golf Channel provided meaningful undergirding to the game's world tours, an unprecedented stage on which the game could be fully exploited. What golf fan of the late 1990s didn't haphazardly stumble onto Golf Channel over Saturday-morning coffee and think, "Hmm, Woosie in the Dubai Desert Classic. OK!"

Finally, by tapping the vast reservoir of orphaned golf content around the globe, Golf Channel allowed the various tours and golf associations of the world to assign a new, heightened value to their product. This benefited everyone from Tiger Woods to Nolan Henke to Michelle Wie in the form of higher purses, and the average golfer has benefited from recruitment or instruction or maintenance programs promoted by golf's organizing bodies.

The network has now been on the air for almost 200,000 hours. The story of how the first hour happened is an unlikely tale that has had a dramatic impact on the golf universe.

A few years in the bustling, land-rush era of cable television had given Joe Gibbs some money in the bank, enough to buy a home in Birmingham's most exclusive enclave, Shoal Creek. With its luxurious residences and a renowned Jack Nicklaus–designed golf course, the area was the acme of Alabama's high-end golf scene. In a very roundabout way, Gibbs' choice of neighborhood would change the course of sports television and how we experience the game of golf.

Shoal Creek was slated to host the PGA Championship in 1990. Given its pedigree, Shoal Creek was a haven for serious players...and Gibbs. The new guy in town had played only six rounds of golf in the year leading up to the PGA Championship and broken 100 just once. But high scores didn't stop Gibbs from pursuing the game and joining in the excitement of the upcoming tournament. Many residents volunteered to host visiting tour professionals, and Gibbs and his wife were no different, offering up their recently remodeled guesthouse. Gibbs was told that his tenants would be Ben and Julie Crenshaw.

At the time, Gibbs' work in franchising cable systems was taking him to London with some regularity. While there in the summer of 1990, he noticed the Open Championship was being contested at St. Andrews. He and his wife made contact with the Crenshaws, took a day off, and flew up to Scotland to introduce themselves. It was the first golf event of any kind that Joe Gibbs ever attended.

As the PGA Championship approached, the all-white Shoal Creek became embroiled in an ugly controversy over its lack of black members. With demonstrations and tempers building locally, Crenshaw was advised not to stay on-site. The Gibbses had lost their tenant. "We had the guesthouse all cleaned and furnished and stocked," said Gibbs.

On the Sunday before the championship, Gibbs and his wife went to a cocktail party. In attendance was Shoal Creek founder Hall Thompson. Gibbs relayed his frustration to Thompson, who then repeated the story to his son, Mike. That was the last time the issue came up until Tuesday's practice round. Little did Gibbs know it, but on that day, his life was to change forever.

As the players and their wives arrived at Shoal Creek, they were greeted by championship staff, who were helping them find their housing, among other things. That Tuesday, one player's spouse was expressing disappointment with her and her husband's hotel. Mike Thompson overheard the conversation and, without even contacting Gibbs, said, "Joe Gibbs wants you to stay with him." The woman's name was Winnie, also known as Mrs. Arnold Palmer.

Gibbs was given the assignment of tracking down Palmer on course and telling him that Winnie had green-lighted the guesthouse. "When Arnold walked up [to the tee box]," said Gibbs, "I put out my hand and told him that I was Joe Gibbs and he would be staying with me that week. He looked at me and cocked his head and said, 'Well, OK. Come on.'"

Now attending the second golf tournament of his life, Gibbs followed along for

Golf Channel was initially offered as a "premium" channel. When it became part of "basic cable" service, viewership exploded.

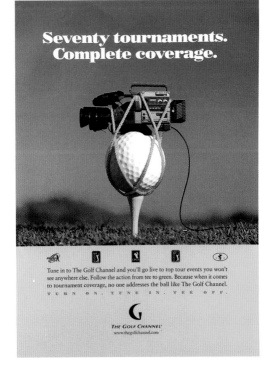

The new network offered an unprecedented breadth of tournament coverage—pieced together one by one by Joe Gibbs and his team.

the rest of the practice round. The man who had little previous experience with the game was soon conscripted into Arnie's Army. "Late that afternoon, there were probably no more than three or four players left on the course," recalled Gibbs. "So, it was Arnold, me, his caddy, and three thousand people following him. Arnold controlled that crowd and told jokes and had a ball. I'd never seen anything like it. He had an amazing ability and intention to connect. He came home that evening with ink marks all over his arms where people were trying to get to him to sign autographs. I was in awe."

For the next four nights, Palmer was in residence chez Gibbs (Palmer would miss the cut and leave town Saturday). Every afternoon, the King would pull his car into the garage and start rewrapping his grips. Gibbs would saunter over, Winnie would serve some cold beers, and there was dinner. Palmer loved it. So did Gibbs. They hit it off. Chris Murvin, a lawyer and a close friend of Gibbs who would play a major role in the rise of Golf Channel, was a guest of the Gibbses that week as well. "Joe and Arnold immediately developed a connection," said Murvin. "I think a lot of it was their background and upbringing. They grew up in smaller towns and did a lot of manual labor. Grew up on the other side of the tracks, if you will, not country club at all."

As he prepared to leave, Palmer thanked Gibbs and invited him and his wife to Florida to repay the kindness. Gibbs thought Palmer was simply being polite, but the King responded in the voice that launched a million pallets of Pennzoil: "Well, you are going to get the invitation, whether you take it is up to you."

A few days later, a letter from Orlando arrived in the mail: The Palmers meant it, and the Gibbses would soon visit. When Gibbs departed Orlando, he reflected on the remarkable sequence of events and the enjoyment had by all, but with zero further expectations. "Yes, we're 'friends,'" thought Gibbs at the time, "but I never expected to see him again."

That was until a quiet Sunday afternoon around Christmas 1990. The phone rang at Shoal Creek. It was Winnie saying, "We just got back from Kennebunkport from the Bushes' and thought we would check in on you and see how you were doing." It was clear to Gibbs that Winnie and Arnold weren't just "friends," they were now friends. Little did Gibbs or Palmer know at the time, but they were about to become business partners, too, in the largest enterprise upon which either of them would ever embark.

Some people do their best thinking in the shower, some in the gym, or even on the practice tee. Joe Gibbs had the greatest idea of his life 40,000 feet over the Atlantic Ocean. In March 1991, he was en route to London, where he and his firm were helping an investor group bid for a cable franchise. He was reading a cable industry trade magazine story about compression technology. The article made it clear that one effect of video compression would be that the capacity for "narrowcasting," or niche programming, already hinted at by all-sports ESPN and all-news CNN, was about to explode. Television, which had spent most of its life proffering three broadcast networks and had blossomed with dozens of cable channels, was poised to enter the oft-predicted 500-channel universe.

As the jet engines thrummed, Gibbs' mind starting churning. "I started thinking, 'Well, what do people want to see that they haven't seen much of?'" He jotted down a list of ideas. At the very top he wrote down a word that had already brought dramatic change to his own life.

"Golf."

Though he was new to the game, what Gibbs had seen in the previous year was the passion of its fans and players. He'd witnessed firsthand how Arnold Palmer, even sapped of his youthful strength, could energize a throng with a simple slash. He'd seen the degree to which a sport could inspire an entire lifestyle. He wrote down "Golf" and thought, "Wow, this might make some sense." A new channel devoted to golf, twenty-four hours a day.

Shortly after returning from London, Gibbs acted on the idea. He contacted the Gallup polling firm and commissioned a national survey of consumers on their interest in televised golf. He helped design the questionnaire and wrote a check for the hefty fee. The survey, which went out in June 1991, identified an underserved market of some 27 million people who played golf and 44 million people who liked to watch it on TV. That was all Gibbs needed to know. "Right then," said Gibbs, "I knew it would work." If only he had a friend in the golf business.

In the meantime, Gibbs, already a successful cable system entrepreneur, was busy expanding his other communications investments. In 1986, he and his cable partners determined that cellular communications would be the wave of the future and started looking for an investment in that space. Very long story short: Gibbs, his partners, and a handful of outside investors acquired a firm they named Crowley Cellular for $20 million. Six years later, they sold it for $270 million.

Gibbs now had the time and money to devote to his new project, an idea he had shared with no one. He rented an office and installed two things: a young Alabama grad with a degree in finance, and a padlock. Phillip Hurst was there to research all things golf. The padlock was to ensure that no one knew what they were up to.

With Gallup's evidence supporting his idea, it was time for Gibbs to pitch the idea to his friend in the golf business, Arnold Palmer, who, as he had been for decades, was the most influential person in the sport. Gibbs called Palmer, saying he had an idea he wanted to talk about. Palmer explained he was busy traveling here and there, but Gibbs cut him off at the pass, saying, "I'll come wherever you are at any time to talk to you about it." Palmer knows about home-court advantage. It's not so much that you need the home court—all you need is the advantage. So Palmer said he'd bring his plane into Birmingham for a meeting. That way he controlled the schedule, and he could come and go as he chose. They'd meet in a conference room at Birmingham's airport.

Gibbs laid out the idea, using the Gallup data and his own research to bolster the proposition. The good news was that Palmer didn't fire up the jet and bolt. On the contrary, the two spoke for nearly an hour and a half. The bad news was that at the end of the session, Palmer was far from sold. He simply didn't know if the idea could make money.

Palmer then said, "I know somebody who can help us." He reached over and picked up the phone to call Mark McCormack. McCormack had essentially invented modern sports marketing and athlete representation. If every professional golfer owes a debt to Palmer for elevating the game, then every pro athlete owes a debt to McCormack for his ability to negotiate contracts and expand off-the-field earning opportunities. McCormack had founded IMG, an agency that today represents hundreds of high-profile athletes and models and produces sports television. Palmer was McCormack's very first client—the agent represented Palmer from 1960 until his own death in 2003.

Needless to say, McCormack took the call. "Mark, my friend Joe Gibbs and I have an idea, and he's going to come see you," said Palmer. Before Palmer left, he gave Gibbs two words of advice regarding McCormack: "Be careful."

Palmer's caveat inspired Gibbs to overprepare. He bought every book that

"It was the right time. There was a thirst for knowledge about the game. There was Tiger Woods. The PGA Tour was big enough, it was diverse enough, and there was worldwide interest in golf instruction. All the game needed was a vehicle."
FRANK NOBILO

McCormack, a Yale Law School grad, had written, including his best sellers, *What They Don't Teach You at Harvard Business School* and *The Terrible Truth About Lawyers*. In December 1991, Gibbs flew to New York and met with McCormack at the sumptuous IMG offices in Manhattan. Palmer's dose of caution was validated when McCormack "allowed" Gibbs to hire him to help construct the business plan. First, McCormack's internal television arm, TWI, was a worldwide leader in sports television production. His people, who put together some of the most-watched sporting events in the world for their broadcast network partners, knew everything about producing sports television and the costs associated with it. Gibbs, who knew nothing about production, had the cable industry covered. Between the two of them, they could arrive at a business plan that made sense. Second, and just as important, was this: If the key to getting Palmer on board was satisfying his agent, then the quarter-million dollars that McCormack charged seemed a reasonable price to pay. Once again, Gibbs paid it out of his own pocket.

Now began a series of monthly meetings of Gibbs, the IMG brain trust—McCormack, Peter Smith, and Barry Frank, IMG's television man, whom Gibbs credits with suggesting Golf Channel's most enduring program, *Golf Central*—and two cable consultants brought in by Gibbs. Meanwhile, Gibbs' future wife, Tina (he divorced and was soon to be remarried), who worked in the offices back in Birmingham, began filing papers for the new enterprise. When she requested a tax ID number in December 1991, she filed simply as TGC, Inc. so as to conceal the nature of the company and its business.

In fact, secrecy was a hallmark of the firm's early days. Phillip Hurst, the sworn-to-secrecy researcher working in the padlocked office, was dating a young woman during the few hours he was not covertly scouring the world for information on golf. After about a year, the young man approached Gibbs with a dilemma. He wanted to get married, but both his intended and her father were more than a little curious to know what he did for a living. "Joe," said the young employee, "I want to marry this girl, but her dad wants to know what I do. Can I tell them?"

Gibbs said no. A month later, the young man again escaped the padlocked office and pleaded that he was very interested in getting married and could he please tell the girl and her father a little bit about what he did? Gibbs relented, sort of, saying, "Will you swear him to secrecy? You can tell him, but only as much as he needs to know." Gibbs' practice of keeping a hush on his plans was maintained right up through the launch of the network. "Look, if ESPN or Turner heard what we were doing, they would have launched [a golf network], and I would have been done, right there," said Gibbs.

Working hand in hand with McCormack and his colleagues, Gibbs finished his business plan in the spring of 1992. It called for Golf Channel to launch as a "mini-pay." Today the network is available on most cable systems' basic tier of channels, but in the early 1990s, the cable industry was operating under heavy government regulation. Cable operators could charge a maximum of only fifty-five cents per basic-tier channel per customer. But they could price anything above the basic tier as they wished. Understandably, the cable operators positioned new channels above the basic tier. Golf Channel had no choice but to launch as a mini-pay, costing subscribers who requested it $6.95 per month.

"It was the only way they would launch us," said Gibbs. "The cable industry was going to dictate." The requirement, instituted by the FCC to protect consumers, would nearly kill the start-up.

"The original concept of Golf Channel being on a [premium] sports tier restricted the number of homes that could receive the network," recalled Rudy Martzke, the longtime sports TV critic for *USA Today*. Once Golf Channel earned basic cable status on multiple distributors—driven by its compelling content and timing of its launch—it had the critical mass to become a success.

Gibbs now needed two things: programming and investors. It was a serious chicken-and-egg situation. How do you pay for expensive rights to golf tournaments when you don't have investors? What kind of investor was going to put money into a channel with no content? So Gibbs needed to scavenge the calendars of every worldwide professional golf tour and buy up any scrap events that weren't already controlled by CBS, ABC, NBC, or smaller networks. Furthermore, he needed to do it on the sly and get all of his contracts in place before the gossipy world of sports television figured out what he was up to.

These were substantial contracts running $10 million, $20 million, $30 million over a period of years. Gibbs didn't have that kind of money. Even Palmer, if he ever agreed to pair up with Gibbs, couldn't invest that kind of money. But Palmer could certainly grease the skids.

Gibbs approached Palmer again. With the certitude that only an entrepreneur can muster, Gibbs told his friend flat out, "This idea is going to work, and I'm going to do it, but I want to do it with you." Now, Arnold Palmer hadn't become the highest-paid sexagenarian athlete in the world by being reckless. His fortune was built on reliable businesses such as car dealerships. He also lent his name to business ventures and his image to product endorsements, but he rarely put up actual cash. He didn't have to. Gibbs wanted to turn that comfortable and effective practice on its ear. He told Palmer he wanted to be his 50-50 partner, but that Palmer would have to go beyond lending his name to the project. He would have to have skin in the game. Gibbs had spent $300,000 of his own money on the venture so far. He offered Palmer half the stock in TGC, Inc., for reimbursement of one-half of what he had spent.

> ## "The power of Arnold Palmer speaks for itself—the most charismatic and probably the most important figure in the game. Combine that with the star power of Tiger and that's an ideal combination for the fastest-growing cable TV network in history."
> KELLY TILGHMAN

BEST
OF THE
MAJORS

BEN CRENSHAW
1995 MASTERS

On the Sunday night before the 1995 Masters, Ben Crenshaw and his wife, Julie, were having dinner with Jack Stephens [then the Augusta National chairman] and legendary golf announcer Pat Summerall when the maître d' handed Mrs. Crenshaw a slip of paper that simply read, "Call Tom or Christy Kite." Julie called Christy and motioned Ben away from the table. It was then that she informed him that Crenshaw's beloved mentor, Harvey Penick, had died back in Austin, Texas, at the age of ninety. Crenshaw flew to Texas for Penick's funeral to honor the man who had given Crenshaw a putting lesson from his sickbed only a week earlier. On Wednesday of Masters week, Crenshaw, who was forty-three and had last won a major eleven years earlier, served as a pallbearer at Penick's funeral. Four days later, Crenshaw miraculously won the Masters.

Ben Crenshaw breaks down on the 18th green at Augusta after winning the 1995 Masters.

"I don't think I've ever seen anything like that in my professional career. To be that close to the end of the tournament and to experience such a low and such a high back-to-back like that was incredible."

DEBORAH VIDAL

1995 Open Championship

Costantino Rocca

Final Round

The 1995 Open Championship will forever be remembered as John Daly's second major championship. But before Daly would be named Champion Golfer of the Year, Melpomene, the muse of tragedy, and Thalia, the muse of comedy, would make dueling appearances. Needing an eagle-two on the home hole to win, Costantino Rocca duffed his pitch shot into the Valley of Sin. Rocca now needed to hole out for birdie to force a playoff. He drained a sixty-foot putt from off the green, and although he would lose in the playoff to Daly, his ups and downs at 18—and his heartfelt reactions to both—won him a lasting place in our hearts.

> ## "We stand for people that like golf, that want to see something nice in sports, and see some competitiveness, too."
>
> ARNOLD PALMER

Gibbs knew that having Palmer fully invested would give him the ability to raise more money. "I want to be able to tell people that you've got your money in here just like me," argued Gibbs.

Palmer said he would think about it. A few days later, he phoned Gibbs from the cockpit of his plane and said, "So where do you want me to wire the money, partner?"

For well over a year now, Gibbs had been operating in utter secrecy and with little outside funding. He could now approach some strategic investors as well as trustworthy, closemouthed friends and neighbors. His goal was to raise $100 million. The funds came in small lumps—$100,000 here, $200,000 there. Gibbs himself put in more money, McCormack invested personally, and soon the company had raised $6 million. It was a decent amount, but nothing even close to what it would cost to acquire the all-important programming rights. Gibbs came up with a brilliant solution, a form of financial triage. He would approach the individual tours and option their idle content.

Charlie Mechem, then the LPGA commissioner, was one of the first tour executives he approached. Gibbs identified 16 "orphaned" LPGA Tour events with no broadcast partner. He wanted the rights to air those events for four years. That package would have cost millions of dollars, but he proposed a new agreement that essentially stated that if Golf Channel raised the funds it needed to launch, the contract with the LPGA would be valid. As a deposit, Gibbs handed Mechem's LPGA a check for $500,000. If he couldn't raise the "big money," the LPGA would keep the half-million. The contract called for Gibbs to raise the necessary funds by December 31, 1993. He had eighteen months to pull together $94 million.

Gibbs used the same model to buy other tournaments as well as satellite transponder time. The PGA Tour was the final brick in the rights-based programming wall. The most visible tour in the world and the most popular in the United States, the PGA Tour would be vital to Golf Channel's plans. In October 1992, Gibbs met with then PGA Tour commissioner Deane Beman and his deputy, Tim Finchem. Gibbs made his now-polished pitch, only to see Beman throw a wrench into the works. He startled Gibbs by saying that the Tour had been looking into just such a television concept for years. After Gibbs' heart started beating again, Beman added that as commissioner, he couldn't spend $100 million of his players' money on such a risky venture.

The Tour would look at the proposal, but Beman cautioned Gibbs that he was not the first one to approach with such an idea. "Turner Broadcasting," Beman explained, "has already been in to talk about a similar concept." Gibbs' head spun as Beman described Turner's proposal, a $2.95 "mini-pay" channel that would consist mostly of news and instruction and just a few tournaments. The PGA Tour would take the two competing proposals under advisement.

As the Tour did its due diligence, Gibbs and Palmer, now used to getting out over their skis, confronted another dilemma. The hallmark of the company's activities had been complete secrecy to keep potential competitors from jumping into the fray. But knowing that Turner was considering a similar channel and hearing through the grapevine that there was yet another entrepreneur contemplating the same idea, Gibbs decided to abandon radio silence and announce his plans to the world. His theory: If there were going to be three or more companies trying to do the same thing, best to be the first one to announce. "I knew that if we waited until we heard back from the PGA, it might be too late," explained Gibbs. He and Palmer staged a press conference during the 1993 Bob Hope Chrysler Classic without a single PGA Tour event under contract.

1995 U.S. Open

Corey Pavin

Final Round

For years, Corey Pavin, the dogged diminutive of the PGA Tour, had worn the cumbersome label "best player never to have won a major." His gutsy 228-yard 4-wood approach into the 18th green at Shinnecock Hills changed all that. NBC's Johnny Miller, who was announcing, exclaimed, "This is the shot of his life!"

Pavin not only beat Greg Norman by two shots but also outpointed an illustrious field of contenders that included Davis Love III, Phil Mickelson, and Tom Lehman.

OOPS

Greg Norman
1996 Masters

With all due respect to Colin Montgomerie, Greg Norman's is the most star-crossed career in the game. It may be a bit of a stretch to say that about a man who won two Open Championships (versus Monty, who went 0-for-the-Majors), but consider this: The man known as the Great White Shark posted thirty top-ten finishes in major championships (twenty of those were top fives) and came away with only two. In 1986, one man led every major championship after fifty-four holes. He left all but one empty-handed. His name was Greg Norman.

But no loss was as endearing or as enduring as his final round collapse in the 1996 Masters. Beginning Sunday with a six-shot lead, Norman's implosion came out of the blue. It began badly with a bogey on 1 and never really got better. Over the course of five holes (8–12), Norman would cough up five shots, giving the incessant, steady Faldo a two-shot lead. Norman's last gasp was his bid to chip in for eagle at 15. Of course, it missed. Norman fell to his knees and tumbled to the ground. Down and out.

It had long been over. Now it was done. There was a moment on the 18th green where even a casual observer could divine the depth of Norman's loss. For Norman, the pain of the loss was matched only by his self-effacing summary. "I screwed up," he said. "It's all on me. I know that. But losing this Masters is not the end of the world.... All this is just a test. I just don't know what the test is yet."

TIGER WOODS
1997 MASTERS

Tiger Woods' domination of the 1997 Masters may be the most stunning performance in a single sporting event over the past twenty years. He shattered twenty records and tied six others, while redrawing the landscape of the modern game (see page 82).

"It marked a very clear beginning to a new era. The twenty-one-year-old Woods began the week with a front-nine 40, then bludgeoned the old ball yard like no one ever had. Hitting 9-irons into par 5s and gradually widening his lead all the way to the finish.

"Woods became the youngest Masters champion ever, by the widest margin ever, with the lowest total score ever.... So they gave out a green jacket and a crown that year."
JOHN HAWKINS

Woods moments after sinking his putt on 18 to win his first major championship, the 1997 Masters.

> "I felt so comfortable, so at ease and really peaceful within myself. And I just let it unfold. I was very patient and I won the tournament, but I couldn't dream of this. I would never have dreamed it would be this hectic and this crazy."
> TIGER WOODS

Tiger Woods
1996 Las Vegas Invitational Champion

Golf World magazine's coverage read in part: "International Management Group, which just happens to represent Palmer, has not only anted up but will also serve as programming consultant. IMG's close cooperation could prove vital to the channel's success."

But doubters abounded, particularly within the golf media. Pete McDaniel was a writer with *Golf World* in the early 1990s. Like many, he questioned both the need for and viability of a network devoted to golf. "I thought the idea of a twenty-four-hour network devoted solely to golf was a stretch," said McDaniel, who would later go on to produce the documentary *Uneven Fairways* for the network. "I was a faithful follower of ESPN but couldn't imagine anyone, even the most ardent follower of golf, wanting to watch it on TV 24/7."

From October 1992 through the following spring, the PGA Tour left Gibbs and Palmer in limbo, and Palmer was getting cold feet. Twice over the life of the project so far, Palmer had called Gibbs expressing concern over the idea's viability and relaying that his advisers were increasingly lukewarm on the concept. The first time, Gibbs got on a plane, flew to Florida, and assuaged Palmer's concern.

The second time was a little more intense. In late 1993, Gibbs, accompanied by Chris Murvin, arrived in the boardroom at Bay Hill Club and Lodge, the golf resort and hotel owned by Palmer. (Murvin was an early investor and is still with Golf Channel, serving as a senior vice president of business affairs.) This time, the King was seated with a table full of advisers. It was clear that Palmer's concern had moved way beyond cold feet. He was ready to walk unless Gibbs could make the closing argument of his life.

"Arnold was at one end of the table," recalled Murvin. "His people were around him, and Joe and I were sitting at the other end. Joe made the case, not knowing what had been said to Arnold. We had been trying to raise the big money at that time, and there was some frustration and doubt as to whether or not we were going to be able to do it. Joe elegantly went through the entire process, what needed to be done, how much progress we had made, and what the opportunities were.

Hal Sutton has never been one to shy away from a challenge. During the lead-up to the final round of the Players, he had made it clear that he wasn't intimidated by Woods and fully intended to beat him. Famous last words. But for Sutton it all came down to the last hole, the par-4 18th. Trailing by one, Woods missed the green with his approach. Sutton's second shot into 18 was a 179-yard 6-iron. As the ball homed in on its target, Sutton voiced his now-famous line, "Be the right club, *tuh-DAY*." The ball landed eight feet from the pin, and Sutton holed the putt.

"Be the right club *tuh-DAY*."
HAL SUTTON

"At the end of Joe's presentation, Arnold looked at all of us sitting around the table and he said, 'Boys, if I hadn't tried to hit it through the trees a few times, none of us would be here.'"

Palmer was in. Gibbs had made the sale. Again. Murvin, who described the boardroom showdown as one of the seminal moments of his own life, has no doubt that had the meeting gone poorly, Palmer would have walked. Instead, the King never wavered again.

Unaware of the drama unfolding in Orlando, the PGA Tour had hired consultants to compare the Turner and Gibbs concepts. Gibbs' grand idea and a boatload of money hung in the balance. "I had the whole business locked up except the PGA Tour and the rest of my money. That's all I needed," said Gibbs. Compared with Ted Turner and Turner Broadcasting, Gibbs had no organization. He had no money. He had no programming experience. Of course, Turner didn't have the most beloved and influential golfer of all time on his side. Having the highly regarded McCormack and the weight of IMG on board didn't hurt either. Ultimately, the PGA Tour went with Golf Channel. The cornerstone contract that served as the foundation of the network was signed Masters week of 1993 at Arnold's rental home in Augusta, Georgia. On the hood of a car in the driveway.

———

December 31, 1993, was rapidly approaching, the witching hour for Gibbs' jury-rigged contracts with the various tours and the satellite transponder. Despite breakneck travel and countless dog and pony shows, Gibbs was still short tens of millions of dollars. He called Palmer and offered three options: sell the idea, quit, or keep at it.

The tables had turned. Palmer was now adamant that he didn't want to quit. So over Christmas 1993, Gibbs managed to raise another $3 million from friends (he invested as well). He went back to all the tours and the transponder firm, negotiated a year's extension for all of the options, gave each of them another check for $500,000, and kept the good ship Golf Channel afloat for at least another year.

Shortly after extending the options, he had a breakthrough meeting with Tim Neher. Neher was in the midst of a long and distinguished tenure at Boston-based

> ## "One thing I hear a lot is, 'Thanks for the Golf Channel. We have something that we really enjoy watching on television.' That may not sound like a big statement, but it is when you think of all the things that are on TV today."
> ARNOLD PALMER

2003 Bank of America Colonial

Annika Sorenstam

First Round

It may have been the most highly anticipated shot in golf history. For three and a half months, ever since Annika Sorenstam's announcement in February that she would accept a sponsor's exemption into the PGA Tour's Bank of America Colonial stop, fans around the world waited and wondered how she would fare. Could the dominant force on the LPGA circuit hang with the best male players in the world? The story transcended golf, and found its way into the mainstream news, which only added to the hype.

The 10th hole, where Sorenstam began, is a 381-yard dogleg right par 4. She and her caddie opted for a 4-wood, Waiting to play, Sorenstam turned to him and whispered, "I've never felt like this. I don't know what I've gotten myself into."

When she teed it up, Sorenstam said during a recent Golf Channel interview, "I was nervous I might not get my ball on the tee. I was shaking."

She drilled her tee shot 255 adrenaline-aided yards down the middle, about thirty yards longer than she usually hit that club. Her swing made her the first woman to compete in a PGA Tour event since Shirley Spork in 1952.

2005 U.S. Women's Open

Birdie Kim

Final Round

Cherry Hills CC has seen its share of historic shots. More than half a century later, people are still awestruck by Arnold Palmer's driving the first hole en route to his win in the 1960 U.S. Open and slack-jawed by Ben Hogan's water balls on holes 17 and 18. But no single major championship swing at Cherry Hills has been so decisive, so lethal, as that played by South Korea's aptly named Birdie Kim in the 2005 Women's Open. Bunkered to the right of the 18th green in two, the South Korean holed her third shot

to stun Morgan Pressel, who was watching from the fairway. It was the only birdie made on 18 all day, and only the fourth for the entire championship. "I saw her in the bunker, and thought, 'Oh, maybe par will win it,'" said Pressel. "That's a tough hole. Anytime you miss the green there you don't know what to expect. She hit a great shot. I was like, I can't believe this is happening to me."

Even Kim knew better than to expect a hole-out. "Tried my best to make par," she explained later. Kim thought if she made bogey, she'd still have a chance. She never thought the ball would go in the hole. "So amazing," Kim added.

Rich Lerner and Kelly Tilghman have been part of Golf Channel from its earliest days, serving as anchors, hosts, commentators, and in other roles.

cable operator Continental Cablevision, an operation that had seen its subscriber base rise from four hundred thousand to four million in fifteen years, and he had an integral role in that growth. Just as important as his stature in the cable industry was his passion for golf. While other cable operators may have viewed the project purely from a business standpoint, Neher, an avid and accomplished player, personified the future Golf Channel viewer.

Neher, who was spending the holidays in Palm Beach, agreed to meet Gibbs for breakfast. He was intrigued with the idea and expressed his willingness to work with Gibbs, subject to meeting with Palmer to determine his commitment. Neher's involvement in and passion for Golf Channel would prove crucial.

"Golf Channel was a three-legged stool," said Gibbs. "Arnold, me, and Neher. No question about it."

Neher wove in Brian Roberts, a close friend and fellow cable industry leader who shared a passion for golf and who ran the cable company Comcast. The two of them took the lead in analyzing from a cable operator point of view a possible investment in the channel. Neher, Roberts, and their consultants spent nearly four months on the project, crafting valuations, conferring with Gibbs, and recruiting other cable operators as investors. Ultimately, they brought into the fold four additional operators, meaning Golf Channel would have six of the nation's top eleven cable outfits willing to invest in and carry it. Their cumulative investment, however, would total only $60 million—giving the network the start it needed, but leaving it $40 million short.

"I said, 'OK, done deal,'" recalled Gibbs. "We took the sixty in April 1994." The cash infusion came on top of the $9 million previously raised by Gibbs. Add in the funds Gibbs and Palmer had invested early on, and the tally was now $69.5 million. Still $30 million short of where they needed to be.

Even so, it was time to build a television network. Gibbs and Matt Scalici, one of the company's seven employees, who had almost single-handedly built a religious TV network, began to shop for studio and engineering equipment. But Gibbs had long since made the decision that Golf Channel would operate not out of Birmingham but from golf-rich Florida.

"I always knew we were going to Florida," said Gibbs. "It is the home office for the PGA of America, LPGA and PGA Tours, and dozens of tour players. Arnold's got a place there, and if we wanted to get on a golf course to shoot something, Florida has plenty. Direct flights to and from all over the country, good weather."

In May 1994, Gibbs and Scalici leased an empty warehouse in Orlando, about two miles from Bay Hill. It was completely barren, its square footage interrupted only by exposed steel columns. Scalici then undertook the task of building out the studio. Not just any studio, but arguably the most technologically advanced television studio that had ever been assembled at that time. In fact, it was the first all-digital facility in the United States. And at $10.5 million, it wasn't cheap. While that might sound a little extravagant for a firm that was still hunting down 30 percent of its funding, Gibbs was certain the expense was justifiable.

"This was 1994," he said. "We were right on the edge of the digital revolution. If we had built an analog set, we would have had to switch over to digital within twenty-four months." This would also prove vital in terms of the look and feel of the channel's sets. Because Golf Channel was going to launch as a pay channel, it had to exude enough quality and value to rationalize the consumer's expense.

That an upstart cable net was technologically lapping CNN and ESPN was a powerful statement. The word "digital" is commonplace today, but in 1994 it had some futuristic cachet, and while most people didn't really know what it meant, the industry did. It didn't take long for tech teams from ESPN and other nets to visit Golf Channel's studios to marvel at Scalici's handiwork.

Scalici's contribution to the early development and growth of Golf Channel was invaluable. But the network would need a lot more than the seven Birmingham employees. Gibbs had more than two hundred positions to fill. He'd also latched on early to HBO's Bob Greenway, who had put the premium channel on the sports television map.

If Gibbs was the patron and Scalici the gallery, then Greenway was the artist. As senior vice president of programming, production, and operations at Golf Channel, Greenway assembled and led the creative team that would develop, write, produce, and direct the channel's programming.

"I had already found Greenway, and he'd been helping build the business plan," said Gibbs. It was Greenway who brought in the rest of the creative and on-air talent. Most of the other senior management was also lined up early. Gibbs' longtime lawyer, Murvin, had legal; Jim Lowrey was chief financial officer, and Del Wood was controller, both from Birmingham; Gene Pizzolato was the original head of marketing; and Jim Bates handled affiliate relations with the cable operators.

> "Arnold looked at all of us sitting around the table and he said, 'Boys, if I hadn't tried to hit it through the trees a few times, none of us would be here.'"
> CHRIS MURVIN

———

With money (most of it, at least), rights packages, transponders, a studio, and a staff in place, Golf Channel's launch date was set for January 17, 1995, a date that held no significance. It was, according to Gibbs, simply the soonest possible date. But in the summer of 1994, only a few months before launch, the FCC deregulated cable television. This was a bombshell. In the long run, it was excellent news for Gibbs and other cable networks and operators. Deregulation meant that there would no longer be artificial restrictions on what a cable company could charge for a network, regardless of whether that network was distributed on the basic tier or not. That was the good news. The bad news was that Golf Channel was only months from launch, and the *entire* business plan was built around a $6.95 mini-pay network, as had been dictated by the FCC.

TIGER WOODS
2005 MASTERS

Tiger Woods gives a victorious fist pump after making the winning putt in Sunday's playoff.

The 2005 Masters might have been remembered as Jack Nicklaus' final Masters. It would take something pretty juicy to overshadow the Golden Bear's exit from his Augusta lair. But juicy is exactly what we got.

Tiger Woods had entered the tournament on an 0-for-10 winless streak in major championships. Chris DiMarco's place in the game was less distinct. In April 2005 he was emerging from journeyman status to that of frequent contender. DiMarco notched three top tens in 2004, including a tie for second with Justin Leonard in the PGA Championship. An impressive T-6 in the 2004 Masters had also tagged DiMarco as a gritty comer.

DiMarco started the Masters strong, ending the second round with a 4-shot lead (and 6 up on Woods). In a third round that stretched from Saturday into Sunday due to weather and darkness, the tables turned. Woods made seven straight birdies to shoot 65, while DiMarco stumbled in with a 74. With 18 holes to play, Woods held a three-shot lead.

The underdog put up a valiant fight. Playing out of his weight class, DiMarco hung in by scoring jabs with his wedges and putters, while Woods tried for knockout blows with his driver. Ironically, the key shot of the tournament was Woods' iconic birdie chip on 16 (see page 96), but Woods uncharacteristically bogeyed the next hole after a poor drive. He came to the 18th tee with a one-shot lead. Neither player hit the 18th green. Woods was in the green side bunker and DiMarco was just short. His chip for birdie was a life-changer, hitting the pin and bouncing nearly ten feet away. Woods' bunker shot left him a fifteen-foot par putt for the win. His miss meant that if DiMarco holed his own par putt, the two would play off. He drained it.

The playoff began on the 18th hole. Woods made birdie to win and kick-started a run of dominance that would end with the 2008 U.S. Open. DiMarco has had only one top ten in a major championship since, but his reputation as bulldog remains intact.

"It was time for me to go out and have a chance to win a tournament, be aggressive and do something." said DiMarco. "I went out and shot 68 on Sunday, which is a very good round, and 12-under is usually good enough to win. I just was playing against Tiger Woods."

Golf Channel's long-term prospects had just dramatically improved. But could it survive the short term?

At 7 p.m. Eastern on Tuesday, January 17, 1995, Golf Channel went live. It reached approximately ten thousand households—though none of them were in Orlando, so most staffers couldn't even watch. It was a proud day for Gibbs and Palmer. But the brightness of the studio lights was countered by the channel's grim finances. Only three months after launch, Gibbs told his board that the current plan would not work. He promised to come back by the end of that summer with a new plan that would fully leverage the new, deregulated environment and Golf Channel's compelling content.

That summer, Gibbs completely rewrote Golf Channel's business plan. In the fall of 1995, the network had grown from ten thousand customers to about one hundred thousand. By the New Year, the number would blossom to 1.5 million. Distribution was moving in the right direction, but money was still a serious issue. The network had a burn rate of about $48 million a year, and by the end of its first year, Gibbs figured it had enough only cash and revenue to last for two or three more months. Golf Channel was confronting mortality.

Golf Channel needed to raise $120 million. Gibbs scratched out $15 million from existing shareholders, enough to buy another three or four months, then headed back out to hunt down a wide-wallet investor. In the summer of 1996, Neher and Roberts helped Golf Channel approach Fox. A possible Fox investment in Golf Channel was brought up during discussions between Comcast, Continental, and Fox for carriage of Fox channels. The end result was a $50 million investment in Golf Channel by Fox. Shortly thereafter, in August 1996, Tiger Woods, the most acclaimed American amateur since Bobby Jones, turned professional. Timing is everything. "Golf Channel gets the timing award," said *USA Today*'s Martzke. "It rode the surge in cable's rise at the same time that Tiger Woods was drawing millions of new fans to golf. That produced new avid golf fans for Golf Channel."

Kelly Tilghman joined Golf Channel in 1996. Little did she or Gibbs or Palmer or Neher know what Woods held in store for the sport. "They had no idea this gift was coming," said Tilghman. "I believe that Golf Channel would still be a success story today if Tiger hadn't risen to the level of stardom he did. But that said, I give Tiger massive credit for how quickly Golf Channel succeeded."

And suddenly, that was it. The Fox investment was the last outside funding Golf Channel ever needed, and any doubts about the channel's future were put to rest. Around that same time, a young broadcaster named Rich Lerner, who had moved from Dallas to Orlando to take a job at the fledgling network, was relaxing at an Orlando ice-skating rink with his wife and young child. Gibbs also happened to be at the rink. The up-and-coming Pennsylvania native had taken the post in Orlando largely at the urging of his mother, who'd told her son that if Arnold Palmer was part of this thing, the young man should get his rear end down there. The chance encounter at the rink presented a rare opportunity to chat socially with the other boss. Gibbs inquired as to where the Lerners were living, and the young man replied that they were renting a place not far away. The plan, he explained, was to buy a home once the financial future of the family and Golf Channel had been secured. At the end of their discussion, as Gibbs was leaving, he turned to Lerner and said, "You buy that house." The network was here to stay.

By the end of 1998, the network was turning a small profit. It had taken ESPN seven years to break even; Golf Channel had made it in only four. The next year, it made $20 million and never looked back. By the time Gibbs left the helm, the channel was making $50 million a year.

> **Little did Gibbs or Palmer or Neher know what Tiger Woods held in store for the sport. "They had no idea this gift was coming," said Tilghman.**

2011 Tour Championship
by Coca-Cola
Bill Haas
Playoff

If you are ever faced with the opportunity to play a shot from the water for $10 million, you might want to take Bill Haas's advice. In 2011 Haas played one of the most stunning shots in PGA Tour history when, on the second hole of a playoff to decide the Tour Championship by Coca-Cola, he found himself in the eponymous greenside lake at East Lake GC's 17th hole.

"We get up there, and I say in my head, 'I have a shot,'" said Haas. "You play it like a bunker shot, for those of you that want to know, if there's a little bit of water, if you don't mind getting your feet dirty. And then blast it out of there. It came out perfect. Lucky."

It wasn't until later that Haas realized he'd hit the daily double, winning not only the Tour Championship by Coca-Cola but also the season-long FedEx Cup and the $10 million that goes with it.

"We went up and did some TV interviews in the grandstands there on 18, and both trophies were there and there was no other player," recalled Haas. "I looked at my wife and she nodded. That was when I realized."

Tiger Woods
2013 Masters

After the second round of the 2013 Masters, the talk of the tournament was fourteen-year-old amateur Guan Tianlang, who was penalized for slow play. Asked to comment on the situation, Tiger Woods said, "Rules are rules."

Woods would have his own run-in with the rulebook in short order. His approach to the 15th green hit the flagstick and ricocheted backwards into the green-front water hazard. Woods chose to drop the ball near his original shot, but failed to heed the part of the rule that required the drop be as close as possible to the spot from which the original ball was last played.

The miscue caught the eye of the wrong guy: David Eger. The former senior director of rules and competition for the USGA noticed Woods' faulty drop on TV. In an attempt to spare Woods a DQ, he called and then texted a rules official who was working the Masters, saying that tournament officials needed to huddle with Woods before he signed his card. They didn't. The soap opera that ensued when Woods later unwittingly volunteered that indeed the drop was illegal engulfed the weekend of the 2013 Masters in controversy. Woods was ultimately issued a two-shot penalty but remained in the tournament.

Today, Golf Channel is 100 percent owned by Comcast—which slowly built up its stake in the network over the years. When Comcast acquired a majority stake in NBC Universal in 2011, Golf Channel joined NBC Sports Group. Together, NBC and Golf Channel have been able to combine their complementary golf television rights to offer Thursday-through-Sunday tournament play across virtually all major tours, the Ryder Cup, instruction, commentary, and news. Given NBC's distinguished history of broadcasting the Olympic Games, NBC Sports Group's presence will only be enhanced further when golf returns to the Olympics in 2016.

It's doubtful that anyone in the game has a more informed perspective on Golf Channel's influence than Tommy Roy, the longtime executive producer for golf at NBC Sports. Roy, the son of a golf professional, has his office TV permanently tuned to Golf Channel just to keep up with the news in his industry. Beyond the news fix and the obvious benefits of corporate synergies, such as footage gathering and graphics design, Roy sees two ways in which Golf Channel has forever transformed the sports TV landscape.

"It has definitely changed things," he says. "With all the early-round coverage, the hours and hours of televised golf keep growing, so for golf fans, that's very meaningful. Plus, when we do our bigger events and we need to add people beyond our normal team, we turn to Golf Channel to get those folks, and they are terrific. They're very sharp, very eager. They're huge golf fans and they're very knowledgeable about the game. That's so incredibly important, and a great value not only to us but to viewers."

As for Palmer and Gibbs, they and their early investors cashed out in December 1999. When Comcast took control of the network, Brian Roberts and his father, Comcast cofounder Ralph Roberts, flew to Palmer's hometown of Latrobe, Pennsylvania, to sign the paperwork that formalized the deal. After signing the papers, Palmer turned to Brian and said, "Take care of my baby."

Gibbs stayed on running the network for another two years until he retired. If you're looking for people who are surprised at Golf Channel's success, count Gibbs out. When he left the helm, Gibbs was confident it was set up for even greater success.

The Pro Game

When historians write about this ten-year stretch, they'll consider the incomparable rise of Tiger Woods, the popular appeal of Phil Mickelson, and the breathy passion of Payne Stewart. They may not call it the best decade ever, but they sure will be jealous.

1995-2004

Every now and then you get to witness a shot or shots played by a great player, and you know that on a specific shot there's only a few guys in the world that could even attempt it, much less pull it off. When they do something like that, you just sit there and you say, "You gotta be kidding me." It's jaw-dropping.

ROGER MALTBIE

In 1997, Ernie Els became the first international player since 1910 to win two U.S. Open titles.

It was as though golf was shedding a skin, ushering out the old and sheathing itself in the new.

Centuries from now, golf historians will draft scholarly tomes about golf in the twentieth and twenty-first centuries. They'll look for inflection points at which the game took a discernible turn, such as 1894, when the USGA was formed; 1930, when Bobby Jones won the Grand Slam; and 1986, when Jack Nicklaus won his final major.

Add to that list 1995. It is too close for us to see right now, but when studied through a longer lens, 1995 may be to golf what 1066 was to military history, or what 1969 meant to both lunar science and rock and roll. After that year, nothing was ever the same. In 1991, 1992, and 1993, Tiger Woods won the U.S. Junior Amateur Championship. Given the low profile of the championship, the achievement barely registered with the average fan. Even toward the end of 1994, Tiger Woods was simply a one-time U.S. Amateur champion. At only eighteen years of age—then the youngest champion ever—his youth surely stood out, but no one could have predicted the career that lay ahead.

Then, in 1995, Woods, who had just completed his freshman year at Stanford, won his second U.S. Amateur title and his fifth USGA championship, and golf has simply never been the same. Tiger Woods had arrived and embarked on his mission to repaginate the record book.

For the next ten years, it was as though golf was shedding a skin, ushering out the old and sheathing itself in the new. The establishment would eke out its share of wins, but aging greats such as Ben Crenshaw, Nick Faldo, Mark O'Meara, and Tom Lehman would soon be overtaken by Woods and enlivened by a cast of other greats.

JOHN DALY
1995 OPEN
CHAMPIONSHIP

John Daly tees off during the final round at the Old Course at St. Andrews.

When John Daly arrived at St. Andrews in July 1995, he was little more than a long-haired, long-hitting curiosity. It had been nearly four years since he had bellied up to the major championship bar with his stunning victory in the 1991 PGA Championship as an alternate, one of the unlikeliest wins in championship history. The four intervening years were hard ones, a bracing cocktail of two parts fame, one part flameout. Sure, there were two tour wins, but also lots of off-course mileage. Battles with booze and diet and wives and lawyers had obscured his blinding talent. He'd played in sixteen events leading up to that Open Championship at St. Andrews with little to show for it: not a single top ten and five missed cuts. The rowdy twenty-nine-year-old, who only a few years earlier seemed destined to overwhelm the game and its quaint golf courses, was suddenly a 66-to-1 underdog. With a few too many ex-wives. Too big a swing. A pack-a-day habit. And a mullet.

But the musty Old Course and the brassy American clicked. A course that came to fame in the featherie era was ripe for Daly's unrivaled aerial assault. He drove par 4s with regularity and reached par 5s in two with the nonchalance of dragging on a Marlboro. But brute force can take a major championship contender only so far, and Daly showed a combination of guts, cool, and touch under pressure. He took a two-shot lead into 17, a hole that has crowned and downed more Open champions than any other. His 6-iron approach came to rest in the most infamous bunker on earth. The soulless Road Hole bunker looks like something out of *The Shawshank Redemption;* its steep sodden walls make it easy to enter and hard to leave. Daly was so close to the front wall that he would have been forgiven, maybe even applauded, for playing backwards out the low side of the pit, but somehow the man who invented bomb and gauge played the ball to the fat part of the green and 2-putted for the clutchest of Road Hole bogeys. Daly then parred the short par-4 18th and waited along with a frazzled television audience to see if Italy's Costantino Rocca could mount a late charge.

After a heroic par save at the Road Hole, Rocca came to 18 needing a birdie to force a playoff. He drove nicely just short of the famed 18th green. All he needed was a chip and a putt. What happened next was something from a tragicomic Fellini-directed farce. He flubbed the chip into the Valley of Sin (agony), then putted in for birdie (ecstasy) to force a playoff.

Daly toyed with Rocca in the four-hole playoff that ensued and was pronounced "the gold medal winner and champion golfer of the year." The game had never seen anything like him and probably never will again.

If only the claret jug could talk.

"I'd like to see the fairways more narrow. Then everyone would have to play from the rough, not just me."
BALLESTEROS

▼ SEVE BALLESTEROS

Spain's incredible matador, gone too soon.

Career wins: 50 on the European Tour, 9 on the PGA Tour

Major championships: 5 (1980, 1983 Masters; 1979, 1984, 1988 Open Championship)

▼ FRED COUPLES

Lowering the Boom Boom! Masters Freddie always seems to be lurking at Augusta.

Career wins: 15 on the PGA Tour

Major championships: 1 (1992 Masters)

"Golf is a game to me. Other players work extremely hard all year long. I work hard before Augusta. I know I get good results when I practice, but it also wears me out. It literally wore me out even when I was in my twenties."
COUPLES

"I don't think I've ever stepped into a gym—they won't let me smoke there. I just thank God Miller Lite isn't as fattening as most beers. If I cut back on beer, though, I'd look anorexic."
DALY

JOHN DALY

Long John Daly takes the Tour by surprise and by storm.

Career wins: 5 on the PGA Tour

Major championships: 2 (1991 PGA Championship, 1995 Open Championship)

▼ ERNIE ELS

One Els of a ride.

Career wins: 43 on the PGA and European Tours

Major championships: 4 (1994, 1997 U.S. Open; 2002, 2012 Open Championship)

"Up to now, I've had a great career. A couple of putts here and there, it could have been a lot better."
ELS

▼ *Member of World Golf Hall of Fame*

1996 U.S. Amateur Championship*
Tiger Woods Championship Match

Tiger Woods was in hot pursuit of history at Pumpkin Ridge GC in Oregon. A win in the thirty-six-hole championship match would mean Woods would become the only player in history to have won three U.S. Ams in a row. Woods had trailed by five holes with sixteen to play, but cut Steve Scott's lead to two with three holes left. Woods birdied 16 and then holed a thirty-foot putt on 17 to draw all square with Scott and ultimately force extra holes; Woods won on the 38th.

*It may not have been a professional win, but it sure was done professionally.

Steve Elkington 1995 PGA Championship (six strokes down)

Nick Faldo 1996 Masters, beats Greg Norman (six strokes down)

Paul Lawrie 1999 Open Championship (ten strokes down)

U.S. Team 1999 Ryder Cup at Brookline after being down 10-6 entering final day

Tiger Woods 2000 AT&T Pebble Beach National Pro-Am (seven strokes down with seven holes to play)

Stewart Cink 2004 MCI Heritage (nine strokes down)

Louise Friberg 2008 MasterCard Classic (ten strokes down in final round)

Y.E. Yang 2009 PGA Championship (beats Tiger Woods, who had been 14-0 in majors with a lead after fifty-four holes)

Charl Schwartzel wins 2011 Masters (finished with four straight birdies)

European Team wins 2012 Ryder Cup at Medinah after being down 10-6 entering final day (above)

TOP **10** PUTTS

1995 Open Championship. **Costantino Rocca** makes a miracle sixty-foot birdie putt on the final hole at St. Andrews to force a playoff. (John Daly would eventually win, see page 26.)

1998 Masters. **Mark O'Meara** holes a twenty-foot birdie putt on the final hole to win.

1999 Ryder Cup. **Justin Leonard** drains a forty-five-footer on the 17th hole to help the U.S. win. (See pages 68 and 215.)

2001 Players Championship. **Tiger Woods** hits a sixty-foot double breaker on 17, prompting NBC Sports announcer Gary Koch's "Better than most!" call. (See page 95.)

2001 PGA Championship. **David Toms** lays up on the final hole, leaving him a wedge in and a twelve-foot putt, which he hits for his only major win.

2004 Masters. **Phil Mickelson** hits an eighteen-footer on the final hole to win his first major title. (See page 70.)

2008 Arnold Palmer Invitational. **Tiger Woods** nails a twenty-four-foot birdie on the final hole to win at Bay Hill.

2008 PGA Championship. **Padraig Harrington**'s breaking eighteen-footer for par beats Sergio Garcia at Oakland Hills.

2010 Ryder Cup. **Graeme McDowell** hits a fifteen-footer for birdie on 16 and goes on to beat Hunter Mahan to win for Europe. (See page 222.)

2014 HSBC Women's Champions. **Paula Creamer** makes a miracle seventy-five-footer for eagle on the second playoff hole to win in Singapore.

DAVIS LOVE III
1997 PGA CHAMPIONSHIP

All these years later, it's hard to recall just how much had been piled on the shoulders of young Davis Love III. His father, the famed instructor Davis Love Jr., had tied for the first-round lead of the Masters in 1964. The son was born the day after the tournament. As his father rose to prominence in teaching circles as a PGA professional, his star student rose too, emerging from the University of North Carolina as a can't-miss PGA Tour player. The father lived long enough to see the son win on the PGA Tour, the 1987 MCI Heritage Classic, but when the senior Love died in a 1988 plane crash, the son lost a father, a teacher, and a friend.

Every player craves major championships. But Love, who emerged with Fred Couples in the 1990s as two of the game's most popular players, had the curse of not only wanting to win them but being expected to win them. When confronted with the chance to win the PGA Championship at Winged Foot (the workshop of champions), Love had to strike the right balance between reason and emotion. He started Sunday's final round tied with Justin Leonard, a friend who had just won the Open Championship a month earlier. Love pulled away early, his emotions now as much a threat as Leonard.

"I was choking up a lot of times out there," Love said. "Every time I thought about winning, every time I thought about what it would mean."

Love's triumph was sealed on the 18th green with an eight-foot birdie putt. As he was preparing to play that last hole, the clouds and rain that had dogged the finale gave way to a glorious rainbow. He holed the putt and reminded us all that there are no rainbows without a little rain.

Davis Love III acknowledges the crowd after winning the 1997 PGA Championship at Winged Foot.

David Duval
1999 Bob Hope
Chrysler Classic
Final Round

After a lethargic session on the range, David Duval carded eleven birdies in the first seventeen holes and then approached the par-5 home hole with a 5-iron to six feet and holed it for eagle. Final score: 59.

It's arguable whether the great shot was the approach or the putt, but the 5-iron gets our vote. "I had 177 yards to the front of the green and 218 to the hole," said Duval. "My main thought was to knock it on and have a putt for it. I wasn't positive I could get it all the way back to the hole. But I felt pretty good about that just because of the adrenaline, really. And, you know, it just looked so good the whole way, and I just was screaming. It had to be up, be back there, and it did."

This being the Bob Hope, after all, Duval had a straight man among the media who asked, "What were the guys in your group saying as the day goes along?"

"They just kept saying, 'Good shot,'" deadpanned Duval.

SERGIO GARCIA

He started tracking a Tiger in a 1999 PGA Championship duel; fifteen years later, he still hasn't caught him.

Career wins: 27, including 8 on the PGA Tour and 11 on the European Tour

Major championships: None

"After thirteen years, today was the day. I don't have the capacity to win a major.... I'm not good enough and now I know it.... After thirteen years, I have run out of options.... You can live without a major."
GARCIA

"He knows his father is proud and that he's with him. That was the rainbow."
PENTA LOVE, mother of Davis, on her son's PGA win and his pain dealing with his father's death in a plane crash

DAVIS LOVE III

Love finds a way, winning the 1997 PGA Championship under a rainbow.

Career wins: 20 on the PGA Tour

Major championships: 1 (1997 PGA Championship)

"You know, I need that cockiness— the self-belief, arrogance, swagger, whatever you want to call it—I need that on the golf course to bring out the best in myself. So you know, once I leave the course, that all gets left there."
MCILROY

RORY MCILROY

Hear him Rors! McIlroy shows he's a major player just like Tiger.

Career wins: 14, including 4 major titles

Major championships: 4 (2011 U.S. Open, 2012, 2014 PGA Championship, 2014 Open Championship)

"Every time I think of the U.S. Open, I think of heartbreak."
MICKELSON

PHIL MICKELSON

Mickelson has been the biggest name in golf during his career, in the category of people not named Tiger Woods.

Career wins: 42

Major championships: 5 (2004, 2006, 2011 Masters; 2005 PGA Championship; 2013 Open Championship)

PAYNE STEWART
1999 U.S. OPEN

"Payne Stewart
could make the
wind blow fresh and
cool and alive. Only
recently it seemed
did he discover
the soothing tonic
of a gentle breeze.
A complex man,
Stewart wore his
emotions as readily
and colorfully as
those plus fours that
made him instantly
recognizable, even
to those that didn't
follow golf. Perfect?
By no means. Real?
Absolutely. Payne
was funny, playful,
mischievous, cocky,
thoughtful, jealous,
intelligent, and
honest."

RICH LERNER

Payne Stewart looking for a
birdie on 17 in the final round of
the 1999 U.S. Open.

If, when you reach the pearly gates, Peter asks why you spent so much time watching golf, sit him down and show him a tape of the 1999 U.S. Open. You may not gain entry, but you'll have given him a hell of an answer.

That's because the 1999 Open was about redemption. Three of the game's leading men—Tiger Woods, Phil Mickelson, and Payne Stewart—were all in contention on Pinehurst No. 2, one of the crown jewels of American golf course architecture. Woods, for all the record-shattering he'd done at the 1997 Masters, hadn't won a major since. Mickelson was major-less for his career, and Stewart, who had finished second twice in the U.S. Open and once in the Open Championship, was desperate to prove a few things. First, that his major championship titles (1989 PGA Championship, 1991 U.S. Open) were not flukes or ancient history. Second, that regardless of the outcome, Stewart himself had evolved. The flashy, impetuous bad boy of only a few years ago had been replaced by a more thoughtful man.

The last three holes were the Payne Stewart Show. Mickelson actually led by a shot until Stewart dropped a twenty-five-foot bomb of a par putt on the 16th green. Mickelson, rocked by the aftershocks, then missed his own par putt. Stewart simply chewed his gum and poker-faced his way to the 17th tee.

"I had had the exact same putt on 16 that Payne had only earlier in the day," said Brandel Chamblee, who finished T-46 that week. "It was up and over a ridge, and I thought it was one of the hardest putts to read that I had ever had. I remember thinking at the time that it was unreadable and un-makeable. And then he came along and made it, and his demeanor never changed. He just kept chomping on that gum. The cadence of his walk didn't change. We were all agog at what he'd just done, and he was just focused on what he was about to do."

Both went pin-hunting on 17. After Mickleson missed his six-footer for birdie, Stewart holed his four-footer to take a one-shot lead to the 18th tee. Phil hit the fairway and the green, leaving himself a twenty-five-foot putt for birdie. Stewart drove slightly right but into the deep, wet rough. After chipping out to safety, he played a 9-iron third into the green. Mickelson, whose wife was expecting and who had pledged to fly to her side if the pager he was carrying buzzed, rolled his putt within an inch or two of the hole.

It was up to Stewart: Hole the par putt and win by one. Two-putt and force a playoff. "I knew my putt was going to go up and go to the right," said Stewart, who would credit his wife, Tracey, with reminding him the day before to keep his head still on putts. "I said, 'This is an inside left putt, just believe that.'

I stood up there and did my routine, and I kept my head still on that putt. And when I looked up, it was about two feet from the hole and it was breaking right in the center, and I couldn't believe it. I couldn't believe that I'd accomplished another dream of mine."

For many who didn't know Stewart, the one-legged, be-knickered fist pump remains the enduring image of that week. For those who knew him, it was his generous embrace of a dejected runner-up that reflected who Stewart really was. He took Mickelson's boyish face in his hands and reminded him that he was about to be a father. That day, as Stewart held the U.S. Open trophy, he was philosophical about the year ahead, focusing far more on family than on fame.

"I think I'm a lot more prepared to deal with everything that goes along with holding on to this trophy for a year," said Stewart at the time. "I don't plan on changing my schedules. I plan on doing the same things that I've been doing that got me in position to win today, which is working out and spending a lot of time at home and playing when I want to play and playing at tournaments that I enjoy playing at. I don't look forward to running after the elusive dollar, because I've been invited to go and play here and here and here and here," he said. "I've had so much fun being at home, being a father, getting up in the morning, making breakfast, taking my kids to school, going to high school athletics. That's what my life is right now."

Payne Stewart, who had matured from a boy to a man and to a two-time U.S. Open champion, died just four months later in a plane crash. Professional golf has never been the same.

"He was irreplaceable," said Chamblee, whose one PGA Tour win came in the 1998 Greater Vancouver Open at Stewart's expense. "The way he looked. The way he swung. His playfulness. You hear the expression 'larger than life,' but Payne really was. He could go into any room and light it up, and light it up the right way. He would make the lowest person on the totem pole feel welcomed. A lot of people go into a room and find the biggest star in the room. Payne wasn't like that. He walked into a room and it didn't matter to him if you were a rookie or a superstar. He got everyone involved, and that's a gift.

"They always say, 'If you want to know who someone is, watch 'em lose,'" Chamblee continued. "But better than that, watch 'em win. Jack Nicklaus was the greatest loser of all time. That always irked him, but that's the tallest compliment. When he *did* lose, he was always so complimentary of the person who beat him. And when he won, he was always so cognizant of the person he beat. That's emotional intelligence. And Payne had that."

TOP: Stewart hits his second shot on the 7th hole of the final round of the 1999 U.S. Open.

ABOVE: Stewart celebrates with his caddie after capturing that Open.

Kenny Perry
1996 PGA
Championship

For most golfers, the 19th hole is the best part of their game. With eighteen holes under the belt, it's time for, well, a belt. But it was the 19th hole that cost Kenny Perry the 1996 PGA Championship. For several days, Valhalla GC's inaugural major championship was like Old Home week, more like My Old Kentucky Home Week—as natives Perry (Franklin, Kentucky) and Russ Cochran (Paducah, Kentucky) hovered near the lead. In fact, Cochran held the fifty-four-hole lead. But when Cochran faded with a Sunday 77, the Bluegrass State's hopes turned to Perry, who obliged by coming to the 18th tee with a two-shot lead. Given that the par-5 18th was playing as the second-easiest hole of the day, Perry's

chances of rewriting what had been a lackluster record looked good. Until he hooked his drive into the deep rough. He ended up bogeying 18 and then, instead of following anxious contender protocol and going to the range to stay loose and await news of a potential playoff, Perry donned a headset and joined CBS Sports' Jim Nantz in the tower at 18.

Whatever supply of mojo Perry had after seventy-two holes disappeared. Mark Brooks birdied the home hole to force a sudden-death playoff, which started at the 18th hole. Perry again pulled his ball left off the tee while Brooks lapped him and birdied the hole for the win. Perry would never win a major. Brooks would never win another.

Perry recently told the *Courier-Journal* that his meltdown "was the worst of anything I experienced on the tour in thirty years, even though I lost the [2009] Masters in a playoff. The one in your home state, what people kind of remember you for, that was a tough one."

OOPS

Jean Van de Velde
1999 Open
Championship

It was the most jaw-dropping slow-motion train wreck in modern major championship history. Jean Van de Velde's roller-coaster play of the 72nd hole in the 1999 Open Championship at Carnoustie still echoes on barstools around the world. It's been so discussed and dissected over the years that it's helpful to revisit Van de Velde's own description of his home-hole hell, beginning with his drive at 18:

"As I came over [the hill], the ball was, like, fantastic. I could not have placed it any better. The only thing I had was 189 to carry the water, which wasn't very demanding. The only thing you didn't have to do was to hit it left.

"The ball was lying so good, I took my 2-iron and thought, 'You're gonna hit it down there. Either you're on the green or just on the right in the bunker or even in the semi or whatever.' I pushed it a little. I didn't hit a very good shot. From what I heard, it definitely carried the water, hit the grandstand, came back, landed off the rocks, and went off. I would have been better in the water, actually, because I would have had to drop it somewhere.... But no, it came back and I had a dramatic lie.

"I couldn't go backwards. I couldn't. I don't think I could have done anything. The only thing that I could try was to go forwards to hit it there because I had to hit it hard. Obviously I didn't hit it hard enough. So it finished in the water. I dropped it again in the rough. It was terrible. And it was lying so poorly, I thought, 'Here you go now. What are you gonna do? You still have to hit it hard. If you hang left and you hit it too hard, you're over there in the grandstand. That's not gonna help either. I'm going to try for the shot—the shot I need to hit it high and land over there and hopefully finish on the green.' It went underneath the ball and finished in the trap. Made a good up and down, mind you. I'm glad I made up and down for 7. At least I played another four holes."

"Then the Frenchman went *Tin Cup* on us. Huck Finn in the Barry Burn. A riverboat gambler who made the slots ring for two heroic, logic-defying days. And then he ran aground. Suddenly an event that might have been rehashed only in France would now be one of the most-talked-about Opens in history. The artistic opposite of Nicklaus vs. Watson at Turnberry in '77, but talked about nonetheless. That was the greatest, clutchest triple bogey putt in the history of golf. Tragic, sad in some ways, but farcical in other ways. Incroyable, as the French would say. Incredible."

RICH LERNER

Sergio Garcia
1999 PGA Championship
Final Round

On the 16th hole at Medinah, Sergio Garcia played his approach from a tenuous lie dangerously close to a towering red oak tree. His courageous shot (he closed his eyes) came to rest on the green, as Garcia himself found out when he famously bounded up the fairway and leaped boyishly in the air for a glimpse of his handiwork. Although the shot still echoes, the tree itself is long gone. Ten years after Garcia's sprightly flirtation with a major championship (he would lose to Woods by a shot), the tree was felled by rot.

"It takes a certain amount of moxie to shake your fist in the direction of the King [Tiger], especially when you just started shaving. Too young to know or care, I guess. Too good to deny. Sergio brings much more than just sublime skill and that boyish bounce. Sergio, oozing the kind of charisma the sport so dearly needs, loves the stage, and that is where Tiger, until now, had yet to meet his match. Had yet to meet someone with fists as big and lethal. Someone with a smile as wide and bright. Sergio devours the moment. This is Formula One golf. Jump for joy golf."
RICH LERNER

TIGER WOODS

2000 U.S. OPEN

What's left to say? What superlative hasn't yet been applied to Tiger Woods' beat down of the field at the 2000 U.S. Open? The guy won by 15. That's what football teams do. Perhaps a fresh approach to the Massacre at Pebble Beach would be the victim's point of view, that is, wipe off the blood and ask how it went. One victim that week was Brandel Chamblee, who was playing in his third U.S. Open. For him, the reality of what was about to happen set in with a thud two days before the tournament proper even began.

Tuesday is a pretty quiet day on the professional golf scene. Even major championship Tuesdays are pretty low-key affairs. For many players it's arrival day. For many others, it's a chance to play the course and work out kinks on the range. That's what Chamblee was doing the Tuesday before the 2000 Open. He'd been playing well, posting some good finishes on tour, and hitting the ball well. As professional golfers are wont to do, he was polishing his swing and convincing himself he could actually win that week. It was then that Woods slipped into the spot directly behind Chamblee on the practice tee. As Chamblee continued with his routine, his friend, who'd been standing with him on the range, quietly interrupted Chamblee. "I know you're getting ready, and I know you feel good about your game," said the friend, "but you need to just stop and turn around. If you don't watch this, you'll be missing the greatest display of golf the game has ever seen."

That'll get a guy's attention. Chamblee turned and cast his eyes on Woods, who was only about twelve feet away. "I watched him take a six-inch divot three inches in front of a ball that took off at a speed that I was unfamiliar with. Every one of [his shots] flew out on the exact same trajectory, reached the same peak, fell the same way, and his swing was, from start to finish, purposeful. There was just no fat in his golf swing. No fat," said Chamblee. "It was that wide, beautiful takeaway, a beautiful transition—nothing quick about it—graceful into the ball, and an explosion, and then he finished like an Olympic gymnast. He stuck the finish. Poised and relaxed. Anyway, I watched it for about thirty minutes, and I felt impotent. I felt less virile. I turned around and started hitting my shots and they didn't make the same sound, and they didn't fly in as tight a line, and they didn't have the same apex, and they weren't as consistent. I felt like my swing, even though I thought I had a good one, didn't measure up. There was no way in hell I could beat that guy."

Woods beat the field by 15. He beat Chamblee by 34.

Woods hits his tee shot on 13 during his Sunday round at the 2000 U.S. Open at Pebble Beach.

BEST
OF THE
MAJORS

TIGER WOODS

2000 OPEN

CHAMPIONSHIP

Woods lines up his putt on the first green during the third round of the 2000 Open Championship.

It's hard to pinpoint the greater significance of Tiger Woods' win here. Was it that he stormed the course, avoiding every single bunker during a seventy-two-hole test? Was it that he blitzed the field winning by eight strokes? Or was it that at the age of twenty-four, Woods completed the career Grand Slam? Coupled with what Woods had done five weeks earlier in the U.S. Open, and what would come in the next several months with his completion of the Tiger Slam, we were seeing something we'd probably never see again.

"It's the greatest stretch of golf anybody had ever seen," said Brandel Chamblee. "It was predictable, and it was astonishing."

"I look forward to coming back here again next year and trying another U.S. Open disaster."
MONTGOMERIE

🛡 COLIN MONTGOMERIE

The Full Monty: Colin Montgomerie came close, but never won an elusive major championship before joining the senior circuit.

Career wins: 43, including 31 on European Tour, ranking fourth all-time

Major championships: 0 (five second-place finishes)

🛡 GREG NORMAN

The Shark attacks, but gags on the Green Jacket in a historic 1996 Masters collapse.

Career wins: 90; 331 weeks as the world's No. 1 ranked player.

Major championships: 2 (1986, 1993 Open Championship)

"I remember when I first came out on tour, it was Greg Norman and Nick Price. We forget how big Norman was, what a presence he was. I remember one of my first tournaments, Greg threw an orange peel down on the ground and some fan ran over and grabbed it: 'This is Greg Norman's orange peel!'"
PHIL MICKELSON

"I was a rookie from a foreign country. You didn't see many Korean golfers on tour. Pretty much everything was new for us. New life, new language, new golf course week to week."
PAK

🛡 SE RI PAK

Pak's good for the Seoul of the game as the South Korean star becomes a pioneer on LPGA Tour.

Career wins: 25 on the LPGA Tour

Major championships: 5 (1998, 2002, 2006 LPGA Championship; 1998 U.S. Women's Open; 2001 Women's British Open)

ADAM SCOTT

Great Scott! Adam takes the baton from Greg Norman as Australia's top player.

Career wins: 27 (11 on the PGA Tour; 9 on the European Tour; 7 on others)

Major championships: 1 (2013 Masters)

"There's one guy who inspired a nation of golfers, and that's Greg Norman. And part of this definitely belongs to him."
SCOTT

BEST
OF THE
MAJORS

TIGER WOODS
2001 MASTERS

Woods approaches the 18th green during the final round of the 2001 Masters.

Tiger Woods is the most dominant player the game has ever known. Furthermore, he will almost certainly retire as the all-time leader in PGA Tour wins. But if it's true that greatness in golf is measured solely in major championships, it's conceivable that a hundred years from now, Woods will be remembered as the second-greatest collector of major championships ever, second to Jack Nicklaus. That distinction, which would leave him squarely in the shadow of the Golden Bear, would be a disappointment to the man who set out as a youngster to topple the Legend.

That said, there is one distinction, that already sets Woods apart from Nicklaus, Hogan, Snead, Player, Watson, Nelson, Palmer, or any of the other greats of the game: He held all four modern major championship titles at one time. No, he didn't win them all in one calendar year, as did Bobby Jones when the Atlanta attorney went on his Grand Slam spree in 1930. Which slam is more impressive is up to the beholder, but as Golf Channel's David Feherty reminds us, "Two of Jones' wins were against amateurs, fer chrissakes!"

Woods had set the table for his slam by winning the 2000 U.S. Open, Open Championship, and PGA Championship. Although he was threatened at Augusta that day, most notably by David Duval and Phil Mickelson, who pulled within two strokes with six holes to play, Woods made a closing statement on the 13th tee. He activated a shot he'd been practicing all week but had kept to himself. Woods called it the "high sweeper," a hard draw that would suit the 13th hole's famed dogleg left in the event that he was being pursued. "I had to pull it out," said Woods. "I had to step up and aim another fifteen yards farther right and hit that big slinger around the corner to give myself a chance." Woods executed the shot to perfection and called it a slam.

"It is special. It really is," Woods said after donning his second Green Jacket. "To win four [majors] in succession, it's just hard to believe.... Some of the golfing gods are looking down on me the right way."

Has there ever been a better putt? In the past twenty years? Hell, in any twenty years, has there ever been a putt like it?

It's one thing to make a putt for first place in a tour event. Sure, there's a million bucks on the line, but the half-million bucks for second is a pretty nice consolation. At a Ryder Cup there's no money. No consolation. Just pride. Worldwide bragging rights.

They say nobody remembers who finishes second. In Ryder Cups they do. Sure, Europe's José María Olazábal had uncharacteristically bogeyed four of the preceding five holes to let Justin Leonard in, but with the match all even on the 17th green and the Ryder Cup in the balance, Leonard dropped a bomb on his wobbly opponent. His forty-five-footer, which Leonard had only hoped to get close, had a nose for the hole and incited a celebration that seemingly echoes still.

BEN CURTIS
2003 OPEN
CHAMPIONSHIP

Ben Curtis tees off on the 1st hole of the final round of the 2003 Open Championship.

In 1913, when word spread that a local kid from the wrong side of the tracks had won the U.S. Open, the refrain must have been something along the lines of, "Who?"

The same went for Ben Curtis, the invisible American who in 2003 won the Open Championship and, like Francis Ouimet ninety years before him, took home a title in the very first major championship he ever played in.

The win by the unassuming, doe-eyed twenty-year-old Ouimet in a playoff over titans Harry Vardon and Ted Ray is remembered as one of the greatest upsets of all time, but one can make a compelling case that Curtis' was even more earth-shattering. Yes, Ouimet was a twenty-year-old fledgling, but Curtis was only twenty-six. Ouimet was an amateur and knocked off two of the most cold-blooded professionals in the game, but in those early days of American golf, the amateur talent pool was comparable to that of the déclassé pros. And while Ouimet turned back Vardon and

Ray, Curtis bested a global field of contenders such as Vijay Singh, Thomas Bjørn, Davis Love III, and Tiger Woods, all of whom finished within two strokes of the lead. Curtis, who was in his rookie year on the PGA Tour and ranked 396th in the world, had never even played a links golf course until he teed it up at Royal St. George's.

Of course, Curtis had some help. No one who witnessed it will ever forget Bjørn's epic collapse on the final four holes, but Curtis could have backed up, too, and didn't. He was the only player among the top five finishers to break 70 on Sunday. His trip from unknown to major champion is reflected by the bookends of his Open experience. On Thursday, his first shot in major championship play was a sour duck-hook into the fescue. By Saturday night, as he was getting into bed, his fiancée asked him what he expected to happen in the next day's final round. His unruffled answer: "I'm gonna win."

Who?

PHIL MICKELSON
2004 MASTERS

"With the weight lifted, Mickelson can now focus on putting together a sustained run at greatness. Even with all the heartbreak, all these years, he has always been entertaining. But never, never more so than he was on this day. His finest hour. Among the finest the sport has ever known."

RICH LERNER

Coming into the 2004 Masters, Phil Mickelson had played in forty-two major championships as a professional without a victory. While Tiger Woods was cornering the markets in sterling silver and green sport coats, many wondered if Mickelson would ever break through. He'd come close before, painfully so, including seven top-ten finishes in the Masters alone, but no cigar. The 2004 tournament began on a sad note, with the news on Thursday morning that Tom Watson's famed caddie, Bruce Edwards, had lost his lengthy battle with ALS, but it ended on a high note, with Mickelson making birdie on five of the last seven holes, including a downhill thriller on the 18th, to beat Ernie Els by a shot. It was one small step for man, one giant leap (not so much) for Mickelson and his legion of fans.

Phil Mickelson celebrates with an exuberant leap after winning the 2004 Masters.

Tiger

It took golf four centuries to even imagine him.
Lean as a boxer. Stanford smart. Cool as the other side of the pillow,
and strong as a shark. It was worth the wait.

Nobody has ever driven it this long and this accurately. Nobody who's ever driven it so well has also had such sublime touch around the greens. Only a few have ever been this completely fearless on a golf course. Only a few have ever been so committed to perfection. Only a few have been so dramatically better than their peers. Only a few have been as mentally tough. Who compares? In some cases, only a few. In many other ways, nobody. **Absolutely nobody.**

RICH LERNER

By 1997, when he won his first Masters, Tiger Woods had become "the show," the focus of any tournament he competed in.

Can an athlete be bigger than his sport? Can one performer be so blessed with skill, charisma, and determination that he becomes a proxy for the very game he plays? If we assume that's possible, the list of performers who've transcended their sport is short. They were—and still are—iconic figures who so overshadowed their competition that their names have attained a time-defying cachet, a near-mythological status. Just three in the past half-century: Muhammad Ali, Michael Jordan, and Tiger Woods.

Tiger's fellow demigods were crystalline reflections of their game and the era in which they competed. Ali embodied and in large part shouldered the racial and social strife of the 1960s and 1970s. He also exemplified the modern conceit of athlete as entertainer. Jordan reflected the athleticism and versatility of the new age of hoops, one in which the confines of position play decreasingly applied.

By contrast, Woods was the antithesis of golf in the 1990s. The first thing that we noticed: He was black. His racial background may have presaged the demographic "browning" of America, but for most of his young life at least, Eldrick Tont "Tiger" Woods was a black kid in a white game. Although he and his father, Earl, often fed on the tension of race, the younger Woods actually took great pains to avoid being pigeonholed as black. Shortly after his stunning Masters win in 1997, Woods appeared on *The Oprah Winfrey Show*, and when asked by Winfrey about his race, he described himself as "Cablinasian" in a nod to his diversity of bloodlines (Caucasian, black, Native American, and Asian). He added that it actually bothered him when people described him as black. When, that same year, he turned down President Clinton's invitation to join him in New York to honor Jackie Robinson, many took it as a restatement of the fact that Woods did not see himself as black even though many fans—black and white—did.

Woods after sinking a birdie putt at 18 to win the 2009 Arnold Palmer Invitational at Bay Hill Club and Lodge.

Race is a huge part of the legend of Tiger Woods. It was of no obvious use on the golf course (other than as fuel for bigoted detractors and, ironically, as motivation for Woods himself), but even to civil fans of the game and unbiased observers of the sport, the color of Woods' skin amplified the revolutionary nature of the athlete within, this despite the fact that decades earlier players such as Pete Brown, Lee Elder, and Charlie Sifford had shattered the PGA Tour's racial barriers.

"He has this multiethnic appeal that's global," says Golf Channel's Brandel Chamblee. "It's mesmerizing. It seems every country in the world looks at Tiger and thinks he's theirs."

Woods' signature win, his 12-stroke romp in the 1997 Masters at the age of twenty-one, served as his introduction to broader fandom, but within golf circles, Woods had been on the radar screen for well over a decade. The product of an African American stage father, Earl, himself a good athlete who had taken up golf late in life, and a Thai-born Buddhist mother, Kultida, Woods was steered to the game before his first birthday. The first shot Woods ever struck was in the family garage on Teakwood Street in Cypress, California. Earl was hitting balls into a net with his toddler sitting in a high chair nearby. When Earl let his son out of the chair, the young boy took hold of a putter and set up in the mirror image of his

TIGER'S 10 BIGGEST MOMENTS

1978	First TV appearance on *The Mike Douglas Show*, plays with Bob Hope
1996	Wins third U.S. Amateur
1996	Professional debut: "Hello, world."
1997	Wins first Masters
1999	Nike "bouncing ball" ad
2000–2001	"Tiger Slam": U.S. Open, Open Championship, PGA Championship, Masters
2005	Chip shot at Masters en route to a victory
2008	Wins U.S. Open
2012	Passes Jack Nicklaus with 74 PGA Tour titles
2013	Wins five times; awarded eleventh PGA Tour Player of the Year title

father—as a left-hander. (Eventually, of course, he turned around and played as a right-hander.)

Earl knew he had something special on his hands when the toddler self-corrected his grip, took aim, and swung. In 1978, after being tipped off by Kultida, local sportscaster Jim Hill did a feature on the young phenom, assuring viewers that "this young man is going to be to golf what Jimmy Connors and Chris Evert are to tennis." He was not yet three years old. Additional jaw-dropping television appearances by the toddler on *The Mike Douglas Show* and *That's Incredible!* formed the foundation of his celebrity.

His father's compelling presence in his life and Woods' own interest and ability would prove the foundation for a towering life in the game. Of course, Woods was not unique in possessing a golf-loving father or even great skill. But Woods had an additional weapon that would threaten to make nearly every competition he entered an unfair fight: He starved for victory, and once obtained he washed it down with dominance.

Whether these were appetites encouraged by an obsessive father, fueled by the ever-growing expectations of his fame, or by Woods' own measure of himself, we'll never know, but by the time he was seven years old, Woods was on a certain path to greatness. By fifteen, he was playing to a plus-4 handicap. He would win every single meaningful title in the youth game and virtually every single meaningful title in the amateur game, wildly surpassing Jack Nicklaus' records. In 1994, while representing the United States in the World Amateur Team Championship in France, Woods attained Jerry Lewis stature. *L'Equipe,* France's sports daily, referred to him as "*Tiger la Terreur,*" while *Le Figaro* drew favorable comparisons to Mozart. No surprise that in 1994, when Tiger Woods was graduating from Western High School in Anaheim, California, he was voted Most Likely to Succeed.

Former touring professional and current Golf Channel analyst Frank Nobilo first crossed paths with Tiger Woods when the New Zealander and the California kid were both playing in the 1995 U.S. Open at Shinnecock Hills. Nobilo had heard about the amateur whiz kid and looked forward to checking out his game in Southampton. But when the nineteen-year-old withdrew early in the second round after wrenching his wrist on several shots from the infamously dense rough, Nobilo thought, "He can't be that good."

Nobilo next came across Woods a year later when the Open went to Oakland Hills. Woods had made his usual mockery of distance, hitting wedges into par-5s. One evening that week, Nobilo was on the practice tee. Another player slid into the slot next to him and began hitting away. It was Woods. Exposed now for the first time to the young phenom, Nobilo became a convert. "At the time, everyone was trying to hit drives like Greg Norman, like an airplane taking off," recalled Nobilo. "But Woods' ball flight was more parabolic, like a semicircle."

Standing with Nobilo was an equipment rep fully versed in the technology of the time. The rep said to Nobilo, "Man, he hits it long."

Nobilo responded by quietly questioning Woods' atmospheric trajectory. "I said, 'No, that ball is falling out of the air.'"

The rep then enlightened Nobilo, telling him that the low boring drive was a thing of the past, that when a ball comes off the face at 2,400 rpm, with a launch angle of 12.5 degrees at 125 mph of clubhead speed, it will fly higher… and longer.

"That was the first time that anybody had explained to me the physics of the modern ball flight," said Nobilo. "You knew he was different."

Tiger Talks Race
Golf Talk Live
December 18, 1996

TIGER: How many kids do you see at the ballpark or at the playground playing hoops who are of all different race? They gather everywhere and they just do it. I want golf to be the same way. It's such a great game, why limit it to just a few, when it can be enjoyed by all?

PETER KESSLER: *Do you remember it being tough and being treated as an outsider a little bit?*

TIGER: Yeah, I was always treated as an outsider. Because the community I grew up in was basically just a middle-class neighborhood, but it was a predominantly white neighborhood. We were the first and only [black family] for many years....

And we had a lot of problems, and I have been denied a lot of things just because of the color of my skin, whether it's at school, socially, or at golf. It's just the way it was, and it doesn't make it right. I have learned to grow with it or grow through it....

People think that because the Civil Rights Act that happened in the 1960s, they think it changed 180 [degrees], but in golf it didn't happen that way. In '61, Charlie [Sifford] broke the Caucasian clause. The tour then made it so [they were] no longer [open] tournaments, they made [them] invitational, so you only could be invited. That policy went on for years and years and years. Unfortunately, it has taken its toll on Charlie, Lee [Elder], and Teddy Rhodes, all African American players, and I owe them a big gratitude of big thanks because if it wasn't for them, players like myself or other minorities couldn't play this game....

I know from personal experience, I'll just briefly go into it. In 1994, in Southern California, I was kicked off a golf club because of the color of my skin.... Real briefly, I was hitting balls and Army guys were hitting balls as well. They were hitting balls [at a] house, and I was actually going in the opposite direction. And this guy phoned in the pro and said, "This little n___ was hitting balls at my house," and the pro comes screaming out there, accusing me of doing this. I said, "Hey, I'm not that bad of a player. I'm firing the opposite direction. How am I going to hit the ball straight over here to my left when it's behind me? If you're that stupid, open your eyes, bud." That incident was pretty tough, as late as 1994. People think that it has changed, but it really hasn't.

"Hello, world."

After a brief but stellar collegiate career in which he set school records for individual tournament wins (eleven), and captured the 1996 individual NCAA championship, Woods began contemplating dropping out of Stanford and turning professional. The decision was made in large part in July 1996 on the northwest coast of England, shortly after the Open Championship at Royal Lytham and St. Anne's. After carding a 66 in the second round, Woods went on to finish tied for twenty-second, good enough for low amateur honors and an indication that he had the stuff.

"I was still kind of iffy about whether I should turn pro or not," said Woods, "but that gave me so much confidence that I could do it at a high level, I could shoot those scores and I could play against the top players in the world on a very difficult track." If there was any doubt in Woods' mind, it was dashed weeks later when he won his third straight U.S. Amateur title, this time in dramatic comeback fashion over 38 holes against Steve Scott.

Hours after the fabled win, Woods told *Sports Illustrated,* "I had intended to stay in school, play four years at Stanford, and get my degree, but things change. It got harder to get motivated for college matches, and since I accomplished my goal of winning the NCAA, it was going to get harder still.... I always said I would know when it was time, and now is the time."

The man-child from Southern California, the lanky twenty-year-old who made long hitters twice his age feel inadequate, the college dropout who subsisted on a steady diet of video games, cartoons, and McDonald's, was about to reorder the golf universe, the sports universe, really.

Before so much as holing a putt on the PGA Tour, Woods signed what was reported to be a five-year, $40 million shoe-and-clothing contract with Nike. The shoe manufacturer that had ridden Michael Jordan to global dominance in basketball was now placing its chips on golf. Woods signed an additional deal to play Titleist balls and clubs, but it was Nike that most loudly trumpeted Woods' debut.

The toothily handsome SoCal kid who was now the darling of media companies from New York to L.A. took his first swings as a professional in Milwaukee. Whatever glitz Brown Deer Park GC lacked was more than made up for by the hype that accompanied Woods' first tour event. TV networks scrambled to air the Thursday and Friday rounds simply because Woods was in the field. At a press conference that Wednesday, Woods breezily, or perhaps naively, played along, beginning his first press conference as a professional with the words "Hello, world." Those two words just happened to serve as the theme in Nike's first Woods commercial, one which artfully underscored Woods' youth and interracial appeal.

The next day, when Woods was introduced on the first tee as a professional, the starter proclaimed that Woods was from Florida. Jeff Hart, who was paired with Woods that day, turned to Tiger and said, "I thought you were from California."

Woods' one-word answer summed up the entire surrealistic scene and the young man's hyper-maturation, at least in certain aspects: "Taxes."

In those early Florida years, before such visits would bring about DEFCON 1, young Woods would mosey over unannounced to Golf Channel's studios from his home in the nearby golf community Isleworth (also home to Joe Gibbs and to an Arnold Palmer–designed course). In addition to casually shooting the breeze with fellow golf lovers, Woods would set himself up in an editing suite and review old tape of major championships and their venues in order to prepare.

"Golf, as we know it, is over. It came to an end on a chamber-of-commerce Sunday evening in Las Vegas when Tiger Woods went for the upgrade: He's not just a promising young Tour pro anymore, he's an era."

GARY VAN SICKLE

Woods' affection and enthusiasm for Golf Channel—and, truly, for everything about the game—may have spurred his long-form appearances in the first years of his career. In December 1996 and again in January 1997, Woods sat down for hour-plus interviews on *Golf Talk Live*.

The buzz surrounding Woods' professional debut at Brown Deer diminished during the weekend as he slogged to a drab T-60 finish and an underwhelming inaugural paycheck of $2,544. The tone of comeuppance for the young whippersnapper was underscored by former PGA Tour star and two-time U.S. Open champion Curtis Strange, who interviewed Woods for ABC Sports. After Woods proclaimed that he always played to win, that second place "sucks," and that third place was "worse," Strange said, with more than a hint of condescension in his voice, "You'll learn."

Woods never did learn. Few recall that Loren Roberts won the tournament that week, but no one has forgotten Woods' fireworks. Whether it was his scene-stealing press conference on Wednesday or his crowd-pleasing ace at the 14th hole in the final round, that week in Milwaukee, Woods set a precedent that survives to this day: Whether he wins, loses, or misses the cut; whether he withdraws, DQs, or doesn't even show, Tiger Woods is the news.

The Show

"He did stuff no one else did, did stuff that was beyond belief," said Golf Channel's Rich Lerner. "He was unfathomable, so it was natural that we then followed every move. He was the show."

Tiger Woods brought a new level of intensity and presidential-level security to weekly PGA Tour events. Lerner compares him to a rock star. "He looked like Mick Jagger coming into Wembley Stadium, and it encompassed everything," he says. "It was Tiger getting out of the car—'There he is!' For about ten years this 'look at him' never really stopped."

Lerner recalls Woods' newsmaking ways during the 2005 PGA Championship at Baltusrol. As the second round played out, Woods was in danger of missing the cut in a major championship, something he'd never done. Of course, Woods would make the cut and finished tied for fourth. "But that was like the most exciting Friday in history," said Lerner. "His rare dicey Friday was as good as anyone else's Sunday."

Woods' goal in that rookie summer of 1996 was to earn an exemption onto the 1997 PGA Tour. He had two possible routes. The first was the nerve-racking path that most aspiring tour professionals reluctantly take: Sign up for the six-round PGA Tour Qualifying School, or Q-School, survive that most pressure-packed of gauntlets, and earn unfettered eligibility for all 1997 PGA Tour events. Sounds easier than it really is.

The second option, one not even imaginable for most young players, was to obtain the maximum number of sponsor's exemptions (seven) into 1996 PGA Tour events and either win one—which would result in a two-year pass into all PGA Tour events—or earn enough overall money to land a spot in the top 125 earners. That would guarantee him a spot on the tour for 1997. Given his star power, Woods would easily get the exemptions other young players could only drool over, so he chose the second option. (Few realize that Woods did send in his entry fee for Q-School that year as a precaution.)

Even with all of Woods' success as an amateur, there were doubters in the

After Woods proclaimed that he always played to win, that second place "sucks," and that third place was "worse," Curtis Strange said, with more than a hint of condescension in his voice, "You'll learn."

Tiger on *Golf Talk Live* with Peter Kessler December 18, 1996

PETER KESSLER: *Everybody, including you, expects you to win. It's OK when you expect you to win, but what about the outside pressure? Does that add or make anything more difficult or any less fun for you to play the game?*

Woods and his friend Mark O'Meara during a *Golf Talk Live* appearance.

TIGER: My father has always taught me one thing. He says, "Don't ever live your life for anyone else but yourself." I said, "Why?" He says, "If you ever get caught up in people's expectations of yourself, then you will never be a human being, you won't ever live for yourself." That doesn't mean you're very selfish or anything like that. That just means that whatever your goals internally are, you strive for those because only you know what you can and can't achieve. You go for them, and if you do accomplish your goals, it's amazing the self-worth that you feel when you achieve these things.

wake of his failure to win in Milwaukee. Earl Woods, who'd nonchalantly assured the golf media that if his son was given entry to seven PGA Tour events he'd surely win at least one, was looking more like a salesman than a father. Then, six weeks after turning pro, Woods did it. He beat Davis Love III, then one of the tour's biggest stars and longest hitters, in a sudden-death playoff to win the Las Vegas Invitational. Woods had some help when Love fizzled down the stretch, but Tiger, who started the final round four shots off the lead, carded an 8-under-par 64 on Sunday. His game plan would prove familiar to his victims for the next two decades and lead to his utter domination of professional golf: Thoroughly digest the par-5s. In Sunday's final round, he hit irons into all four of them, eagling one and birdieing the other three.

The Woods we've come to know over the past twenty years, the biggest, longest, coolest, toughest player ever, was born that day at TPC Summerlin. Veteran golf writer Gary Van Sickle may have summarized the proceedings best. "Golf, as we know it, is over. It came to an end on a chamber-of-commerce Sunday evening in Las Vegas when Tiger Woods went for the upgrade: He's not just a promising young Tour pro anymore, he's an era."

The 1997 Masters

Tiger Woods' 1997 Masters really began in 1996. For starters, it was Woods' stunning performance on the tour in his rookie summer of 1996 that assured him a spot in the tournament.

Secondly, it was at the 1996 Masters, his last as an amateur, that he received an unexpected stamp of approval from the very two men he was trying to supplant: Jack Nicklaus, the greatest player of all time, and Arnold Palmer, the most popular player of all time. After playing a practice round with Woods, Nicklaus assessed his heir's future in terms that were somewhat expected and yet still stunning considering the source. "Arnold and I both agreed that you could take his Masters titles [four] and my [six] Masters, and add them together, and this kid should win more than that," said Nicklaus.

In pure heft, the words ranked up there with the compliment paid to Nicklaus himself some three decades earlier when the Golden Bear's idol, Bobby Jones, was asked to comment on Nicklaus' own astounding 9-shot win in the 1965 Masters. "He plays a game with which I am not familiar," drawled Jones.

In that 1996 Masters, Woods, perhaps feeling the weight of Nicklaus' imprimatur, missed the cut. His return trip in 1997 didn't start out very promisingly either. He bogeyed the first hole. In fact, his front-nine 40 had a lot of observers writing him off, until he countered it with a dazzling 30 on the back.

Gene Sarazen may have fired "the shot heard round the world" in the 1935 Masters, but he didn't do it on live television and on the cusp of the digital age. On that Thursday afternoon in 1997, it was the impossibly lithe young Woods who pushed Sarazen and every other player from the past into the margins. He fired the opening salvo in the nascent battle between a new generation of long-hitters and the unsuspecting golf courses that would host them. When Woods hit driver-wedge into the revered 15th hole at Augusta on Thursday, he put the field, the course, the entire sport on notice. The metrics by which the game had long been measured had lost their relevance. Hitting a wedge into the green on 15 was a little like running the mile in three minutes...backwards. If his tension-free swing and the resulting ball flight hadn't seduced us, if the sound at impact had not sounded

Woods with the giant check after his first tour victory at the 1996 Las Vegas Invitational.

Woods was mobbed by the media at his first pro tournament, the 1996 Greater Milwaukee Open.

so sweet, we might have thought the show gaudy, but Woods' performance that week was the most mesmerizing moment golf had ever known.

While his former classmates at Stanford were on spring break, Woods trailed by three after Thursday. But by sunset on Saturday, Woods led by a positively demeaning nine shots. Colin Montgomerie, at the time the finest player in Europe, was in a flabbergasted group twelve shots back. He put it quite matter-of-factly when he was asked by a math-challenged scribe whether or not he still felt he had a chance. "There is no chance," said Monty. "We're all human beings here, and there's no chance humanly possible that Tiger Woods is going to lose this tournament. No way."

The suspense had been drained from the Masters and replaced with unadulterated human drama. It wasn't a nail-biting, three-footer-for-birdie drama, because the final round wasn't really even golf. It wasn't even sport. It was part walk in the park, part coronation, part audiovisual aid for the reality impaired. Here you had the youngest winner ever of the Masters winning by the largest margin ever recorded and with the lowest total score ever tallied. Over four days in the spring of 1997, a game that had been played for four centuries evolved right before our eyes. With every step, every swing, and every fist pump, with every fiber of that Smithsonian-worthy red sweater, Woods was telling us that not only was the 1997 Masters over, the game as we knew it had ceased to be. That metamorphosis was underscored near dusk, when the British veteran Nick Faldo, who had the previous year won the last of his three jackets, placed on the muscular shoulders of the young American rookie his first of four.

Historians will note that there was one genuine battle fought that day, a pitched contest for second place among Tom Kite, Tommy Tolles, and Tom Watson. Kite

"This young, talented player goes out in 40 [on the front 9], and we dismissed him very, very quickly. Then it became a record-setting performance. It's arguably one of the best 63 holes of golf ever played in a major championship."

FRANK NOBILO

Nick Faldo helps Woods don his first Green Jacket at the 1997 Masters.

held the duo off to pick up the silverware awarded annually to the runner-up. Kite seemingly knew that on that day—and perhaps for decades to come—the field was playing for second. After his anticlimactic finish, he cheekily told assembled reporters, "I won *my* tournament."

Tiger Slam 2000-2001:
2000 U.S. Open, 2000 Open Championship,
2000 PGA Championship, 2001 Masters

A decade and a half later, it's difficult to fully capture the emotions of the world at the dawn of a new century. We still lived in the naive comfort of a pre-9/11 world. Whatever fear we felt was mostly inspired by the passage of time and compounded by a Y2K panic that proved more neurosis than threat. For years leading up to January 1, 2000, futurists and technophobes alike fueled concerns that the inner workings of the digital-industrial complex would be unable to process the change from 1999 to 2000, and the gears of the modern wired world would grind to an apocalyptic halt. Or not.

But 2000 did validate a few predictions. Tiger Woods, who had for his first three and a half seasons on tour met ridiculously high expectations, actually began to exceed them. Through May 2000, Woods had been playing professional golf for three and a half years, and he'd won two major championships. Not too shabby, but slightly short of messianic. Bubba Watson won just as many majors in a shorter period from 2012 to 2014. Make no mistake, Woods was dominating the weekly tour events, but not the major championships. Coming into the 2000 Players Championship, Woods had won ten of his past seventeen tour starts, but "only" two of his last twelve majors. In fact, during the 2000 Players, veteran tour player Hal Sutton, then thirty-nine and emerging from a slump, did the unthinkable: He took on the notion that Tiger was unbeatable. Sutton led wire-to-wire that week, and the only other player who had a chance was Woods. But from his pre-tournament comments right through Sunday, Sutton tried to pierce what he might have described as the irrational exuberance surrounding Woods. "I can beat him," said Sutton. "I did beat him. Last time I played with him I beat him." He then went on to beat him by a shot to win his second Players.

Coming into the Masters, Woods was the prohibitive favorite. But sloppy driving and a cold putter led to an impressive but disappointing fifth-place finish. As he looked ahead to the next major championship—the U.S. Open at Pebble Beach—Woods, who'd been tweaking his swing, could not have been confident. That led to a pretty intense week of preparation leading into Pebble, including three days with his then instructor Butch Harmon in Las Vegas and a focus so intense that Woods blew off the memorial ceremony honoring the previous year's winner, Payne Stewart. Whether it was heartlessness, hard work, or the focus, it paid off. If it's safe to say that Woods obliterated the field in his 1997 Masters romp, then he humiliated the field at Pebble. NBC's Roger Maltbie summed up the tournament, during the live broadcast with a line that became famous: "This is not a fair fight."

For most of his adult life, Woods had been pursuing and rewriting records written in the 1960s and 1970s. When he won the 2000 U.S. Open, fellow competitors were turned to stone, and sportswriters were turned into archivists, futilely flipping through media guides and record books to find some sort of historical context for the slaughter. There was none. The only guy who came close was Old Tom Morris. He won the British Open by thirteen shots with the old featherie ball, which Golf Channel's David Feherty describes as "a badger's testicles filled with seagull feathers." In 1862. To underscore the sense that times were changing, this was Jack Nicklaus' final U.S. Open. In fact, in a poetic bit of stage direction, the USGA had Nicklaus wrapping up his day as Tiger was beginning his. On a golf course that Nicklaus had often said was his favorite, the sixty-year-old Golden Bear went out in style. On Friday, his last-ever hole in U.S. Open competition, Nicklaus reached the par-5 18th in two shots. It was a last gasp from a generation that had inspired Woods and was now being consumed by him.

"Woods had a par putt late in the final round," remembers Rich Lerner. "He was already leading by 100, but he grinded over that putt as if he was tied for the lead. It epitomized Tiger at that moment in a way that none of his mind-blowing shots ever could because it revealed this will, this refusal to even for a moment accept anything less than excellence. Woods was standing on the shores of Pebble Beach, and the rest of the field was in rafts off the coast of Australia."

Woods set course for the season's next major, which just so happened to be slated for the Old Course at St. Andrews, home of the recently trod-upon grave of one Old Tom Morris. For a golfer with even a glancing appreciation for history, St. Andrews is the great cathedral of the global game. It's *the* must-play for anyone who calls himself a historian of the game and its courses. For world-class competitors, it's often been said that in order to be considered a great player, you must win at St. Andrews.

Woods arrived in the Auld Grey Toon with an impressive résumé: a twelve-shot Masters win in 1997, a one-shot PGA Championship title over upstart Sergio Garcia (in 1999), and, most recently, one shiny U.S. Open trophy (probably should have given him two) from Pebble Beach. Suddenly three discussions arose among the game's chattering class: First, with a win at St. Andrews, Woods, who was only twenty-four years old, would complete the career Grand Slam, something Nicklaus didn't do until he was twenty-six. The second discussion built on the first. If Tiger won the Open Championship, could he keep it going, win the PGA Championship at Valhalla, and then, who knows, go on to win the Masters in April 2001? Third was this question: If he did all of that, what would we call it? These were hyper-hypothetical discussions. No one had ever won four modern professional majors in one calendar year. In 1953, Ben Hogan came close with his famed "Triple Crown." He won the Masters, the U.S. Open, and the Open Championship, but in a wacky quirk of fate, the 1953 PGA Championship was scheduled for the same weekend as the British. Even Hogan couldn't manage to play on two continents at once.

The point is, slams don't happen. Discussing them is about as tethered in reality as looking up supermodel Kate Upton in the phone book. This is the extent to which observers of Tiger Woods had become crazed as the 2000 Open Championship approached: They were scrambling for the best way to describe a feat that had never occurred and almost certainly never would.

While the scribes hunted for new descriptives ("Slamapalooza" was a personal favorite), Woods was focused. He knew that St. Andrews played into his unique strengths far more than any major championship venue. Most of the trouble at the venerable Old Course comes in the form of bunkers—many of them recently deepened in a feeble effort to Tiger-proof the old place. They're located, on average, about 270 yards off the tee. The course also features firm, small greens. Woods, who could easily carry the bunkers off the tee, would have a huge advantage over the field. In a preview of the Open for *Golf World,* Michael Bonallack, the secretary of the R&A, golf's governing authority outside the U.S. and Mexico, said, "If Tiger Woods does not win the Open this year, there ought to be a steward's inquiry."

The stewards could relax. Woods wouldn't score worse than 69 all week. The rough summer for Old Tom Morris continued. Woods decimated the poor guy's Open scoring record by six shots. Woods had muscled another record book and another shiny trophy, the famed claret jug, from the field. These were not surprises. By now, the shattering of records set during the Lincoln presidency was old hat for Woods. But what set this win apart, what will make it stand out (forever?), was the surgical insouciance with which Woods dissected the game's grandest test. All these years later, Scottish golf fans, the most knowledgeable and least impressionable on earth, are still shaking their heads over the fact that in his first Open Championship at the ancestral home of the game, Woods played seventy-two holes under the toughest conditions and against the finest field of the year and never once played a shot from a bunker. St. Andrews is bunkers. Like most great links-style golf courses, it lays on a natural sand bed. The bunkers here are like neighbors. They have names from an *Our Gang* episode: Hell, Principal's Nose, Road, Spectacles. They are a key defense against par. Consider David Duval. During Sunday's final round, Duval climbed into semi-contention against Woods, but the four shots he needed to extricate himself from the Road bunker did him in. For Woods to play a record-setting seventy-two holes and not even step in one was like winning the Kentucky Derby without ever leaving the paddock. It can't be

The eight-week stretch of golf played by Tiger Woods between June and August 2000 was simply the greatest exhibition of skill the game had ever seen.

2000 Canadian Open

Tiger Woods

Final Round

Just for the record, there are some people who don't necessarily believe this shot belongs on this list. Golf Channel's Brandel Chamblee is one of them. "I happen to know that he pushed it," argues Chamblee. Most observers, however, will rank it top 20-worthy when they consider the context: final round, final hole, par-5 fairway bunker, 216-yard carry, all water, a one-shot lead over Grant Waite, and Waite was already on the green in two. "I had already hit mine on the green," said Waite, "and I remember thinking to myself, 'Let's see what he can do.'"

With Waite looking at a possible eagle, Woods had no choice. "Grant forced my hand, " said Woods. "He was a guaranteed birdie, if not possible eagle....Since he put the ball on the green, I had to go for it."

Waite stood watching with his caddie as Tiger made his move. "I said, 'This ball's going right at the flag,' and what can you say," said Waite. "I mean, to have the mindset, the poise, the calmness inside his body to be able to make that swing and hit that shot, you know, just shows you where he's got such an advantage on probably the rest of the players."

Woods' shot landed about twelve feet past the hole and came to rest in the right-rear fringe. He later critiqued the shot. "I didn't hit the green, I hit it over the green," said Woods, with a twinkle in his eye. "So it wasn't really that good."

Maybe Chamblee was right.

done. "Everything you thought never would happen now was in play," said Lerner. "Four straight, eighteen majors, nothing was impossible."

From the sea-soaked history of Pebble Beach and St. Andrews, the Tiger Woods Magical History Tour took a turn inland. The Valhalla Golf Club outside Louisville hosted the 2000 PGA Championship. Woods, who was only twenty-four years old, was still maturing as a player. In fact, after four years as a professional, Woods claimed he was still acclimating to the rigorous cycle of major championships.

"When I grew up playing junior and amateur golf, there was only one tournament a year that you wanted to win; that was either the U.S. Junior or the U.S. Amateur. Those were the only tournaments. You peak one time a year," said Woods. "But when you turn professional, it's four; you have to peak at four different times.... I'm starting to understand what I need to do to get ready for each one; what it requires, mentally and physically, emotionally.... Each year I have gotten better at getting ready and peaking for majors. It is just a matter of learning a little bit more and, hopefully, I can keep repeating the process."

Woods' pairing at Valhalla was made for TV. Tiger, who was now on track to rewrite a record book authored by Jack Nicklaus, would play alongside the Golden Bear for the first time ever in competition. The pairing was a microcosm of the duo's relationship: Young vs. Old, Now vs. Then, Ohio vs. California, digital vs. analog, black vs. white. Each step Woods took on the 7,167-yard, Nicklaus-designed track was another attack on Nicklaus' historic flank.

The outing would prove to be Nicklaus' final appearance in the PGA Championship, an event he'd entered thirty-seven times and won five. Woods was playing in only his fourth PGA and was en route to his second win. Poetic

"It revealed this will, this refusal to even for one moment accept anything less than excellence. Woods was standing on the shores of Pebble Beach and the rest of the field was in rafts off the coast of Australia."

BRANDEL CHAMBLEE

Woods takes a swing at the U.S. Open at Pebble Beach, the second stop on his "Tiger Slam."

Woods tees off on the 18th hole at St. Andrews en route to a victory at the 2000 Open Championship.

that Woods' record win at Pebble two months earlier came in Nicklaus' final U.S. Open. The youngster's attempt at a third consecutive major championship win would take place in the very shadow of the man who'd most recently done just that, the man Woods was so driven to dethrone.

The final hole on Friday provided Shakespearean drama. The Old Man, beloved and respected, hobbled by age and injury, was under siege from a young challenger for whom it all appeared too easy. In defiance of Time, the Legend summoned the strength for an object lesson in pecking order. Needing eagle to make the cut, Nicklaus' sand wedge from seventy-two yards hit the green, spun backwards, and briefly considered Nicklaus' mandate. Alas, the ball rolled quietly by. Nicklaus' 77-71=148 missed the cut by an inch. He was going home. Meanwhile, Woods' rounds of 66-67=133 had him alone in first place and on a trajectory to eclipse his pairing partner as the greatest player the game had ever known.

Come Sunday, Woods, who'd been compared to deities such as Jones and Nicklaus for most of his young life, was making a serious bid for the third leg of what was now being described as the "Tiger Slam." (It couldn't be a Grand Slam, since the four majors weren't lined up in the calendar year. A distinction for the ages.) The only man standing between Woods and that bid was not Phil Mickelson or Sergio Garcia or Davis Love or Fred Couples or any of the other stars of the day. It was Bob May. No, the other Bob May. There are two. One was an actor who stood inside the robot costume in *Lost in Space*. He was the better-known Bob May. *This* Bob May spent his childhood picking balls off the range at Big Tee Golf

Center in Buena Park, California, for the privilege of hitting them back out again. Every Sunday, May's father would drive his son an hour to Los Angeles for a one-hour, 7 a.m. lesson with legendary instructor Eddie "the Little Pro" Merrins. At sixteen, May became the youngest player ever to qualify for a PGA Tour event when he gained entry into the 1985 Los Angeles Open. (Years later, Woods would play the L.A. Open at sixteen as well, but on a sponsor's exemption.)

"Unknown" is a strong word for a guy with May's competitive background; "unheard of" may be more like it. As it turned out, the only guy at Valhalla that week who knew anything about May was Woods. They'd known each other back in junior golf. In the 1980s, May, who is about seven years older than Woods, was the dominant player in California junior golf. Woods idolized him. "I just wanted to hopefully one day win as many tournaments as he did," Woods later said.

Woods entered the final round with a one-shot lead over May, and the duo comprised the final pairing. Most contenders who play alongside Woods on Sunday of a major championship get splattered. But May, a virtual unknown who to this day has never won a PGA Tour title, earned the respect of millions around the world when he faced down the game's most intimidating player. Both played brilliant golf—each shot 31 on the back nine Sunday with no bogeys. Woods carded an impressive 67, but May cheered journeymen everywhere when he answered with a cool 66 to force extra holes.

That year, the PGA of America had instituted a new playoff format for the championship: three holes (16, 17, and 18), aggregate score. The situation, the principals, the amount of history that lay in the balance, even the dappled Kentucky sunlight, made it one of the most memorable three holes ever played. Woods, who seemed to feed off the energy of the moment even more than May,

CALLER: Tiger, I'm 13 and you're one of my role models. I was wondering how you stay so consistent?
TIGER WOODS: How did I stay so consistent? I guess one reason is I have the fire and the drive. I would never quit, and I would never [accept] failure. I would always learn from my failures and apply them later. I think that's the key. That's how you can stay consistent. If you could learn from every round that you play, whether it's a weekend round with your buddies or after school or in a tournament, if you can learn from each and every round something, then you can always apply that later when you really need it.
GOLF TALK LIVE

TODAY ❂ THRU 15 ❂ TOTAL

❂ PGA CHAMPIONSHIP ❂

TODAY	LEADERS	HOLE	TOTAL
E	WOODS	15	E
E	MAY	15	E
	PLAYOFF		

ABOVE: Woods celebrates his putt during the playoff round of the 2000 PGA Championship.
LEFT: Woods' approach shot on the first hole of the final round of the 2001 Masters.

eked out the victory, but May made him earn it. Afterward, Woods described it as "one of the greatest duels I've ever had in my life."

Woods had now won three straight major championships. Could he win a fourth? It's been said that a good Notre Dame squad is the best thing that can happen to college football. Success for the Irish gives their legion fans something to root for and their legion detractors something to root against. Same for Woods and golf. The phenom now stood on the edge of uncharted greatness. In the eight months to come, golf households all over the world would engage in debates about calendars, metrics, and semantics. All winter long, sportswriters and pundits would invoke Bobby Jones, Hogan, and Nicklaus. It was all up for debate, but what was never in doubt was Woods' supremacy. The eight-week stretch of golf played by Tiger Woods between June and August 2000 was simply the greatest exhibition of skill the game had ever seen.

So what would it be: Grand Slam? Great Slam? Pretty Good Slam? Near Slam?

Words matter, of course, but deeds matter more, and what Woods was about to do at Augusta National mattered far more than anything the pundits had to say. A win would mean four professional majors in a row, backwards, forwards, up, or down, no matter how you counted or discounted them.

Woods' opening round 70 was solid if not spectacular. He'd played worse golf at Augusta, notably his sloppy 40 on the front nine in 1997, and surely this student of Nicklaus knew that the Golden Bear had won in 1986 despite a 74 on Thursday. Even if Chris DiMarco was at the top of the leaderboard early, Woods remained in touch, trailing by only two on Friday night.

On Saturday, Woods logged a 68 and climbed into the lead. The only clear contenders come Sunday morning were David Duval, Ernie Els, and Phil Mickelson. As Woods emerged from the clubhouse that afternoon to make his way to the first tee, his mother, Kultida, was standing two feet from the doorway. You couldn't miss her. Woods' focus was so deep, his blinders so firmly strapped on, that he walked past his own mother without even noticing her. "He was gone already," said Golf Channel's Lerner. "Wherever Tiger went mentally so that he could do the things he did, he was already there."

Aside from Duval's impressive 67, the group put little pressure on Woods. Duval crept within three shots but never made a legitimate charge. The Slam arrived with a whimper, not a bang.

The world knew on that Sunday afternoon, as Woods approached the 18th green, that he was walking irrevocably into a new level of celebrity. He holed his fifteen-foot birdie putt to win by two strokes over Duval. As Mickelson, who was paired with Woods that day, prepared to finish his own round, Woods walked to the side of the green and pulled his Nike cap over his face to hide the tears. It was an emotional acknowledgment that he had done the impossible. He had carved out a niche in golf history that will probably never be equaled. "I don't have any more shots to play," realized Woods. "I'm done."

"I don't give a damn whether they count it as a slam or not," said Feherty. "It's the single greatest achievement in golf history and arguably the single greatest achievement in the history of sports."

They used to throw ticker tape parades. Both Jones and Hogan had them after their respective dances with immortality. Woods got a call from President Bush.

> ## "I don't give a damn whether they count it as a slam or not. It's the single greatest achievement in golf history and arguably the single greatest achievement in the history of sports."
> DAVID FEHERTY

Woods celebrated securing the 2001 Masters with his by then trademark victory fist pump.

2001 Players Championship

Tiger Woods

Third Round

Three years into his professional career, young Tiger Woods had already completed the career Grand Slam. His place in golf history had been excavated and the cement poured. But there was still the odd matter of the Players Championship. Major? No. Major-ish? Definitely. The PGA Tour's own championship was the only significant title that had to date avoided Woods' sticky grasp.

On the strength of a final-round 66, Woods notched his first Players win by bypassing Jerry Kelly and outlasting Vijay Singh and Bernhard Langer over the rain-addled final two days. But it was his birdie putt on Saturday at the 17th hole where Woods made history and declared his intentions. His sixty-foot snake of a putt on one of the most dynamic greens in all of golf was accurately and famously described by NBC Golf analyst Gary Koch: "Better than most!"

Every star has "that one." That spectacular fusion of physics, kinetics, and timing that becomes the go-to refrain for every autograph seeker and interviewer. Woods' list of candidates for "that one" is longer than any active player's. But no shot has ever been more viewed, more emailed, more talked about than his chip onto the 16th green during the final round of the 2005 Masters.

Woods came to the 16th leading Chris DiMarco by one shot. As the final twosome walked up to the 16th green, DiMarco had a makeable birdie putt, while Woods had missed the green long and left, leaving himself a very difficult chip. It was about thirty feet to the hole. The green broke severely right and back toward him. It was a bad leave at a bad time. "You're not supposed to hit the ball over there," said Woods. He was facing a possible bogey.

Woods' objective was not so much to hole it as it was to get his chip inside DiMarco's ball. "If I can get inside Chris, even if Chris makes it, I can still make my putt to be tied for the lead," explained Woods.

Woods aimed about twenty feet left of the hole and left the rest to Isaac Newton. The ball slowly tracked down and to the right. "All of a sudden, it looked pretty good," said Woods. "Then all of a sudden it looked, like, really good, and it looked like how could it *not* go in, and then how did it not go in...."

The ball, a Nike in case you hadn't noticed, stopped on the lip for a few seconds of discounted global marketing before dropping softly, like Danny Noonan's birdie bid on the final hole at Bushwood in 1980. "Somehow an earthquake happened and it fell in the hole," said Woods with a wink.

"It was the perfect combination: the magnitude of the stage, the intensity of the duel, and the style of the shot," says Kelly Tilghman. "It had flair. It required skill and creativity and willpower for the ball to take that last little baby turn, the logo flashes, and it drops."

And Augusta National called Tom Fazio to activate the panic button. It was time to proceed with the Tiger-proofing that had been in the planning for some time. Then-chairman of Augusta National, Hootie Johnson, announced on the eve of the 2001 tournament that the club planned to make "significant" changes before the 2002 Masters. Asked how many yards might be added to the course, Johnson responded tellingly, "All we can."

Most every great golf course has made some accommodation to technology and/or distance over the years, and Augusta has made dozens of changes over the decades. For instance, in 1999, not long after Woods barnstormed to his first Masters title by hitting driver-wedge into the famed 15th hole, the club reduced that hole's fairway mounding and planted pine trees both left and right to tighten the landing area. But the changes to Augusta after 2001 were even more widespread: sixteen changes in total, adding approximately 270 yards in length. Woods won again in 2002, becoming only the third player to win back-to-back Green Jackets. Other changes followed, but Woods won again in 2005.

2008 U.S. Open at Torrey Pines

Woods is the dominant figure in the past twenty years of golf. He's dominated not only on the golf course but also off. He dominated by both skill and intimidation; he dominated in dollars and in sense, in wins, in ratings, in endorsements won and lost and won again. By any measure he is not only the straw that stirs golf's global drink, but he's the ice, the gin, the tonic, the lime, the glass, the coaster, and the table it sits on. He's dominated fanhood, too, often ranking both among the most beloved and the most reviled of sports figures of our time.

From the time Woods began to nip at the heels of Jack Nicklaus' records, he cleaved the golf world in two. On the one side, to generalize, were the younger fans, some avid golfers, many not, and followers of other sports who only began to consider golf when they recognized that Woods was the lead story on *SportsCenter* four nights a week. On the other side were the Jack partisans. They tended to be older,

> **"It was as if Tiger had been sitting around thinking, 'OK, what haven't I done? Hmm, let's see, I haven't won a major on one leg. Let's see how this goes.'"**
>
> RICH LERNER

whiter, more khaki than crimson. Ironically, their fealty to Nicklaus was not unlike their own fathers' loyalty to Arnold Palmer when young Nicklaus was the upstart.

The dynamic began in August 1996, when Woods passed Nicklaus' total of two U.S. Amateurs, and has continued since unabated, save for a few days in 2008. That's when it all changed. For four days that June, Woods healed the game's great schism with an unadulterated show of guts. For more than a decade, Woods had beaten his opposition with superior skill and focus. That's what favorites are supposed to do. Combine Woods' seemingly breezy domination with his failure to win a single major championship in come-from-behind Sunday charge fashion, and one can see how Woods had become pigeonholed by his own record as a front-runner. The wins kept coming, but to some doubters and deniers, Woods always had something more to prove.

Two days after the 2008 Masters, Woods, then thirty-two, underwent arthroscopic surgery on his left knee. It was the second such procedure in five years, and Woods' third left-knee surgery overall. (In 1994 he had a benign tumor removed.) The recommended recovery period wiped out much of Woods' spring schedule and put his competing in the U.S. Open at Torrey Pines, a course on which Woods had won eight times as a professional, in doubt.

But Woods wasn't about to miss a major. As Feherty, who is a commentator for CBS as well as for Golf Channel, says, "The guy would find a way to stick the club between his ass cheeks and clinch it" to play in the U.S. Open. A few days after the procedure, Woods began working with physical therapist Keith Kleven. The two found a balance between Woods' preferred "all out" rehab style and Kleven's more cautious approach. Between workouts and watching his daughter toddle around the house, Woods slowly set his sights on the National Open. By the time the Memorial came and went without him in the field, Woods knew he was ready. The doctors weren't so sure. With little regard for doctor's orders, he returned to Torrey, a beloved childhood hangout, and flinched, winced, and lurched his way into contention. The pain was apparent, searing the knee after impact on virtually every full swing. Even teeing up the ball or picking up a used tee was a tax on Woods' left leg. Woods, who had never had any use for excuses, gutted it out. That alone was impressive. Had Woods limped backwards on Saturday, the world would have understood. Instead, he grimaced his way to the third-round lead.

Woods not only eschewed excuses, he refused to manufacture a swing that might have been less painful, saying, "If pain hits, pain hits. So be it. It's just pain."

The world knew that Woods was recovering from the April arthro, but the truth would come out a few days later.

In Sunday's fourth round, he hobbled to a 73, but his cool, clutch putt on the 72nd hole forced a playoff with Rocco Mediate. That Mediate was in a playoff for the U.S. Open was news enough. Here was a jumpy, balding forty-five-year-old Pennsylvanian who unquestionably led the league in loquaciousness, but had more missed cuts than top fives in major championships. In fact, Mediate, who'd missed eight of ten cuts earlier in the year, was best known for becoming the first player to win on the PGA Tour with a long putter in 1991.

Mediate was ranked No. 158 in the world, 157 slots behind Woods. But you wouldn't have known it judging by the galleries. For one day in the decades-long reign of Tiger Woods, Rocco Mediate was the most beloved player in the world.

"Rocco was so popular and so likable," said Golf Channel's Kelly Tilghman. "He had enough of a name that people knew who he was and knew what a great guy he was, and people rooted for him. For most of Tiger's career, people rooted for Tiger. He was the dynasty. He was Michael Jordan or the Lakers. He was that guy. Rocco was the perfect foil for him from a rooting standpoint. That's what made that playoff stand out."

On paper, it was a colossal mismatch, but Mediate was more than game. After Woods holed his tying putt on Sunday afternoon he walked over to Mediate, who'd been watching in the wings, and said, "We have a game tomorrow."

Mediate replied, "Yeah, I'll see you in the morning, big man."

The two then cornered the market on ice for their swollen, aching bodies.

The USGA is the only one of the game's major championship-sanctioning bodies that still breaks a 72-hole tie with an 18-hole Monday playoff. It's undoubtedly a hassle. Players, TV people, fans, media, volunteers all have lives, and a Monday playoff can cause havoc for thousands. But if ever there was evidence in support of the format, it was the finale staged on Monday, June 16, 2008.

"It was as if Tiger had been sitting around thinking, 'OK, what haven't I done,'" said Lerner. " 'Hmm, let's see, I haven't won a major on one leg. Let's see how this goes.' "

Mediate was thirteen years older, and his back problems had been well documented. There was no facet of the game in which he could best Woods. Save for a sense of humor. When Mediate got dressed that Monday morning he had only one clean shirt left. It was red. Tiger red. As Mediate walked up to Woods on the practice tee to say good morning, Woods looked him up and down and said "Nice [*expletive*] shirt." As Mediate wrote in his 2009 book, he responded to Woods, saying with a smile, "I thought you only wore red on Sundays."

There seemed a certain fatalism in Mediate's laugh track. It wasn't unlike Lee Trevino's nervous snake routine before he and Jack Nicklaus did battle at Merion in 1971. Only underdogs need humor, right? But Trevino won that day.

"Rocco was using Everyman tactics to get inside Superman's head," said Tilghman.

Apollo Creed led by three after the opening nine on Monday. Rocco Balboa

Nicklaus and Woods during a practice round at the 1996 U.S. Open.

A Rocky Road to 18: Tiger vs. The Bear

Childhood dreams have a head start on reality. How many of us at ten years old fully expected to play centerfield for the Yankees? When Tiger Woods was growing up in Cypress, California, he was too young, too gifted, and too dedicated to know just how presumptuous his dream was. In his bedroom was a poster of Jack Nicklaus and a list of the Golden Bear's record eighteen major championships. The kid's goal: Jump the Bear.

Will Woods ever surpass Nicklaus's record in major championships? In 2008, Frank Nobilo thought it was a sure thing. He remembers:

> On Golf Central's *Live From...* we used to play Tiger vs. the Field early in the week. I would always take the Field and that night Kelly and Brandel took Tiger, and I said, "You're crazy. The game's too hard." I just couldn't get my head around 10 for 10, and I certainly couldn't get my head around the prospect of 11 for 11. Lo and behold, Tiger won. I thought from that point on that it was a foregone conclusion.

For him to be so clear-minded to make the right shots and the great putts and not be scared of failure, I just came to believe that it was a done deal and there was only one thing that could ever stop him: the unthinkable. Nothing's ever sure in an athlete's life, but he was the closest thing to a sure bet.

Woods was thirty-two years, five-and-a-half months old when he captured the 2008 U.S. Open at Torrey Pines, his fourteenth major championship. By the same age, Nicklaus had only eleven majors to his credit. But the comparisons between Woods and his idol were apples and oranges, Tiger and Bear. They always assumed a happy and fulfilling off-course life for Woods as well as the same modicum of physical health enjoyed by Nicklaus. Neither would be the case. In fact, Hall-of-Fame golf sage Dan Jenkins wrote in 2001, "Only two things can stop Tiger—injury or a bad marriage."

Since winning that 2008 U.S. Open, Woods has seen twenty-six major championships, a wife, several ligaments, some cartilage, a disc, and several sponsors come and go without a win. Nicklaus' longest major-less streak was twenty. Woods is not only battling Nicklaus, he's battling his own body.

The fact that Jack's body won a major at forty-six and Tiger's seems to be running out of gas at thirty-eight is cautionary.

Tiger has been pounding golf balls mercilessly since he was three. The repetitive stress injuries we're seeing now are no surprise.

It's not just the pounding, it is also the way he's done it, the swing itself. Watch Jack's swing in his prime. There's very little stress on the front leg because Nicklaus had a way of bowing out his left knee—his kneecap facing the target—to ease the strain. Then look at Tiger in his prime. Woods spent years hyperextending his left knee—posting up with his kneecap facing perpendicular to the target line—to derive maximum power. This source of endless *oomph* is now a source of endless *ouch*.

Jack himself recently admitted that he could have worked harder during his career, but other pursuits and family often got in the way. Unlikely that Tiger could have worked any harder, on course or off. A workout fanatic, Woods had been known early in his career to work out two or three times in one day. During the 2000 U.S. Open at Pebble Beach—the one he won by fifteen shots—there was a rain delay that forced most contestants into easy chairs in the clubhouse. Woods ran six miles. This is the same guy who in 2007 asked to join in Navy SEAL training. It's been widely reported that the underlying injury to his knee was actually sustained during this endeavor.

"I still believe he has a great chance to break Jack's record," says Tilghman. "It's sad that Tiger has lost so much time, but I think he's so focused as an individual that he still has plenty of time—a good forty majors left in the tank—to make it happen. That's plenty of opportunity for him to spark something. Say he wins the 2015 Masters. Boom, all of a sudden he's at fifteen. Everyone's going to come back onboard. It's just going to take that little spark."

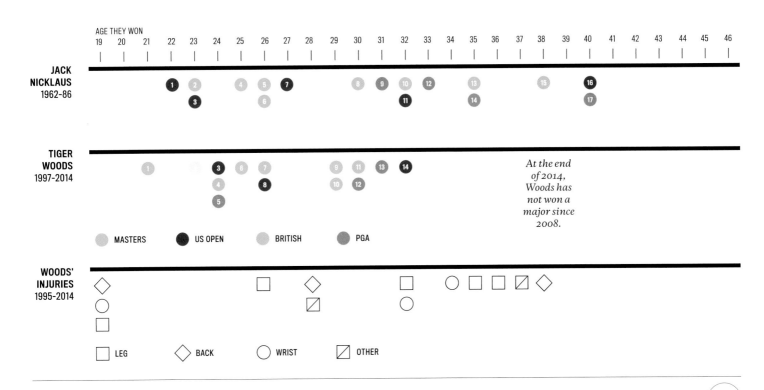

Unrivaled: Tiger & Phil

Ali-Frazier was a rivalry. Yankees–Red Sox is a rivalry. The Hatfields and McCoys is a rivalry. A genuine rivalry requires certain ingredients. Friction is helpful. The second element is obsession. In the minds of genuine rivals, the rivalry transcends the competition at hand. Nicklaus-Palmer is the greatest rivalry golf has ever known. Nicklaus has said that the two icons' obsession with beating each other often led them to lose sight of the match.

Third, you need a record. Ali and Frazier only went head-to-head three times. Two of them were for the heavyweight championship of the world. One man prevailed.

Does Tiger and Phil qualify? No question they are the biggest personalities in world golf over the past twenty years. In the mid-1990s, during his formative years on Tour, Mickelson seemed destined to be the world's dominant player. Then Woods came along. One can argue that Woods' co-opting of the global game hurt Mickelson more than any other professional golfer. How many more titles would Phil have won? It's hard to say, but a dozen seems low. Beyond trophy theft, there's the obvious difference in their personal style. Mickelson

oozes good cheer, and much like Palmer did, he willingly engages with fans and galleries. Woods, save for his wild, showboat swings from deep rough and his fist-pumping celebrations, can seem a joyless figure during competition.

There have been some kerfuffles. Remember in 2003 when Phil described Woods' Nike equipment as inferior? Or in 2008 when Tiger's then caddie Stevie Williams was quoted as saying: "I wouldn't call Mickelson a great player, 'cause I hate the prick"? Or re-run the tape of the 2004 Ryder Cup when in a fit of tone-deafness Hal Sutton paired them in the first match on Friday morning. It was like watching Cain and Abel play in the backyard.

But Woods-Mickelson lacks major heat. In 72 major championships since the 1997 Masters, Tiger-Phil have finished 1-2 only once, at the 2002 U.S. Open, and that was a virtual dud.

Woods held the No. 1 ranking for 683 weeks, more than thirteen years. Mickelson never got there. As much as we may have wanted a Tiger-Phil tension-fest, there wasn't one to be had.

"There were some real duels, but everybody—Phil, Ernie, Vijay—was always on the receiving end," says Frank Nobilo.

clawed back to lead after the 15th hole. At that point Mediate reflected on a conversation he'd had with Paul Azinger the previous day. Azinger's tidbit: When you regain the lead, don't be shocked.

"In the playoff I thought the same thing: 'When you get the lead, don't be shocked, run with it,'" said Mediate. "All of a sudden I'm 3-down, then I go to 1-up in five or six holes. But I was ready for it. I kept trying to make him play."

Mediate led by a shot with one hole to play. Reports came in from around the country; people were gathering on the streets, watching TV in store windows and clogging airport bars to see the finale. After seventy-two regulation holes and seventeen playoff holes, golf's heavyweight, the man who had completed his 500th week as world No. 1, was on the ropes. Still, Woods reached the par-5 18th green in two and two-putted for birdie. Mediate could only eke out a par after missing a twenty-foot birdie putt that would have won him the U.S. Open. The format now shifted to aptly named sudden-death. They teed it up on the 7th hole, and after Mediate pulled his drive into a bunker and failed to hit the green in two, it became clear that he and fate were going their separate ways.

"Great fight," said Woods as the combatants embraced on the 91st green.

The man who hadn't even played eighteen holes since April had hobbled through ninety-one holes in obvious pain. It was one of the great spectacles the game has ever staged. Tommy Roy, longtime executive producer of golf for NBC Sports, says the 2008 U.S. Open, for which he and his team won the Emmy for live sports special, ranks right up there with the 1999 Ryder Cup miracle as the twin peaks of his broadcasting career. As dramatic as the script was, Roy doesn't doubt for a minute that Woods' feature role was the key.

"I would certainly say that if it was another athlete doing that, I'm not necessarily sure we would have won the Emmy," says Roy. "Even with the same drama and situation and an injured leg and playoff, if it's someone other than Tiger, we might not have that Emmy." In fact, at the end of Saturday's riveting telecast, Roy sat back and told his colleagues, "Imagine if that was a final round," only to see Saturday outdone by Sunday's dramatics. "The next day we got it topped by Tiger having to make birdie on the 72nd hole to force the playoff, and we did nail it on that putt and capturing his emotional reaction and the crowd's going absolutely ballistic, and Rocco back in the scoring area saying, 'I knew he'd make it.' It was pretty good stuff."

All week Woods had deflected opportunities to bemoan his condition or make excuses. After the Championship, he mentioned that he planned to take some time off, and when asked if the coming month's Open Championship was his next event, Woods coyly said, "I hope so."

Then came the following exchange:

Q. Did they tell you, though, that (if you played here) you could further injure it, Tiger?

Tiger Woods: (Nods head affirmatively.)

Q. Yes?

Tiger Woods: (Nods head affirmatively.)

Q. Did you?

Tiger Woods: Maybe.

We should have known. All week, Tiger's then coach Hank Haney had been telling media behind the scenes that he was unable to reveal the truth about his client's leg, but what he *could* say was this: "When you guys find out, you're not going to believe it. You have no idea how tough this guy is."

Days later, the sports world learned the painful truth: Woods had played in

2008 U.S. Open

Tiger Woods

Final Round

"Pretty amazing," says Golf Channel on NBC commentator Roger Maltbie, who counts Tiger Woods' birdie at the 72nd hole of the 2008 U.S. Open as one of the most memorable moments he's had covering Woods for the past twenty years.

"I was behind the green," said Maltbie. "You stand there, and you know that every single person watching, a) wants him to make it and, b) fully believes he's going to make it, and you know as a player that most players in that situation wouldn't make it. That's a big ask. Sure enough, he pours it in, and [NBC golf anchor] Danny Hicks called it: 'Expect anything different?' The answer of course is no! Nobody did. Everybody expected that putt to go in. It's unbelievable when you really sit down and think about it."

The fifteen-footer forced an eighteen-hole playoff, and then a sudden-death playoff, which Tiger won by a stroke.

"**Hats off to Rocco Mediate. He was just about to put together a fairy-tale ending. But, as we know, Tiger does not do fairy tales. He is in the cold business of winning major championships.**"

RICH LERNER

"It was just, it was horrific."

"It's going to be my actions over time. I'm trying to become a better person each and every day. The proof in the pudding is over time, and that's what I'm trying to do."

Kelly Tilghman: Tiger, you've been a master of control your entire life. How did things get so out of control?

Tiger Woods: Going against your core values, losing sight of it. I quit meditating, I quit being a Buddhist, and my life changed upside down. I felt entitled, which I had never felt before. Consequently, I hurt so many people by my own reckless attitude and behavior.

KT: Were there moments you thought you should stop, but didn't?

TW: Yeah, I tried to stop, and I couldn't stop. It was just, it was horrific.

KT: For a man who's so disciplined physically and psychologically, why couldn't you say no?

TW: I don't know. Now I know. It's part of what I learned in treatment. Being there for forty-five days, you learn a lot. You strip away the denial, the rationalization, and you come to the truth, and the truth is very painful at times,

and to stare at yourself and look at the person you've become…you become disgusted.

KT: You went from becoming recognized as the greatest golfer in the world to becoming a punch line. How did that make you feel?

TW: It was hurtful, but then again, you know what? I did it. I'm the one who did those things, and looking back on it now with a more clear head, I get it. I can understand why people will say these things, because you know what? It was disgusting behavior. As a person, it's hard to believe that was me looking back on it now.

KT: America was concerned when the world's greatest golfer was lying on the ground with no shoes at 2:30 in the morning, bleeding. What happened that night?

TW: It's all in the police report. They investigated it, and they have it on public record. There's a lot of stuff between Elin and I that will remain private, and that's about it.

KT: How did you crash the car?

TW: I wasn't going very fast, but unfortunately, I hit a few things.

KT: If your father were here today and looked back on these last four months, what would he say to you?

TW: He'd be very disappointed in me. We'd have numerous long talks. That's one of the things I miss. I miss his guidance. Wish I could have had his guidance through all this to have him help straighten me up. I know he would've done it.

KT: What do you think he would say?

TW: Can't say it on air, but he would've been very direct. Basically said, "You need to get your life headed in the right direction again."

KT: For the twelve-year-olds and the parents out there who looked at you as a role model, what do you have to say to them to make them believe in you again?

TW: It's going to be over time. It's going to be my actions over time. I'm trying to become a better person each and every day. The proof in the pudding is over time, and that's what I'm trying to do. I will continue to do that.

KT: Based on all that has transpired, what do you want your legacy to be when all is said and done?

TW: Just like I wanted before. I felt that golf was a vehicle for me to help a lot of people. My dad had always said something that I never really quite understood until these times. In order to help other people, you first have to learn how to help yourself. Going into a treatment center for forty-five days, I learned a lot. I learned how to help myself, and that's the way I can help others down the road.

and won the U.S. Open with a ruptured anterior cruciate ligament (ACL) that had been hampering his left knee for more than a year. Furthermore, he had a double stress fracture in his left tibia or shinbone, the latter likely caused by an intense rehabilitation program fueled by his insistence on playing at Torrey Pines. Woods, who could have undergone the ACL surgery in April when he had the cartilage cleaned out, had postponed the procedure because it carried a long recovery time. He would have missed the Open at Torrey Pines, and so would have we.

Real heroes sacrifice life and limb for others. It's a stretch to describe playing golf for millions of dollars, even in pain, as a heroic act. But what Woods did that week was inspiring, perhaps the gutsiest major championship win since Ken Venturi's dance with death in the 1964 U.S. Open (when he almost collapsed from severe dehydration). Woods gave the world an object lesson in determination and perseverance. He did the impossible that week. Sure, he won on one leg, but in doing so he humanized himself and glorified the game we love.

————

As these words are written, it's been six years and two months since Woods' win at Torrey Pines. What a long, strange trip it's been. Woods' body has been battered by age and his reputation tarred with personal problems. Gallons of ink and gigabytes of data have been spent analyzing his swing, his game, his mind-set, his relationships, and his entire anatomy. The bottom line: We don't know. He showed glimpses of the old self in 2013 when he earned PGA Tour Player of the Year honors (for the eleventh time), but it wasn't the same. At this point, Tiger winning tour events (he won five in 2013) is the essence of underwhelming. As he approaches his fortieth birthday, we know it's all about eighteen majors, and he knows it's all about eighteen majors. The rest is wrapping paper.

Maybe the quest for eighteen did end for Tiger on that 91st green at Torrey Pines. If so, there are worse ways to go out. Hank Aaron batted .229 in his final season. Joe Namath's last pass was an interception. If Woods' last major came on one good leg, in the shadow of his childhood innocence, on a verdant, breeze-blessed expanse of familiar cliffside, would that be so bad?

Woods in the rough on the first day of the 2014 Open Championship. He was sixty-ninth in his second tournament following back surgery.

The Course

*Golf architecture has seen a dramatic return to a
minimalist philosophy that defined the
very first courses: "Less Is More."*

Pinpointing the turning point for golf architecture over the last twenty years is not a simple matter. A number of restorations, new course designs, and provocative writings awakened the golf world to the merits of nature-based, lay-of-the-land design after two decades' worth of big, brawny, and branded "championship" courses. The exact origin of the spark is not important. What matters most is that the recent shift in tastes has set golf architecture on a path to a sensibility harking back to the game's most timeless designs, characteristics, and sustainable playing values.

GEOFF SHACKELFORD

Jack Nicklaus, one of the most influential golf course designers of the era, sketching out Baha Mar in the Bahamas.

"I don't think there's anything really new in golf course design. We've been designing and redesigning golf courses for something like five hundred years, and I think we've pretty much covered it all." Those are the authoritative words of Jack Nicklaus, one of the most prolific golf course architects working today.

He's right. The fundamental elements of golf course architecture are pretty constant, but the underlying philosophy behind their deployment has undergone an enormous evolution. Today, players are enjoying the beauty and challenge of a new approach to course design, one that both harks back to the Golden Age (1910 through World War II) and earlier, and that stands in sharp contrast to the Age of Big Golf. That was the bygone 1980s and 1990s, during which designers were struggling to keep up with demand. The in-boxes of Nicklaus, Tom Fazio, Rees Jones, and others were clogged with requests for the biggest, longest, or toughest course in _____ (fill in your state or country).

The fruits of the Big Golf era are courses such as Hallbrook CC in Leawood, Kansas, designed in 1988 by Tom Fazio to be the hardest golf course in the state. Another example is the mind-bendingly difficult Ko'olau GC near Honolulu. Opened in 1993 and designed by Richard Nugent and Jack Tuthill, the course is reputed to be the toughest in the nation. In fact, when the USGA sent a rating team to assess it, they suggested a slope rating of 152. Dean Knuth, who at the time oversaw the USGA's handicap and course rating system, couldn't believe that a course could be that hard. He assessed it himself and did change the rating: to 162.

So what has changed? First, overbuilding. In 1988, the National Golf Foundation estimated that the United States would need to open a golf course per

Some describe today's trend as "minimalism," others as an outright return to the Golden Age of course design.

day for the entire decade of the 1990s in order to sate the demand of retiring baby boomers. This seemed far-fetched until the industry actually exceeded that goal in 1999, opening 398½ golf courses (in eighteen-hole equivalents). But rather than spread the new courses over the breadth of the country, the bulk of the development was in a few markets.

Second was the financial collapse that began in 2008. Financing for big, long, tough real-estate–driven-golf courses dried up overnight. Soon, more courses were closing nationwide than opening. Course design firms pared staff, and some simply closed their doors.

Third, the era's architectural trends—very long courses, target golf—that pushed the elite player eventually frustrated the higher handicapper. Acclaimed Canadian golf course designer Ian Andrew argued that frustration has been expressed in reduced participation in recent years. While 3.7 million people took up the game in 2013, 4.1 million golfers quit, a net loss of 400,000 players. "We moved so much dirt, and golf was becoming so hard and long and time-consuming, that people kind of lost interest," said Andrew.

Maybe it was time to go in another direction. It might have been a general feeling that courses had gone too far. Maybe it was a by-product of environmentalism. Or perhaps it was nothing more than the inevitable change of tastes and styles that seems to wash over the sport every generation or two. Whatever the reason, the era of course architecture that began in the late 1990s and early 2000s harked back to the great designs of the Golden Age and brought in a breath of fresh, links-style air to the sport.

If the Golden Age had three main characteristics, they'd be, first, that the great courses from Shinnecock to National Golf Links of America to Winged Foot to Pebble Beach were designed as core golf courses. That is, there was no real estate component, no houses to sell. Second, because most Golden Age courses were built before the wide availability of diesel power, there was a limit to what developers and designers could do in terms of shaping the land. Third is the emphasis on options. A great Golden Age course afforded the player, whether highly skilled or not, various ways of playing a given hole. A perfect example is the famed Cape hole at National Golf Links. A short par 4, even for the early 1900s, the Cape doglegs left around an inlet of Bulls Head Bay. How much of the inlet a player wants to try to carry off the tee and how much he'd like to contend with on his approach is entirely his decision. Both options offer risk and reward as well as...fun.

If the current era has anything in common with the Golden Age, it is the core principle that "Less Is More." Less movement of earth, less emphasis on residential real estate, less investment in a clubhouse. Less reliance on difficulty and yardage. And in many cases, less need for water and chemicals and less maintenance. Some describe today's trend as "minimalism," others as an outright return to the Golden Age of golf course design, a time when the limits of earth-moving technology put more emphasis on finding the golf course within the land as opposed to laying one on top of it. Whatever you want to call it, we're in it.

"The modern view of golf course architecture was that you present a challenge. In its most basic form it's the Golfer vs. the Architect," said Andrew. "Whereas

Coore & Crenshaw's design for Sand Hills Golf Club in Nebraska helped start a new era of golf course minimalism.

when you look at the classical origins of golf, it was more about finding your way and deciding on options. What we are running into right now are architects who have started to put aside the idea of direct challenge and difficulty—the buzzwords of the previous generation—and who are looking more at creating something that's fun. And what they're trying to do now is give the golfer the ability to choose their own route or pick their own level of difficulty by building a different style of golf course. It's the Golden Age revisited."

Golf course design is a big tent. Unlike baseball fields and tennis courts, each golf course is a creative work of imagination and strategy with influences both overt and subconscious. Nicklaus may have had it right—there's nothing new in golf course architecture—but the following golf courses and architects have surely had an outsize influence on the state of the game, nudging it back to the future.

The Most Influential Golf Courses *of the* Past Twenty Years

Sand Hills Golf Club
Mullen, Nebraska
ARCHITECTS: Coore & Crenshaw
OPENED: 1995
Private
YARDS: 7,089, par 71
SIGNATURE HOLE: 17th, 150 yards, par 3

The evolution back to minimalism started quietly, virtually unnoticed, in the windswept swales of central Nebraska. Dick Youngscap had developed Firethorn GC, a well-received Pete Dye golf course in Lincoln, Nebraska, in 1986. For Youngscap, the experience of building Firethorn deepened his desire to get closer to the linksy roots of the game. For golf's previous four centuries, "linksy" meant one thing: coastal. In fact, one of the defining characteristics of genuine linksland is that it is situated near the sea. But what Youngscap found in desolate Mullen, Nebraska (population 509), was wind-riddled, kettle-and-kame topography with perfectly sandy substrate. Farmers in the region had long known the land to be useless for raising either crops or cattle, so it had never even been plowed. That allowed Youngscap to acquire the land for only $150 an acre. He was buying perfect linksland without the waterfront premium.

He recruited the then-little-known design team of Bill Coore and Ben Crenshaw to lay out a private eighteen-hole golf course. Crenshaw has remarked that the hardest part of the process was deciding which eighteen holes to build, as the duo had identified 136 possible holes on the tract. The combination of the land and the delicate touch and impeccable eye of Coore-Crenshaw makes for one of the world's great "links" golf courses. (While not located near the sea, Sand Hills, with its sandy stratum—residue of long-gone bodies of water—is as linksy as any course in the world.) The palpable remoteness of Mullen helps make for an almost mystical golf experience.

The physical plant is minimal and exists only in service to golf (that said, the food and the wine list are superb). But the most telling aspect of Sand Hills' creation, and the one that inspired the current generation of minimalist-destination golf courses, can be found in the information booklet made available to visitors. Written in understated plain English, it reveals the secret sauce of the minimalist era:

"Fairways, greens, and tees were developed in 1994, using the following procedure: 1) mowing existing vegetation to ground level; 2) tilling all areas to a depth of 6'; 3) doing some minor finish grading on the greens—rough grading expense was less than $7,000—primarily with a small power rake; and 4) applying seed fertilizer and water."

To put all this in financial perspective: The cost to construct a green at Sand Hills was about $300. The average cost of a new putting surface built to United States Golf Association specs is about $40,000.

In the twenty years since Sand Hills opened its doors, the golf course has vaulted into the pantheon of America's most highly regarded layouts alongside much older, much more famous sandy-soil brethren such as Pine Valley GC and National Golf Links of America. In 1999, *Golf* Magazine called it "the greatest golf course of the last 50 years." The course fueled the trend toward spectacular, minimalist golf experiences far from cities and real estate developments. In fact, Sand Hills might be the most remote great golf course ever built. But more important, Sand Hills tapped a nascent desire in the twenty-first century golfer to draw closer to the roots of the game.

Bandon Dunes Golf Resort
Bandon, Oregon

ARCHITECT: David McLay Kidd
OPENED: 1999
Public
YARDS: 6,732, par 72
SIGNATURE HOLE: 16th, 363 yards, par 4

Bandon Dunes opened in 1999, four years after Sand Hills. It was not a copycat project, more a parallel project celebrating the same themes: simplicity, Golden Age design, and remoteness. The essential difference is that while Sand Hills is intensely private, Bandon, a resort, is open to the public.

Bandon owner Mike Keiser was an early investor in Sand Hills. He considered hiring Coore & Crenshaw for his first course on the Oregon coast but didn't want Bandon to be seen as an imitation. The job instead went to David McLay Kidd, a Scottish son of a greenskeeper. Kidd was only twenty-seven years old the first time he set foot on Keiser's raw property. His assignment was to travel back in time and build a genuine Scottish-style links course.

Coore & Crenshaw were eventually brought in to design Bandon Trails, the third of the four regulation courses that now comprise the resort; and its Preserve, a spectacular thirten-hole par-3 course. Each is a paean to long-ago links-style golf.

The Bandon Dunes course, famed for its Pacific vistas, earned the resort a reputation as the premier destination golf resort in the United States. But even as its spectacular sister courses Pacific Dunes, Bandon Trails, and Old Macdonald came on-line, the original course had no trouble holding its own. Its option-filled golf (the old-school run-up shot is almost always offered) and its beauty fulfill the promise of the resort's tagline: "Golf as it was meant to be."

Golf Channel travel guru Matt Ginella ranks Bandon as "far and away my ultimate buddy-trip destination, not just in the United States; it rivals St. Andrews in Scotland and the southwest coast of Ireland."

Augusta National Golf Club
Augusta, Georgia

ARCHITECTS: Alister MacKenzie and Bobby Jones
OPENED: 1933
Private
YARDS: 7,435, par 72
SIGNATURE HOLE: 13th, 510 yards, par 5

Augusta is the most influential golf course in the world because, as the annual host of the Masters, it's the most viewed golf course in the world. With an unlimited budget for greenskeeping and water management (the course is equipped with a SubAir system of underground fans that suck excess water from the turf), Augusta sets an unrealistic bar for the average club. Each spring, lush images of the Masters send local golf committees into paroxysms of insecurity over every brown patch of grass at their course.

As a club, Augusta is a cultural icon and a bellwether for the game. In 2002, when Martha Burke leveled charges of gender discrimination in golf, she targeted Augusta National, then the highest-profile all-male golf club in America. (In 2012 Augusta National welcomed two women as members.) The decision by Augusta and its chairman, Billy Payne, to extend an automatic invitation to the winners of the Asia-Pacific Amateur and South American Amateur will pay enormous dividends in two areas of the world that have tremendous potential for golf growth.

Yet it will always be as a golf course that Augusta wields most of its influence. Designed by the legendary Alister MacKenzie in consultation with Bobby Jones, the course remains a lens through which we can reflect on MacKenzie's Thirteen Principles of Golf Course Architecture:

1. The course should have beautiful surroundings.
2. The course, where possible, should be arranged in two loops of nine holes.
3. There should be a large proportion of good 2-shot holes, and at least four 1-shot holes.
4. There should be little walking between the greens and tees.
5. Every hole should be different in character.
6. There should be a minimum of blindness for the approach shots.
7. There should be infinite variety in the strokes required to play the various holes (with every club utilized).
8. There should be a complete absence of the annoyance and irritation caused by the necessity of searching for lost balls.
9. The course should be so interesting that even the scratch player is constantly stimulated to improve his game.
10. The course should be so arranged that [all levels of players can] enjoy the round in spite of...piling up a big score.
11. The course should be equally good during winter and summer, the texture of the greens and fairways should be perfect, and the approaches should have the same consistency as the greens.
12. There should be a sufficient number of heroic carries.
13. The greens and fairways should be sufficiently undulating.

Streamsong Resort
Streamsong, Florida
ARCHITECTS: Coore & Crenshaw (Blue),
Tom Doak (Red)
OPENED: 2012
Resort
YARDS: 7,176, par 72 (Blue), 7,148,
par 72 (Red)
SIGNATURE HOLE: 7th (Blue), 203 yards,
par 3; 16th (Red), 208 yards, par 3

"If you build it, they will come."

What started twenty-five years ago as a baseball man's fantasy has evolved into the traveling golfer's truth. Sand Hills and Bandon Dunes have long since proven that when it comes to "destination golf," quality trumps location. Still, when the Mosaic Company, which operates massive phosphate mines in the Sunshine State, announced plans to venture into the golf resort business in central Florida, whose golf industry had been brutalized by the most recent recession, some were dubious. Mosaic was beginning to face limits to its decades-long practice of harvesting central Florida's phosphate mother lode. Urbanization and environmental concerns were closing in. Meanwhile, endless acres of sand discarded in the mining process sat with no obvious future use in mind. In an attempt to derive revenue from the sandy soil, the company took a whack at golf.

Much has been made of golf course architecture's return to minimalism. In reality, the return to sand may be more accurate. There are many great golf courses built on parkland soil, but a preponderance of the great golf courses of the world have one thing in common: sand. The core of these linksy gems is sandy soil that supports flowing design, firm turf, and perfect drainage. What's more, since these sandy surfaces are most often found near large bodies of water, salt air and wind complete the trifecta.

Mosaic put the sandy wasteland to work. It hired Coore & Crenshaw to build one course, the Red, and Tom Doak to build the other, the Blue. The result is otherworldly. Imagine that Pinehurst No. 2 had been abducted by aliens, forced to mate with hoary Royal St. George's (think Maiden bunker), and their mounded, fuzzy, bumpy, sprawling offspring was laid out in a foreign-looking region. This can't be Florida, but it is.

Streamsong is the next evolution of minimalism.

Old Works Golf Club
Anaconda, Montana

ARCHITECT: Jack Nicklaus
OPENED: 1997
Public
YARDS: 7,705, par 72
SIGNATURE HOLE: 4th, 195 yards, par 3

The golf course industry has plenty of critics who deride it for the reckless use of natural resources. Not at this course. Old Works sits at the nexus of golf and sustainability. In an era when environmentalists can be critical of golf, the very existence of Old Works is a powerful response.

In the 1880s, this site housed a bustling copper mine and smelting operation. After a modern smelter rendered it obsolete, the site remained an idle eyesore and an environmental hazard until 1983, when it was identified by the U.S. EPA as a Superfund cleanup site. At the time, no Superfund site had been usefully reclaimed, but in 1989, local citizens formed a group to promote the construction of a "world class" golf course. Through unprecedented cooperation among the community, along with ARCO (the gas company that owned the site) and state and federal agencies—and a dazzling creative effort by Jack Nicklaus—the Old Works was reborn.

The existing property had to be essentially wrapped in a huge plastic bag to permanently prevent runoff of the harmful smelting residue. The property was also riddled with decades-old piles of black slag from the smelting operation. Once lab tests confirmed the slag was harmless, Nicklaus, out of curiosity, tested the surface for use as bunker sand. "To my amazement," he wrote years later, "it performed beautifully." The bunkers at Old Works are black as night, a visually stunning way to include the history of the mine in the golf course.

The golf course, with its wide, accepting fairways, is among the most popular in the state. And it reflects the maturity of its designer. Early in his career, Nicklaus was often criticized for designing golf courses that only he could play, meaning that because he played a fade, he intuitively designed courses that required a fade. By the 1990s, Nicklaus had long shaken off this predilection, and it shows at Old Works.

Oakmont Country Club
Oakmont, Pennsylvania

ARCHITECT: Henry Fownes
OPENED: 1903
Private
YARDS: 7,255, par 71
SIGNATURE HOLE: 18th, 484 yards, par 4

Oakmont has been influencing golf ever since the early 1900s, when its founder and designer, Henry Fownes, set out to build the hardest golf course in the game. But that's not why Oakmont is on this list. In recent years it has been enormously influential in agronomy, particularly among American parkland-style golf courses.

Trees can be lovely and useful things on golf courses, which is why so many clubs actually planted trees in the 1960s. But too many trees can suck the water out of the turf, prevent sunlight from getting through, and mute freshening breezes. This combination was quietly holding back thousands of great golf courses from attaining their optimum conditions.

Enter Oakmont. In the mid-1990s, the club began to restore the course to the original look and feel envisioned by Fownes. This required the removal of the many trees that had taken root in the intervening nine decades. At first the club's leadership, aware of tree-lovers among the membership, undertook the removals in secret,

cutting down trees between 4 a.m. and dawn. Members eventually caught on to the covert project, which would eventually remove well over 5,000 trees, but the clearing continued.

The new Oakmont debuted when the club hosted the 2007 U.S. Open. The shorn golf course received rave reviews from players, fans, and architecture critics alike. There had been tree-clearing programs prior to Oakmont's, but Oakmont's generated so much attention that other clubs—some well-known, others less so—began following Oakmont's lead. Today, as a result of Oakmont's leadership, hundreds of golf courses are in better condition. "I was asked a few years ago, what's the most important thing that's happened in the last ten years in golf course architecture," recounted ASGCA member Ian Andrew. "I said Oakmont. When they stripped out all the trees, it justified all the people like myself who work with old historic clubs. We started to get more leeway in tree removal."

**Trump National Doral
Golf Club
Miami, Florida**
ARCHITECT: Dick Wilson;
redesign by Gil Hanse
OPENED: 1962, redesign 2012
Public
YARDS: 7,288, par 72
SIGNATURE HOLE: 18th, 424 yards, par 4

In this day and age, if you love golf you've got to like a guy who is investing in a sport from which most others are running. Donald Trump now owns sixteen golf properties from California to the Caribbean to Scotland. His most recent acquisition was the spring 2014 purchase of Scotland's famed Turnberry Resort. Trump's unceasing efforts to land a men's major championship on one of his courses paid off in May 2014, when the PGA of America announced that the 2022 PGA Championship will be contested at Trump National Golf Club in Bedminster, New Jersey, and the 2017 Senior PGA Championship will be held at Trump National Golf Club in Washington, D.C.

The news came on the heels of Trump's purchase of and well-received changes to Doral and its legendary Blue Monster golf course. His hiring of Gil Hanse, one of the leading young minds in golf course design, showed a surprising understanding of the art. This was underscored in 2012 when Hanse was selected—over the biggest names in the

business—to design the Rio de Janeiro golf course that will host the game's triumphant return to the Olympic stage in 2016.

The rehabbed Doral debuted in the 2014 WGC-Cadillac Championship to rave reviews. Hanse estimated that his changes raised the tough-o-meter from a seven to a nine. Jason Dufner, 2014 PGA Champion, wouldn't disagree. "I think the changes make the holes extremely difficult compared to what they were," said Dufner. "In general, they have brought a lot of strategy into play on the golf course. This used to be a golf course where you grabbed your driver on every hole, swung for the fences, and played from there. You can't get away with that at Doral anymore."

Donald Trump was, for decades, golf's odd man out. Oddly enough, he is now one of the game's leading men.

The Old Course
St. Andrews, Scotland

ARCHITECTS: Several.
Daw Anderson and Old Tom Morris are
the most notable.
OPENED: 1552
Public
YARDS: 7,305, par 72
SIGNATURE HOLE: 17th, 455 yards, par 4

Sure, she's hundreds of years old, but that's precisely why she's so influential today. If you're not at least thinking of St. Andrews when you design your golf course, you're probably off track. In a recent essay for *Golf Inc.* magazine, Ian Andrew wrote about the influence that one round at the Old Course had on his own work. He'd played a round in strong wind and realized that the layout of the famed links did little to punish poor shots but rather did plenty to encourage smart play. "It's greatest asset," wrote Andrew, "was that it offered freedom to choose." Ever since, he added, "I've tried to provide the same freedom to choose in my own architecture."

The Old Course's influence stems in large part from her direct link to the ghosts of the game, legends such as Old Tom Morris, who ruled golf at the Auld Grey Toon in the mid-to-late 1800s, and his son, Young Tom. But the Old Course has a much more tangible link to modern golf and golf course architecture. In the early 1900s, Charles Blair Macdonald, who was born in Canada, attended Scotland's University of St.

Andrews before settling in the United States. Upon his return to Chicago, Macdonald realized that the States had nothing comparable to the Old Course. Around 1906, he set out to build his "ideal golf course" with two goals: to create a great golf course for his friends, and to import features and concepts from the great holes of Scotland and England so that these characteristics would take root and serve as models for future golf course design in the Americas. He succeeded on both fronts. The result of his efforts is the famed National Golf Links of America in Southampton, New York, several holes of which—notably the 6th, 7th, and 13th—draw directly from St. Andrews. National remains one of the great clubs in America and stands as the inspiration behind many of today's minimalist architects, most notably Coore & Crenshaw, who are leading the charge back to the Golden Age.

**Reserva Marapendi
Golf Club
Barra da Tijuca,
Rio de Janeiro, Brazil**
ARCHITECTS: Gil Hanse
and Amy Alcott
WILL OPEN: 2016

Course designer Gil Hanse, a former shaper for Tom Doak, assembled a portfolio of excellent redesigns and restorations before laying out the minimalist classic Rustic Canyon (with Geoff Shackelford and Jim Wagner) in California and Boston Golf Club and TPC Boston (the latter with native New Englander Brad Faxon). Hanse rose to greater acclaim in 2009 with his unveiling of Castle Stuart GC in Inverness, Scotland (codesigned by Mark Parsinen). The course was named the top new international golf course by *Golf* Magazine as well as Golf Course of the Year by Golf Tourism Scotland.

Hanse's seemingly inevitable rise to the status of "most influential golf course architect in the world" continued when he was hired by Donald Trump to renovate the famed Blue Monster at Doral. But Hanse will likely never have a project as significant as the recent design of Reserva Marapendi GC in Rio. The soft-spoken Pennsylvania native won the most hotly contested design job in history when he and Amy Alcott were selected ahead of a Who's

Who of global golf course architecture to design the course that will stage golf's long-awaited return to the Olympic Games.

The stakes are high for the course and for Hanse. A successful golf competition in the 2016 Olympic Summer Games will clearly benefit the sport, not only in South America, which has very low levels of participation, but around the world, particularly in growth markets such as China and India. That may explain why Hanse has planned a dramatic finish for his Olympic course: a short par 4, a short par 3, and a reachable par 5.

The National Golf Links of America
Southampton, New York

ARCHITECT: Charles Blair Macdonald
OPENED: 1908
Private
YARDS: 6,873, par 73
SIGNATURE HOLE: 17th, 375 yards, par 4

Since its founding in the early 1900s by Charles Blair Macdonald, the National has quietly and proudly reigned as the father of American golf course design. Macdonald, a Chicagoan by way of Canada, who studied for a time at St. Andrew's, realized upon his return to the United States in the 1870s that the few American golf courses existing at the time were inferior to the golf he'd enjoyed playing in Scotland. Eventually he set out to build the National, using the great holes of the United Kingdom as a model. National would provide recreation for the club, but just as important, in Macdonald's view, was his intention that it would serve as a template for future golf courses in the Americas.

The list of designers and developers spawned or inspired by Macdonald's magnum opus ranges from Seth Raynor (whose first involvement with golf came as Macdonald's surveyor at National) to Bill Coore and Ben Crenshaw, the dynamic design team of the current age, who infuse all they do with Macdonald's thinking. When Macdonald entered—created, really—the field of golf course architecture, it was at a time when most American golf courses were plain vanilla. Flat rectangular fairways were followed by motionless pancake greens. Macdonald brought risk and reward, strategy and intention to the art. While most of his golf courses are quite beautiful, they can all be described as fun. His exposure to the great golf courses of the United Kingdom in the late 1800s gave him a reservoir of knowledge that he routinely adapted to his course design projects in the U.S., leaving a trail of genius that is still revered.

National ascended to new heights of influence in 2013, when the club, which has operated very quietly and privately for more than one hundred years, welcomed the prestigious Walker Cup amateur competition back to the sandy shores of Peconic Bay. For the first time ever, eager aficionados of golf course architecture could see the famed layout on television.

Pinehurst No. 2
Pinehurst,
North Carolina

ARCHITECT: Donald Ross
OPENED: 1907
Semi-private
YARDS: 7,565, par 70
SIGNATURE HOLE: 18th, 453 yards, par 4

The American golfing public may seem a progressive lot, but golf is often more tethered to yesterday than tomorrow. The addition of a bunker or deletion of a tree can send howls of objections to the green chairman's office.

Tradition and expectation trump change and risk. Credit Pinehurst with overcoming that inertia. The No. 2 Course, a 1907 Donald Ross gem, spent a century at the apex of American resort courses. After the famed course hosted the U.S. Amateur in 2008, course owner Bob Dedman and course president Don Padgett held a review with the USGA's Mike Davis. "We felt like we'd become too much like everybody else," said Dedman. "It was wall-to-wall green. It was really monochromatic out there. I think it had become part of the homogenization of the game of golf. We lost the uniqueness of being part of this beautiful thirty-mile-wide, eighty-mile-long [stretch of] sand hills of North Carolina."

It was time to help restore the character Donald Ross intended. Dedman minimized the risk by hiring Bill Coore and Ben Crenshaw. They were

handed a three-point assignment: Make No. 2 more authentic. Make it more strategic. Make it more ecologically sustainable. Oh, and if you can land us some future USGA championships, great.

The most notable of Coore & Crenshaw's changes was the insertion of sandy wire grass into what had been rough. The trademark of U.S. Open play for the better part of a century had been impenetrable rough, but now players got a dose of local flavor when they missed the fairway: sandy scrub. Other key aspects of the redo are wider fairways and fewer heights of grass-cut for easier, cheaper maintenance. Today Pinehurst manages forty fewer acres of turf and has reduced its watering system by 700 sprinkler heads. "We spend a lot less on chemicals now," says Dedman.

And yes, the course did host another Open— two, in fact. In June 2014, No. 2 became the first course ever to host the U.S. Open and the U.S. Women's Open in back-to-back weeks.

Castle Stuart Golf Links
Inverness, Scotland

ARCHITECTS: Mark Parsinen and
Gil Hanse

OPENED: 2010

Public

YARDS: 7,009, par 72

SIGNATURE HOLE: 11th, 144 yards, par 3

If you think American golf course design is handcuffed by tradition, consider Scotland. Whether it's the musty halls of the R&A or the fact that a simple modernizing edit to the Old Course is treated like a high crime, the cradle of golf sometimes does less to nurture the game than to suffocate it. That's why Castle Stuart is so important. It showed students of golf course architecture on both sides of the Atlantic that new is not necessarily bad. In fact, Castle Stuart, codesigned by Gil Hanse and the developer Mark Parsinen, adds considerably to the Scottish Highlands portfolio headlined by the time-honored Royal Dornoch and Nairn.

Castle Stuart's influence lies in its seamless confluence of new and old. If the course has one trademark, it's the unusually wide fairways—seventy-five yards in places—but the width is rooted in one of architect Alister MacKenzie's dearest tenets: "There should be no single thoroughfare to the green." The width allowed Hanse and Parsinen to use distance as a wedge. Castle Stuart is designed to tempt and test the longer-hitting player, while giving the shorter hitter safer options. Parsinen likens it to a more uniquely American game. "As the three-point line in basketball mitigates the advantages of pure height, Castle Stuart's width of play mitigates the advantage of length off the tee by offering different lines of play with advantages to players of lesser length," he says. "We want our course to test your perceptual ability, decision making, and emotional poise. We want it to be more interesting and engaging than it is difficult."

Tobacco Road Golf Club
Sanford, North Carolina

ARCHITECT: Mike Strantz
OPENED: 1998
Public
YARDS: 6,554, par 71
SIGNATURE HOLE: 14th, 194 yards, par 3

When a course that's just over a decade old breaks the top fifty in *Golf Course Architecture* magazine's top one hundred global golf courses, one ought to pay attention. Students of golf course design will not be surprised that this headline-stealing layout was designed in 1998 by the late Mike Strantz, one of the most imaginative golf course designers of the past twenty years. Strantz began with an old sand mine that had produced material for ball fields and construction sites. Rather than lay out a classical Carolina-style parkland golf course, he crafted an otherworldly collection of mounds that were just too big and greens that were just too oddly shaped or too small or too shallow. The end result is a course that has been embraced by highbrow critics and is beloved by the everyday golfers who play it. It may be bizarre and even visually jarring, but the only word that really matters is the adjective most often applied: fun.

As fellow golf course architect Brandon Johnson wrote in a recent *Golf Course Architecture* review of the course: "This is the most fresh and unique twist or interpretation of golf course design I have experienced....The visual intimidation or 'play on optics' burned images in my mind that are still crystal clear almost ten years later. Truly a masterpiece."

Bethpage Black
Old Bethpage, New York

ARCHITECT: A.W. Tillinghast
OPENED: 1936
Public
YARDS: 7,468, par 71
SIGNATURE HOLE: 4th, 517 yards, par 5

If you played golf in the New York area in the 1970s and 1980s, you knew Bethpage Black. You knew—maybe you lived—the tale of parking overnight to get a tee time. You heard about the difficulty of a golf course that came with a warning label, an infamous sign on the first tee that reads: "WARNING: The Black Course Is An Extremely Difficult Course Which We Recommend Only For Highly Skilled Golfers."

Bethpage was the worst-kept secret in New York-area golf, but almost unheard of beyond the tristate region. It probably would have stayed that way if not for David Fay. In 1995, Fay, then the executive director of the United States Golf Association, paid an impromptu visit to Bethpage to answer a question: For all its downscale reputation, balding turf spots, and crowded parking lots, could it be a worthy host for the U.S. Open? In classic Bethpage tradition, Fay snuck on the course for a peek.

His answer: Yes. The bones of greatness remained. With some TLC and a full-on restoration by Rees Jones, Fay had no doubt that the Black could host a U.S. Open, and in doing so fulfill his dream to bring the national championship to a truly public course, where real public golfers played genuine public golf.

Fay and the USGA pulled it off; Bethpage hosted the 2002 U.S. Open, the first national Open since the terrorist attack on the World Trade Center. The top-five finishers that week were Tiger Woods, Phil Mickelson, Sergio Garcia, and Nick Faldo, and it's arguable that the 2002 U.S. Open was the most successful, affecting major championship ever staged. The legacy of what is now referred to as "The People's Open" is that public golf courses have been permanently added to the championship's unofficial rota. Of the ten U.S. Opens between 2008 and 2017, six have been or will be contested on courses anyone can play.

**The Shore Course
Monterey Peninsula
Country Club
Monterey, California**
ARCHITECTS: Robert E. Baldock and
Jack Neville, redesign by Mike Strantz
OPENED: 1961, redesigned 2003
Private
YARDS: 6,914, par 72
Signature hole: 11th, 181 yards, par 3

This coastal jewel, Mike Strantz's final golf course, may be his finest work. The original Shore Course, a slapdash low-budget affair designed in the late 1950s by Robert E. Baldock and Jack Neville, had a long history of drainage issues. It was also outshined by the club's sister course, the famed Dunes, designed by the legendary duo of Charles Blair Macdonald and Seth Raynor in the 1920s.

Around 2001, the club hired Strantz to transform the course. He conjured a new routing, removed acres and acres of tedious ice plant, and capped the property with a layer of sand to assure better drainage and ease maintenance. Strantz reimagined not only the forsaken land but his own work, too. His maverick use of mounding and bunkering (on his Tobacco Road golf course, nearly half of the greens require blind approaches) would not have worked here, and he knew it. His serene layout with broad fairways and more traditionally sized and shaped greens was a huge hit. He managed to install his usual array

of options off the tee and into the green, but he did so in a more subtle, classic manner.

"The Shore shows that a golf course can be more than redesigned. It can be fully reimagined," says Golf Channel contributor Geoff Shackelford.

Pebble Beach Golf Links
Pebble Beach, California

ARCHITECTS: Jack Neville and
Douglas Grant

OPENED: 1919

Public

YARDS: 6,828, par 72

SIGNATURE HOLE: 18th, 543 yards, par 5

Pebble Beach's 1919 layout, originally designed by Jack Neville and Douglas Grant but since rehabbed and tweaked by no fewer than a dozen men, is the king of America's resort courses. It's often been said that the Masters is the game's first official breath of spring, but for many, it's Pebble Beach and the old Crosby Clambake that coax the frozen faithful out to play temporary greens.

Pebble remains American golf's greatest seaside course. Its influence is immeasurable. When it hosted the U.S. Amateur in 1929, the course underscored the western migration of a growing game. After nearly a century, it remains the standard for oceanside golf. Jack Nicklaus, who redesigned the course's 5th hole in the mid-1990s, has often said that if he had one round to play, it would be at Pebble Beach. All that stature comes at a price. Eighteen holes here runs about $500, but for many, Pebble tops the bucket list.

"I have to put Pebble Beach at the top of the list," said Golf Channel's Kelly Tilghman. "It's a masterpiece from both a visual standpoint and a playing standpoint, but the great X factor for Pebble is that it's open to the public. I know it's pricey, but it's a slice of heaven on earth and anyone can walk through those gates if they save up. I love that about Pebble."

Whistling Straits Golf Club
Kohler, Wisconsin

ARCHITECTS: Pete Dye and Alice Dye
OPENED: 1998
Public
YARDS: 7,790, par 72
SIGNATURE HOLE: 17th, 223 yards, par 3

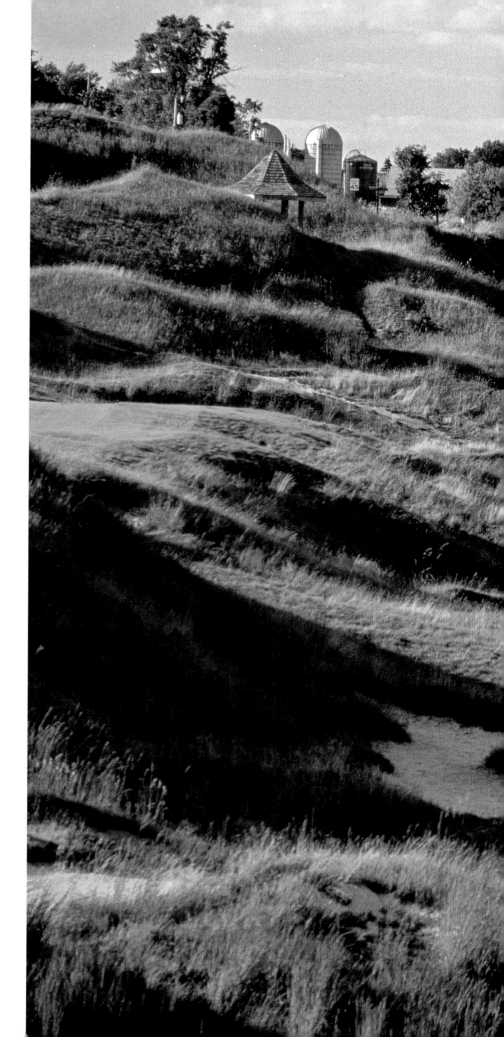

When this Pete Dye design opened for play in 1998, it was a stunning departure from anything the modern game had ever produced. We had seen world-class golf alight in out-of-the-way places (Sand Hills). We'd seen homages to the great golf courses of the United Kingdom (National GL). We'd even seen a great Pete Dye–designed golf course in Kohler, Wisconsin (Blackwolf Run). But in the mid-1990s, when developer Herb Kohler first took Pete Dye to a flat former army base and landing strip in the Badger State, he gave the designer marching orders that would change not only the appearance of the land but also the face of golf course design. "Next time I see this land," said Kohler, "I want it to look like Ballybunion."

Dye failed magnificently. Aside from ribboned topography and its juxtaposition by the water, Whistling Straits looks nothing like Kohler's Irish muse. The Straits Course, with its countless man-made bunkers (one of which famously trapped Dustin Johnson in the 2010 PGA Championship) and its over-the-top artificial mounding, was sui generis. A first-time visitor recently commented, "I don't think it feels like Ireland. It looks like a bomb went off in Ireland."

Perhaps the most remarkable aspect of Dye's mammoth exercise in dirt-moving was how he sliced a sheer seventy-foot cliff in half, sloughing nearly one million cubic yards of dirt from the top to the bottom to create a usable lakeside terrace on which he could place several golf holes and then build the rest of the course in echelon. Those who flinch at the pitted, potholed slopes miss the fact that Dye's greens are enormous, thus easing the pain of playing all day from side-hill lies and sheep's grass rough.

TopGolf
22 locations around the world

ARCHITECT: Steve and Dave Jolliffe
OPENED: 2000

It's not exactly a golf course, but that's precisely why Topgolf has the potential to be among the most influential developments in the modern game.

There was a time when playing golf and being a member of a private club were among the most aspirational aspects of American life. But that was then. In the 21st century, young families are looking for multimedia experiences that appeal to both parents and children, and young couples are less inclined to join a club. As any parent with a fifteen-year-old knows, the idea of being stranded without a smartphone for four or five hours is anathema. Enter Topgolf, a growing chain of high-end driving ranges. But calling a Topgolf facility a driving range is like calling Disney World an amusement park. Each facility offers a broad array of food and beverage options, bars, lounges, and family-friendly dining. Imagine that the luxury suites at your local sports arena were outfitted with dozens of climate-controlled hitting bays, and golf balls equipped with microchips provided immediate feedback on distance and accuracy. Flat-screen TVs abound, so rather than competing with televised football or *SpongeBob SquarePants*, golf is integrated with the entertainment.

Topgolf began on an ordinary driving range in Watford, England, in 1998. Twin brothers Steve and Dave Jolliffe grew bored with simply beating balls and imagined a facility that would add levity to the range experience while improving their games. The result may prove to be the missing link that connects today's nongolfers or lapsed players to the royal and ancient game. Topgolf, which boasts nineteen facilities in the United States and 2.7 million annual visitors, just purchased a $7 million property near midtown Atlanta, and has proven that it can attract serious players, casual golfers, and those who have never been on a course to its wonderland. The Topgolf facility in Allen, Texas, is a great example. Since opening in 2011, more than 50 percent of the entire city's population of 90,000 has visited.

"I've been around golf for twenty-five years," says Golf Channel's Matt Ginella. "I'd heard about Topgolf, but until I walked in and saw it and felt the energy, I couldn't believe it. I walked back into the network office in Orlando and told people, 'Guys, I just found the future of golf.' This format addresses the issues that golf has: slow play, too expensive, too hard, inaccessible. This is the opposite of all those."

**Harbour Town
Golf Links
Hilton Head,
South Carolina**

ARCHITECTS: Pete Dye and Jack Nicklaus
OPENED: 1969
Public
YARDS: 7,101, par 71
SIGNATURE HOLE: 18th, 472 yards, par 4

Maybe one day we'll find a manuscript coauthored by Shakespeare and Milton, or a painting jointly crafted by Kandinsky and Monet. Until then we'll have Harbour Town. One of the grandes dames of American resort courses, Harbour Town has hosted the PGA Tour for so long that we sometimes forget the historic nature of its creation. It is the only course ever codesigned by titans Pete Dye and Jack Nicklaus, and the first golf course on which Nicklaus ever worked in an official design capacity.

In 1967, a local golf course developer took a flyer on a little-known golf course designer named Pete Dye. Dye, then forty-two, laid out the golf course and, before completion, asked a fellow Midwesterner and friend to critique it. Although the twenty-six-year-old Nicklaus had never really considered golf course design, he had no qualms telling Dye what he thought of certain holes. He described one green as "Mickey Mouse." Not in a good way.

Their collaboration on Harbour Town came at a time when golf courses—new and old—were beginning to be stretched out to accommodate the modern player. Dye, ever the iconoclast, and Nicklaus, the forthright long-ball hitter, zigged when the rest of the industry was zagging. They designed a 6,655-yard golf course (6,973 today) with microscopically small greens that have minimal contour even after Dye's 2000 update. Harbour Town serves as a reminder that golf, even at the PGA Tour level, is more than length or massive roller-coaster greens. The Dye-Nicklaus design stresses accuracy and course management over power and distance.

"You really have to shape your ball around the golf course, position yourself in the right spots," said Matt Kuchar, who won the RBC Heritage here in 2014.

South Cape Owners Club
Namhae Island, South Korea

ARCHITECT: Kyle Phillips
OPENED: 2013
Resort
YARDS: 7,313, par 72
SIGNATURE HOLE: 16th, 223 yards, par 3

South Korea is often called a hotbed for twenty-first-century golf. That's an understatement. Consider that as recently as 1980, the entire nation featured only twenty-four golf courses, which hosted 750,000 rounds of golf per year. Today, South Korea boasts more than four hundred golf courses and four million rounds a year. With that kind of passion, it's no surprise that the smallish nation has emerged as a force in the global game.

Since its opening in 2001, Nine Bridges golf course, located on the volcanic island of Jeju, off the country's southern coast, has been considered the foremost course in the country. But the recently opened Kyle Phillips-designed South Cape Owners Club, etched into the jagged waterfront along Namhae Island, in the southeastern part of the country, is likely to displace Nine Bridges and assume the mantle of most influential course in golf's most influential Asian nation. Phillips, who has gained worldwide acclaim for his course designs at Kingsbarns in Scotland and Yas Links in Abu Dhabi, has brought a dose of links-style golf to decidedly unlinksy terrain. The 11th through 16th holes, Phillips' so-called promenade to the sea, feature two holes that will remind visitors of the renowned 7th at Pebble Beach and the unrivaled 16th at Cypress Point.

The course represents the maturation, or at the very least the increasing sophistication, of the nation and the region's view of the game.

The Architects

Their work covers vast expanses, often dozens of acres at a time—not to mention the verdant fields of our daydreams— but their ranks are surprisingly small. The American Society of Golf Course Architects lists fewer than 200 members. And while golf course development has contracted in recent years, putting pressure on the profession, a handful of designers have shown an ability to adapt and maintain their standing or emerge as influencers of the art.

Bill Coore & Ben Crenshaw

Bill Coore and Ben Crenshaw founded their firm in 1986 more as a passion-driven hobby than as a business. With layouts such as Sand Hills, Bandon Trails, Bandon Preserve, Streamsong Red, the redesign of Pinehurst No. 2, and the 2018 U.S. Open prep for Shinnecock, they've become the undisputed godfathers of neoclassical golf course design.

By the time he partnered with Coore, Crenshaw was a brand name in golf, known as much for his silky putting stroke as for his professorial devotion to golf history. His deep passion for and knowledge of the game and its touchstones such as Shinnecock makes his involvement in the revival of Golden Age design almost predictable. Less well known was Coore, but his own background is equally rooted in Golden Age landmarks. A native North Carolinian, he played a lot of his early golf at Pinehurst (whose No. 2 course he would restore with Crenshaw) and the mystical Old Town Club in Winston-Salem.

Tom Doak

Tom Doak, who came to fame in 1986 for *The Confidential Guide to Golf Courses*, a now-rare critique of golf courses, has emerged as a classical iconoclast or, as golf writer Daniel Wexler put it, "a cutting-edge traditionalist." His work as an architect first gained notice as a codesigner (with Gil Hanse) of the Old Course at Stonewall Golf Club in eastern Pennsylvania. Since then, he and his firm, Renaissance Golf Design, have designed or codesigned some of the most important contemporary courses, including Pacific Dunes, Cape Kidnappers, Barnbougle Dunes, Ballyneal, Sebonack (with Jack Nicklaus), Streamsong Blue, and Old Macdonald.

Doak worked early in his career for Pete Dye; that may be where he gets his rebellious streak. As Doak wrote in his autobiography, "I've been called a lot more names than most golf course architects. Iconoclastic. Cerebral. A traditionalist, and a radical."

If Pete Dye is the most innovative designer of recent decades, Tom Fazio is the most artistic.

Jack Nicklaus

Jack Nicklaus remains the most in-demand golf course designer (he eschews the term "architect") in the world. Nicklaus's early work—he began designing in the late 1960s—was criticized for mandating his style of play, i.e., the high power-fade. The legend admitted to that long ago and corrected the tendency. Although his baby is the frequently updated Muirfield Village GC near his hometown of Columbus, Ohio, which he codesigned in 1974 with the late Desmond Muirhead, Nicklaus's finest work has undoubtedly come in the past twenty-five years, with notable efforts including the Bear's Club in Jupiter, Florida, and his heralded codesign of Sebonack GC with Tom Doak, a project that many believe had a beneficial impact on both men. With more than three hundred golf courses in the ground on virtually every habitable corner of the earth, Nicklaus remains the global face of golf course design.

Pete Dye

If there hadn't been a Pete Dye, golf would have had to invent him. Creative, risk-taking, flinty, Dye is in many ways the anti-architect. If the popular notion of golf course designer is someone who ponders elegantly drawn sketches and blueprints, then count Dye out. Even at eighty-eight, Dye is as hands-on as it gets, the original finger-in-the-dirt, two-hands-on-the-bulldozer golf course charmer.

Herb Kohler, the golf-loving billionaire who hired Dye to design the four existing courses at the American Club in Wisconsin, told Golf Channel's Matt Ginella, simply, "In my mind, he's clearly the strongest living architect."

Frank Nobilo agrees. "No question," says the analyst. "He's one of the great designers of all time. It doesn't mean you have to like his work, but if you're going to talk about influence, you have to talk about things that have been done differently. That's Pete Dye to a T."

What stands out to Nick Faldo about Dye is his ability to do equally outstanding work with both dynamic landscapes and flatter properties. "People want to play his golf courses. They can be outrageous and different and 'Dye-abolical,'" Faldo says. "Look at what he did at Whistling Straits. On the first hole alone, he used more land than most designers would use for three holes. He was very fortunate to have a canvas like that. Designers die for that sort of no-holds-barred, do-what-you-want-to-do opportunity. But he's also very good with dead-flat property. That's quite an art. Look at TPC Sawgrass, which is like an ironing board. He has a great ability to create strategy on either type of land."

Tom Fazio

If Pete Dye is the most innovative designer of recent decades, Tom Fazio is the most artistic. He hasn't designed the most courses—in fact, he rarely accepted a project that required him to miss a night at home with his family. But in the 1990s, a decade when beauty sold golf courses and beautiful golf courses sold real estate, no one designed more eye-catching layouts than Fazio. "Fazio's a real artist," says Nick Faldo. "He's always come up with good-looking stuff."

Fazio dominated the annual lists of best new courses for years. He created newsworthy Xanadus such as Shadow Creek in Las Vegas while also serving as consultant to some of the most tradition-bound clubs in the game, such as Pine Valley, Oakmont, and Winged Foot. When Augusta National tried to contain Tiger Woods in the early 2000s, they relied on Fazio to come up with the renovation. And when historic gems such as Saucon Valley, Merion, or Oak Hill have welcomed major championships in recent years, Fazio has been on call.

Gil Hanse

Gil Hanse bridges the classic and the modern eras. A graduate of Cornell, he won the William Frederick Dreer Award, which funds a year in the U.K. studying golf course architecture. During his time in Britain, Hanse interned with Hawtree and Son, one of the world's oldest design houses. Hanse has shown his ability to work with the iconoclastic and brash Donald Trump (at Doral), yet draw inspiration from the work of classicists such as Charles Blair Macdonald, Alister MacKenzie, Colt and Alison, and neoclassical designers Coore & Crenshaw, as well as his onetime design partner, Tom Doak.

Hanse is another of the frontline leaders of the growing minimalist school. His impact is being felt not only in the work he's putting in the ground but also in the craftsman-like way he approaches it. Like Coore & Crenshaw, who have eschewed the global, corporate, multioffice model and have succeeded by keeping design a passion, Hanse prefers to design fewer courses and focus more closely on each.

Mike Strantz

The late Mike Strantz was the rare golf course designer capable of combining a radically creative streak with the traditional tenets of golf course architecture. That's borne out in the descriptive most often given to his design at Tobacco Road: "Pine Valley on Steroids." Strantz, whose firm was aptly called Maverick Golf, was named 1998 Architect of the Year by *Golf World* magazine on the heels of Tobacco Road's opening.

Robin Hiseman of European Golf Design wrote in *Golf Course Architecture,* "Tobacco Road...was the course that transformed what I understood to be possible with golf course architecture....Mike Strantz had the nerve and the commitment to try things that others would never dare to do. He was the Evel Knievel of golf architects, always looking to jump more buses than anyone thought possible."

Rees Jones

Rees Jones learned his trade from a genuine master: his father, Robert Trent Jones Sr. Jones the elder, who died in 2000, was probably the most influential American designer from the late 1940s through the late 1970s. While prolific—it's estimated he designed more than five hundred golf courses—Jones was also a pioneer. Not only did the elder Jones impact his field through his heroic view of the game and his "hard par, easy bogey" philosophy, but it was Jones who, while working with amateur legend Bobby Jones on the latter's beloved Peachtree GC, bridged the Golden Age and Modern Age of golf course design.

His impact on the game continues today in the work of his son Rees, who has designed some two hundred courses and was named Golf Architect of the Year by *Golf World* magazine in 1995. In recent years, Rees, too, has had a massive impact on the game through his specialty of preparing golf courses for the U.S. Open. Also nicknamed the "Open Doctor," like his father, Jones has prepared legendary layouts such as Baltusrol, Bethpage, Pinehurst, Congressional, and Torrey Pines for major championship play. His tests, always strategically exacting, have affected the outcome of several major championships and have drawn their share of complaints from frustrated tour players, notably Phil Mickelson, who has had six second-place finishes in the U.S. Open.

Just as his father did before him, Jones shrugs it off. It was Sr. who answered such gripes with a trademark dismissal: "Golfers complain a lot."

Kyle Phillips

The Robert Trent Jones legacy strikes again. Kyle Phillips, a former protégé of Rees' brother, Robert Trent Jones Jr., hung out his own design shingle in 1997 after working for Jones Jr. in Europe. The posting had given Phillips broad exposure to the historic links and parkland golf courses of the region.

Still, when he began work on Kingsbarns in Scotland, people thought he was crazy. Local politicians assumed that the region, home to The Old Course at St. Andrews and six other courses, had all the great golf it needed. Due to the perseverance of developers Mark Parsinen and Art Dunkley, Kinsgbarns opened in July 2000. In a masterstroke of timing, the new course opened the same week as the Open Championship, which was being contested only seven miles away at ancient St. Andrews. While Tiger Woods' domination was the story of the Open, Kingsbarns, with its emphasis on old-style contours and landforms, was the talk of the Toon. When *Golf Course Architecture* magazine had its readers rank the top one hundred golf courses in the world, only three post-1960 golf courses were included on the list. One of them was Kingsbarns. (The other two were Sand Hills and Pacific Dunes.)

Ed Seay

While a student at Wake Forest University, Arnold Palmer and his teammates carved out a rudimentary practice facility near the Winston-Salem, North Carolina, campus. Later, when he served in the U.S. Coast Guard at Cape May, New Jersey, Palmer was asked to fashion as nine-hole course on the base. These were the beginnings of a remarkably successful career in golf course design that would begin to truly blossom in 1972 when Palmer began to work with golf course architect Ed Seay.

Seven years later the duo formed Arnold Palmer Course Design Company and they quickly became a force in the business. Seay, who served as president of the American Society of Golf Course Architects from 1976-1977, designed, built or promoted more than 350 golf courses worldwide, 250 of them designed by Arnold Palmer. Seay died in 2007, but among the many honors he received was the 2006 during his Distinguished Service Award from the ASGCA Board of Governors.

David McLay Kidd

David McLay Kidd was a virtual unknown when he was tapped by Mike Keiser for the job of a lifetime: designing the initial golf course for Keiser's grand vision for coastal Oregon golf, Bandon Dunes. Looking at the spectacular setting today, it's hard to imagine just how inhospitable the gorse-covered property once was. But Keiser had an unerring vision for a simple, throwback golf course. Kidd had a similar vision, and the rest is history.

Kidd designed a course with broad appeal, providing a balance of challenges for both the better and the weaker players, all amid a difficult climate. The course echoed the simplicity of its spiritual cousin, Sand Hills. Anyone who has visited Keiser's first golf course, the nine-hole Dunes Club, a paean to Pine Valley in southwestern Michigan, knows that he craves simplicity. Evidence the Dunes' one-room clubhouse with self-serve sandwiches.

Kidd's work and Keiser's vision helped launch the minimalist age into high gear. The tradition for first-timers at Bandon is to hit a ball into the fog-smothered ocean off the 17th tee. It's a metaphor for the blind leap the two took on a grand vision in this faraway place.

Kidd now has twelve courses to his credit, including the Castle Course at St. Andrews.

Lee Schmidt and Brian Curley

There are more than 1.3 billion people in China. If one in twenty took up golf, there would be more than twice as many golfers there as in the U.S. That's called potential. Add in golf's return to the Olympic Games in 2016 and China's appetite for gold medals, and it's easy to see why designers such as Jack Nicklaus are spending so much time in the country. Nicklaus has eighteen courses open for play in China and another nineteen under development.

But Nicklaus is overshadowed in China by a former protégé. After apprenticing under Pete Dye, Lee Schmidt worked for seven years as a senior design associate for Nicklaus Design. His design partner, Brian Curley, has more than thirty years of design experience. Together they have all but cornered the market for American designers in China. To date, their firm has completed more than forty courses there. One of them, the Sandbelt Trails Course, hosted the inaugural event of the newly formed PGA Tour China in April 2014. How big can golf get in China? The sky's the limit, but there is no question that the courses to come will be descendants of Schmidt and Curley's pioneering work.

The Pro Game

*Just when you thought you'd seen it all, Tiger wins a U.S. Open on one leg,
Bubba wins two Masters, and Rory eyes a slam.
Did that decade really happen?*

2005-2014

Tiger was digital in an analog age. He was one of the very few athletes I can think of— LeBron?—who came out with massive hype and not only lived up to his hype but outran it, like Usain Bolt. He just blew by it. We naturally followed his every move. I make no apologies for how we've covered him. He warranted it. He absolutely did. First warm-up shot through final putt until he got in the car. You couldn't miss a second of it. And it was a helluva show.

RICH LERNER

Phil Mickelson tries to get back to the 17th fairway, from the 15th, during the third round of the 2010 Masters. He won the tournament.

For students of human drama, the past ten years of golf have been replete with triumph, tragedy, and redemption. The most obvious example is the implosion of Tiger Woods's personal life in 2009. Combine that with Woods' debilitating injuries and the loss of his father in 2006, and you get a sense of the dramatic underpinnings that marked the past decade in the game.

Beyond the salacious headlines of Woods' struggles was more affirming drama of the highest order. Consider the case of Northern Ireland's Darren Clarke, who, after losing his wife in 2006, rebounded a few weeks later to play a leading role in Europe's emotional Ryder Cup win at the K Club, and then his own moving Open Championship title in 2011. Who wasn't stirred by fifty-nine-year-old Tom Watson's charge toward a sixth Open Championship in 2009? Or new father Bubba Watson's emotional win at the Masters in 2012?

In terms of pure golf, the feel-good story of the decade may have been Phil Mickelson's entirely unexpected win in the 2013 Open Championship only weeks after swallowing a runner-up finish in the elusive U.S. Open for a record sixth time.

There was plenty of heartbreak, too. Has there ever been a more numbing finish to a major championship than Dustin Johnson's bunker madness at Whistling Straits in 2010? Or Adam Scott's self-liquidation during the final round of the 2012 Open Championship?

If the decade from 1995 to 2005 was the era of Tiger's vertical ascent, the past ten years have seen the bruised legend move slightly aside, affording a whole new flock of champions the fore.

BEST
OF THE
MAJORS

TIGER WOODS
2008 U.S. OPEN

Woods tees off on 16 in the final round of the U.S. Open.

For Tiger Woods, who has now lived outside of California for nearly as long as he lived in the Golden State, Torrey Pines is as much of a home game as he gets. Coming into the 2008 U.S. Open, he had already won eight times at Torrey Pines dating all the way back to the Junior World Championship in 1991. In fact, among the aging photographs on the walls of the clubhouse is one of young Eldrick Woods, who essentially grew up at the place. Golf nearly got in history's way. After seventy-two holes, Rocco Mediate was tied with Woods for the lead. It was hard to tell who precisely was the spoiler. Was Mediate, he of the aching back and crutch-length putter, spoiling Woods's homecoming? Or was Woods raining on Mediate's long-awaited major championship parade? It would take nineteen more holes of mesmerizing golf to get the real answer. The biggest winner that Monday afternoon was the game. (For more on the 2008 U.S. Open, see page 98.)

"I had a chance today to walk inside the ropes with Reggie Jackson, Mr. October, one of the clutch performers in baseball history, and he compared Tiger to Michael Jordan and Bill Russell, men who just refused to lose. He compared him to Bob Gibson, who willed himself to victory. He compared Tiger to Sandy Koufax, who willed himself through pain."
RICH LERNER

⛳ VIJAY SINGH

Singh, at home on the range and on the course, occasionally plays the role of villain.

Career wins: 34 on the PGA Tour, former World No. 1 player

Major championships: 3 (1998, 2004 PGA Championship; 2000 Masters)

"But in the end, it's still a game of golf, and if at the end of the day you can't shake hands with your opponents and still be friends, then you've missed the point."
STEWART

"Maybe it was asking too much for me. Maybe I should have laid up. The ball was laying so well. Next time, I hit a wedge, and you all forgive me."
VAN DE VELDE

"If you think about it, the golf ball doesn't know what country you're in."
SORENSTAM

⛳ ANNIKA SORENSTAM

How Swede it is! Sorenstam dominates the LPGA Tour.

Career wins: 72 on the LPGA Tour

Major championships: 10 (2001, 2002, 2005 Kraft Nabisco; 2003, 2004, 2005 LPGA; 1995, 1996, 2006 U.S. Women's Open; 2003 Women's Open Championship)

JEAN VAN DE VELDE

Burn, baby, burn! Van de Velde tangles with the Barry Burn, and it leaves him all wet as he disintegrates on the final hole of the 1999 Open Championship.

Career wins: 2 on the European Tour

Major championships: 0

"I just love the feeling of hitting good golf shots."
SINGH

⛳ PAYNE STEWART

The tragic loss of Stewart remains palpable fifteen years after his death.

Career wins: 11

Major championships: 3 (1989 PGA Championship; 1991, 1999 U.S. Open)

The Changing Tour

When PGA Tour Commissioner Deane Beman announced his decision to retire in 1994, the organization went through the typical gyrations to assure that the search for a successor would be wide open. A search committee was formed. Lists were compiled and debated. Backroom lobbying heated up. But in the end, there was only one genuine candidate. Tim Finchem had been Beman's most indispensable aide since joining the PGA Tour in 1987.

An attorney by training and steeled in some of Beman's signature causes—notably the quixotic legal battle against Ping's U-grooved clubfaces—Finchem had also overseen all tour operations for half a decade. Finchem, who had served as deputy adviser for economic affairs in the Carter administration, assumed the post on June 1, 1994. Beman, the man who took the PGA Tour from the relative dark ages of media and promotion to the precipice of the digital age, had set the table for the fully groomed Finchem. He knew all about the tour's operations, its sponsor relationships, and its TV deals. He knew the players and the media partners. What he didn't know was that a skinny high school kid nicknamed "Urkel" who had just enrolled at Stanford was about to take the game into the stratosphere. When Finchem took the reins, the yearly PGA Tour's total purse was $56.4 million. Today that figure is over $300 million.

By any measure, Finchem's reign has been a remarkable success. Sure, he's the Phil Jackson of golf: You're supposed to succeed when you have Kobe Bryant or Tiger Woods on your team. But Finchem's legacy will transcend Woods'. His visionary decision to institute the FedEx Cup, a season-long points race that

PGA Tour Commissioner Tim Finchem, standing between the PGA Championship and Presidents Cup trophies, announces that San Francisco's TPC Harding Park will host the 2020 PGA Championship and 2025 Presidents Cup.

leads to a series of limited-field playoff events ("Playoffs! Did you say playoffs?") changed everything. The FedEx Cup made professional golf, which for decades had ceased to matter after August's PGA Championship, relevant year-round.

Then there's the wraparound schedule. Since Neanderthal times, the PGA Tour season started in January and ended in the fall. In order to give greater stature to overlooked fall events and to help the tour combat the oxygen-stealing nature of NFL and college football, Finchem created a wraparound schedule. The tour season now starts in October and runs into the fall, ending neatly, dramatically, and logically with the Tour Championship by Coca-Cola.

Finally, there are tours abroad, developmental tours, and Q-School. In 2014, the PGA Tour launched PGA Tour China, which hosted twelve tournaments in its first year and is slated to reach fifteen next year. PGA Tour Latinoamérica was formed in 2012 and now hosts eighteen tournaments in eleven countries. And in late 2012, the PGA took over the Canadian Professional Golf Tour, now known as the PGA Tour Canada and hosting twelve tournaments.

What's known today as the Web.com Tour was originally founded in 1989 as the Ben Hogan Tour. During Beman's tenure, the Ben Hogan Co. put up $15 million in prize money over three years to host what amounted to a Triple A minor-league circuit for aspiring tour players. When, after the 2012 season, Nationwide decided to not renew its title sponsorship of the developmental tour, Finchem and company found a way to add value to a tour that had seen sponsors come and go: Make it essential. It became the gateway to a coveted PGA Tour card. In essence, the developmental tour would replace the storied PGA Tour Qualifying School, which had been the gauntlet for aspiring tour pros since 1965. Now, the top seventy-five players on the Web.com Tour will qualify for their own playoffs—a four-tournament series against the players ranked 126–200 on the PGA Tour's FedEx Cup points list. The top fifty coming out of that series earn Tour cards for the coming year.

It may have been a casualty of growth or a necessity, but Q-School had something of the Marine Corps about it. The few, the proud. It was Everyman's shot at a dream. "In a sport that focuses so heavily on greatness at majors, Q-School was The Desperation Open," says Rich Lerner, who covered plenty of them. "Players may have loathed it, but fans and press loved it, and they miss it."

In 2014, Finchem named Jay Monahan deputy commissioner of the PGA Tour. Whether or not the forty-three-year-old sports marketing maven succeeds Finchem, the next commissioner will likely have a tougher job than either Beman or Finchem did. Both had their critics, but they undeniably fulfilled their primary responsibility: increase purses and playing opportunities for the players on the PGA Tour and its allied tours. Tiger Woods gets the assist for the past twenty years, but as he ages out of dominance, the PGA Tour will have some huge shoes to fill.

Twenty-five years ago, the LPGA hired the avuncular Charlie Mechem, retired CEO of Taft Broadcasting and Great American Broadcasting, to drag the tour out of the rough. Mechem may have succeeded precisely because he had nothing to prove. His rescue of the LPGA Tour had little to do with salary or status—it was born of a passion for women's golf and for doing things right. Mechem came aboard when the association was at its nadir. The schedule was anemic and weakening. Sponsor interest was fading. The tour had very little television presence, and the bankable stars it had produced in the 1980s—certified icons such as Nancy Lopez and Jan Stephenson—were nearing the end of their careers. Morale was in the tank. Mechem did the one thing he could do. He showed the flag. Whereas his predecessor had refused to even move from California to Daytona Beach, Florida, to be nearer to the headquarters, Mechem never stopped moving. Over the course of his five years as commissioner, Mechem logged roughly three million miles on Delta. Under Mechem's care, the LPGA made genuine progress. Total purse money grew nearly 40 percent to almost $25 million, and for a the former broadcast executive left office with twenty-six of his thirty-eight tournaments on TV.

It's no exaggeration to say that Mechem ushered in the contemporary era of professional women's golf. In the years since his retirement in 1995, the LPGA Tour leadership has seesawed. The brassy tenure of Mechem's successor, Jim Ritts, who beefed up the LPGA schedule to a modern-era high of forty-three events, was followed by the steady, brotherly approach of Mechem disciple and LPGA Tour general counsel Ty Votaw. Under Votaw, who introduced the controversial "Five Points of Celebrity," average tournament purses nearly doubled to $1.4 million. In fact, by 2005 and the end of his six-year stint as commissioner, Votaw had put such a shine on the LPGA that there were reports that the PGA Tour was considering a merger with the women's tour. Those rumors only heated up in 2006 when, after leaving the LPGA Tour, Votaw joined the PGA Tour, where he is now executive vice president and chief global communications officer.

Votaw was succeeded by Carolyn Bivens, a media industry executive with little golf background. From her early effort to exert control over the work of print media covering LPGA Tour events to her plan to suspend foreign players who didn't speak English, Bivens was a divisive force. She was essentially forced out in a 2009 coup. Interim commissioner Marsha Evans was succeeded in early 2010 by Michael Whan, a Procter & Gamble–trained executive with oodles of sports industry experience and a modest bearing. Whan has succeeded by putting the players first and building consensus. His first act: ripping out the sign in the tour headquarters parking lot that read "Reserved for LPGA Commissioner." It's hard to imagine Ritts or Bivens inspiring LPGA Tour players to play an LPGA Tour event for no pay. Under Whan, the players did just that in 2011. Even though there was no purse, the ladies played in the 2011 Founders Cup. The next year, RR Donnelley funded the purse and the charity. Risk and reward. When Whan joined the LPGA Tour, there were twenty-three events on the calendar. Today there are thirty-two.

"I say this to our players a lot, that you can't dream big and be afraid of making mistakes," Whan told Golf Channel in 2014. "They are not mutually exclusive."

Whan is a risk taker. He shocked the golf world in 2014 when he salvaged the flagging LPGA Championship by enlisting KPMG as a sponsor and the PGA of America as a partner, renaming the event the KPMG Women's PGA Championship. He flouted tradition when he unilaterally named the Evian Championship as his tour's fifth major championship. In 2013, he awarded then sixteen-year-old Lydia Ko a special exemption onto the LPGA Tour despite the tour's minimum age requirement of eighteen. She validated Whan's call with her first LPGA Tour win as a professional on the weekend of her seventeenth birthday.

The South Korean–born youngster represents a wave of dominance washing over the LPGA Tour by Asian players and others born outside of the United States. Whan sees only possibilities in the internationalization of the tour. In 2014, he gamely jumped onboard the USGA's bold plan to host the U.S. Women's Open immediately after the U.S. Open at Pinehurst No. 2. "Some of them won't work, but you've got to be able to take chances. You have to be willing to fail," Whan said.

There's irony inherent in the PGA European Tour, which is headed by executive director George O'Grady. It's headquartered in the United Kingdom, the home of golf. The Scots invented the game but have seen other nations produce deeper talent pools, better weather, and larger purses. As a result, there's been a healthy tension as Europe's best players have tried to determine which of the tours best

LPGA Tour Commissioner Michael Whan with Shanshan Feng, the first player from mainland China to win a tour event.

suits them and their financial futures. Virtually every great European Tour player has moved at least temporarily to the United States to cast his lot against the deepest bench in the game. Whatever pride the United States might take from that is seemingly negated every two years when the European side wins the Ryder Cup.

Ken Schofield, who served as executive director of the European Tour from 1975 to 2004, oversaw a period of tremendous growth and growing pains. During his tenure, the tour grew from seventeen events to forty-five, expanded around the world, and added the Challenge Tour and European Senior Tour. Much of that growth derived from the "Co-Sanction Programme" instituted during Schofield's directorate, where the Euro Tour co-sanctioned events with other worldwide tours such as the Asian Tour and the South African PGA Tour. The Euro Tour reached Australia in 1996 with the playing in Perth of the Heineken Classic. The 1999 Malaysian Open also came from this program, which continues to flourish today.

Perhaps the greatest on-course accomplishment in Europe over the past twenty years was the outstanding play of Scotland's Colin Montgomerie, who led the Euro Tour money list seven successive years (1993-99) and again in 2005. Then there was Padraig Harrington, who claimed three major championships in just over a year—including the PGA Championship in 2008—the first European in nearly eighty years to do so (if you count Tommy Armour, who won in 1930 as a Scot). Graeme McDowell and Justin Rose closed out the period in style by winning the U.S. Open at Pebble Beach (2010) and the U.S. Open at Merion (2013), respectively. And most recently, Rory McIlroy's stellar 2014, with wins at the Open Championship and the PGA Championship.

But it was a seemingly small decision made in the early 1990s that, Schofield says, reshaped not only European golf but also the global golf landscape. Through 1993, only the leading money winner on the European PGA Tour was guaranteed a spot in the U.S. Open. Before the 1994 U.S. Open at Oakmont, however, the USGA agreed to expand that number and allow fifteen European Tour players. "It allowed the European Tour to retain many players based in Europe who then knew they could get into a U.S. major while competing in Europe," said Schofield. In the very first year of the expanded access, Ernie Els won the U.S. Open at Oakmont in a playoff over Loren Roberts and Els' fellow European Tour standout Colin Montgomerie. Since then, the impact has only grown. In the eighty majors played between 1973 and 1993, non-Americans won twenty-five major championships: 31 percent. In the seventy-eight majors played from 1994 through June 2014, non-Americans have won thirty-five: 45 percent.

Although it is not a governing body, there is another organization that has brought enormous and far-reaching change to the sport: Augusta National Golf Club. Over the past twenty years, the club has taken on a broader mission. Its focus has widened from host of the Masters to charitable force, supporter of youth golf, influencer on equipment, and global ambassador. (One measure of Augusta National's new mission is that in 2012, the club welcomed its first two female members.) Much of Augusta's evolution is attributable to Billy Payne, who assumed the chairmanship of the club in 2006 and brought with him a global view honed during his presidency of the Olympic Games in Atlanta. Sensing the game's budding potential in Asia, Augusta helped create the Asia-Pacific Amateur and awarded the winner a spot in the Masters. The club did the same thing with the Latin American Amateur, which will premiere in 2015. A long-time supporter of The First Tee, Augusta National under Payne created the highly successful Drive, Chip & Putt in partnership with the PGA of America, USGA, and Golf Channel.

USGA

In the 120 years since the USGA's founding on a chilly night in New York City, the organization has been engaged in virtually every single meaningful issue confronting the game. For starters, they are the rule-making body for golf in the United States (and Mexico). Anyone who's followed the debates on balls or the long putter is aware of the USGA's stands. But the purely legislative view of the USGA is a narrow one. Through myriad sections and services, the USGA does far more than police the game; it sanctions national championships and helps the game grow, thrive, and mature. On a practical level, if you need to grow grass, the USGA Green Section is at your service. On a more philanthropic level, if you need funding for your youth golf program, the USGA Grants Initiative has awarded millions over the past seventeen years.

To the extent that the USGA has a personality, it's reflective of its three most recent leaders: the late Frank Hannigan; David Fay, who retired in 2010 after thirty-two years with the USGA; and Mike Davis, who currently serves as executive director. All three shared the requisites for the job: passion for the game, a moral compass, a willingness to take risks, and a sense of humor.

The seminal administrative figure in the USGA—maybe even the game—over the past two decades was Fay. He had been steeled in the USGA's bruising battle with PING (see page 192) but emerged unabashed and unafraid. Aside from the broad web of relationships he wove within the sport, the bow tie-favoring Fay may be best remembered for ushering the USGA's premier championship, the U.S. Open, onto truly public golf courses. The effort began in 2002, with the arrival of the national open at Bethpage State Park's Black course, and he has since brought the championship to Torrey Pines, with visits slated for Chamber Bay in 2015 and Erin Hills in 2017.

The USGA's Mike Davis, Bill McCarthy, and Tom O'Toole Jr. confer at the 2007 U.S. Amateur Championship.

PGA of America

The PGA of America is the grassroots patron of the game. Where people want to learn it, the PGA, through one of its 27,000 professionals, is there to teach it. In fact, the PGA of America was integral to the launch of Golf Channel when it helped create Golf Channel's *Academy Live*, a one-hour interactive golf instruction show featuring top PGA teaching professionals. To this day, *The Golf Fix*, hosted by Michael Breed, PGA's 2012 National Teacher of the Year, closes with a PGA of America logo.

For most golf fans, the PGA of America, which was founded in 1916, has been best known for hosting the PGA Championship, the fourth and final major championship of the year. Since its creation in 1916, the championship has been a marquee event, but in recent years another PGA property, the Ryder Cup, has skyrocketed in popularity (see "The Ryder Cup," beginning on page 206).

The PGA has been infused in recent years by the visionary leadership of president Ted Bishop, who has forcefully represented the interests of the PGA of America and its professionals, and chief executive officer Pete Bevacqua, who succeeded longtime CEO Joe Steranka.

The R&A

The R&A is not only Royal and Ancient, but simply put, it is the most influential golf organization in the world.

Responsible for the administration of the Rules of Golf everywhere but North America, where the USGA reigns, the R&A is not only Royal (having earned its designation from King William IV in 1834) and Ancient (having been founded in 1754), but simply put the R&A is the most influential golf organization in the world. For 250 years the private club known as the Royal and Ancient Golf Club oversaw the Rules, hosted championships such as the Open Championship and the Amateur Championship and fostered the game in emerging markets. But in 2004 the club reorganized, cleaving the private club known as the Royal and Ancient, which makes its home at the Old Course at St. Andrews and the administrative body, now known as the R&A, which manages rules, championships and grow-the-game initiatives. The two key figures in recent R&A history have been Sir Michael Bonallack, who retired as Secretary of the Royal and Ancient in 1999 and his successor, Peter Dawson, who is slated to retire in September 2015 as both chief executive of the R&A and secretary of the Royal and Ancient. Dawson is also president of the International Golf Federation and played a vital role in golf's upcoming return to the Olympic Games at Rio de Janeiro in 2016.

2006 Kraft Nabisco

Karrie Webb

Final Round

It had been four years since Karrie Webb's last major championship and two since her last LPGA win. She had carded a 76 on Saturday. No worries.

"When I was playing a lot of my good golf, my practice used to be really, really bad, and I would...[wonder] what sort of game I was going to have for the tournament, and then I got a win," said Webb.

Precisely. Webb blitzed the field with a 65 in the final round and capped it off with the shot she has called the greatest of her career. She was trailing Michelle Wie by a shot. As the veteran approached the par-5 18th hole on the Dinah Shore Tournament Course at Mission Hills CC, she needed birdie to have a shot at a playoff. She sized up her 116-yard approach and selected a wedge. She flushed it for an eagle. Four soft little baby hops followed by a disappearing act.

Webb's eagle gained her a spot in a playoff with twenty-four-year-old Lorena Ochoa, which Webb won on the first hole. It was her second splash in Poppie's Pond but her final major championship win.

OOPS

Phil Mickelson
2006 U.S. Open

Phil the Thrill came to Winged Foot with only a driver and a 4-wood in his tool kit. Regrettably, as he stood on the 18th tee, he opted for the driver and blocked the ball badly to the left, but managed a good bounce and decent swing on his second shot. Absolved of his original sin, greed, Mickelson went for gluttony, as in glutton for punishment. A par would have won him the elusive Open, and a bogey would have earned him a playoff against Geoff Ogilvy. With 210 yards to the hole, Mickelson could have punched out right and had an unobstructed view to the hole. Instead he went up the tree-filled left. "In hindsight, if I hit it in the gallery and it doesn't cut, I am fine," said Mickelson. "I can still make bogey, even par. I ended up hitting the tree."

When his third shot found a fried-egg lie in the right front bunker, the ending to the tragedy was already written. The cheers of "Let's go, Phil!" rang a little empty. And as the spin-less ball ran across the green into the far rough, Mickelson was down to his last shot. If you needed someone to hole a chip from deep rough, Mickelson would be a pretty good choice, but it was too much to ask. He ran his chip past the hole and to the right. It never had a chance.

"I am such an idiot," said Mickelson. "I just can't believe I couldn't par the last hole. It really stings. As a kid I dreamt of winning this tournament.... I just can't believe I did that."

BRANDEL CHAMBLEE: **Well, this was nothing new. All day long, we saw Phil Mickelson struggle with the driver. This bounces off the tent, with a 1-shot lead, comes back into the gallery. And then, seeming a good break, ends up on the matted straw. We don't know what happened here. Bounces around up in the trees and falls down right in front of him. Again, same area here, trying to hoist it up over the trees from the matted-down lie. And this one plugs in the bunker short and left of the green.**
KRAIG KANN: **At this point, Geoff Ogilvy is in disbelief.**
CHAMBLEE: **Just a horrid shot right here. Trying to stab it out. It releases and runs off the green. Right here you knew Geoff Ogilvy had won the U.S. Open.**

OOPS

Woody Austin
2007 Presidents Cup

At the 2007 Presidents Cup at Royal Montreal, Woody Austin and his partner, David Toms, were 1 down to Rory Sabbatini and Trevor Immelman on the short par-4 14th hole of the Blue course. With Sabbatini staring at a ten-foot putt for eagle, Austin felt compelled to take a risk. After hitting his drive into the lake guarding the left side of the hole, he decided to play the shot from the water rather than take a drop.

"I knew deep down I probably couldn't pull the shot off. But between wanting really badly to pull it off and having my caddie urge me on...he kept saying, 'You've got to try, you've got to try, you've got to try.' I was doing OK until I stepped on a rock, and once I stepped on the rock, I lost my balance."

Suffice it to say Austin made a splash that day. After swinging wildly at the ball, the barefoot Austin lost his footing and fell face-first into the water.

What is often overlooked in all the hilarity over his fall is how well Austin played that day overall (eight birdies on his own ball), especially after the dousing. In sopping-wet clothes, he birdied the last three holes to earn the United States a half-point.

"I can't tell you how much the competitive fire burns in me," said Austin. "It didn't douse it. I was still fired up and ready to go."

BEST
OF THE
MAJORS

TOM WATSON VS. STEWART CINK
2009 OPEN CHAMPIONSHIP

Tom Watson has made more than his share of history at The Open Championship. With five Open titles to his name and a passion and respect for links golf that is unequaled among his compatriots, Watson is the bar by which all American Open champions are judged. He nearly raised that bar in 2009 when he returned to Turnberry, the stage for his memorable 1977 victory against Jack Nicklaus in the famed "Duel in the Sun."

Galleries could have been forgiven for expecting a creaky golf swing, a missed cut, and a nostalgic tip of the cap as the fifty-nine-year-old legend exited the game's great stage, but even Watson seemed surprised as the week wore on. "The first day here, yeah, let the old geezer have his day in the sun, you know," said Watson, as he recalled the week on Saturday night. "The second day, you say, 'Well, that's OK, that's OK.' And now today, you kind of perk up your ears and say, 'This old geezer might have a chance to win the tournament,'" said Watson, who sat on the third-round lead. "I don't know what's going to happen, but I do know one thing. I feel good about what I did today. I feel good about my game plan. And who knows, it might happen."

"It" did happen, but not the "it" Watson fans had been hoping for. This "it" was the dicey putting stroke that had dogged Watson on and off under pressure for years. Left with an eight-foot putt for the win and a certain place in Ripley's, Watson yipped. He never released the putterhead and blocked the ball to the right. It never had a chance. The only time all week that Watson acted his age was during the ensuing playoff with Stewart Cink. Watson was clearly physically and emotionally spent. It was bittersweet for both Cink, who snatched his first major from the weathered hands of a man he greatly admires, and for Watson, who nearing the age of sixty had the anachronistic experience of treading up the home hole a contender.

"Coming up the 18th hole again," Watson said. "Those memories are hard to forget. Coming up in the amphitheater of the crowd and having the crowd cheering you on like they do here for me.... That warmth makes you feel human. It makes you feel so good."

Tom Watson just after missing an eight-foot putt that would have secured the Open Championship.

Y.E. YANG
2009 PGA CHAMPIONSHIP

If one was looking to punctuate the 2009 major championships, he might want to consider a question mark. There were plenty of great shots and drama, but each result left viewers wondering, "Did that just happen?"

That was just prologue. When Tiger Woods is leading a major after fifty-four holes, they ought to call the final round and let everyone catch early flights. It'd be like the mercy rule in Little League. But it's a good thing for golf historians that they played the final round of the 2009 PGA Championship. It would prove to be the only time that Woods had taken a fifty-four-hole lead in a major and failed to deliver. Furthermore, the man who beat him, the little-known Y.E. Yang of South Korea, became the first Asian to win a men's major championship.

After thirteen holes on Sunday, the duo was even. At the short par-4 14th, Woods drove into a greenside bunker, while Yang hit the fairway. Yang coolly holed his chip for eagle. Even though Woods sandied for birdie, he was 1 down with 4 to play.

They arrived at the 18th with Yang still one ahead. The South Korean played a 3-hybrid approach that had to navigate a copse of trees, some greenside bunkers, a back pin, and the air-sucking presence of Woods. The shot and the circumstances around it were daunting. Under intense pressure, Yang played a flawless shot to ten feet. When he holed his ten-foot birdie putt, he secured a place alongside Jack Fleck as one of the least-known great spoilers in golf history. Furthermore, he replaced the season's question mark with a boldface exclamation point.

Y.E. Yang celebrates his upset victory over Tiger Woods.

2010 Shriners Hospitals for

Children Open

Jonathan Byrd

Playoff

There have been countless playoffs on the PGA Tour, and they've been won in countless ways. But when Jonathan Byrd made a hole-in-one to seal his victory in the Shriners Hospitals for Children Open, it marked the first time a player had ever won a PGA Tour playoff with an ace. His 6-iron from 196 yards on the fourth playoff hole,

at dusk no less, ended the hopes of Cameron Percy and Martin Laird.

"I put a 6-iron kind of back in my stance and tried to play more of a sweeping draw into that left pin and curve it over to it. It started perfect, it turned perfect, and it was coming right down the flag," said Byrd. "I thought I hit it too good. I thought I hit it too far, and I couldn't see anything. But to hear the reaction as it went in, I was just in shock. I was trying to be considerate of my playing partners because two more guys had a chance to keep playing, and I didn't want to overreact." Needless to say, neither one of them matched his ace.

Kevin Na
2011 Valero
Texas Open

There have been higher scores. John Daly carded an 18 on the 6th hole of Bay Hill in 1998. Legend has it that Tommy Armour once made a 23 in the old Shawnee Open. But the virtuoso high score performance of the past twenty years was turned in by Kevin Na in the first round of the 2011 Valero Texas Open. It was a symphony of misfortune.

Heading into the 9th hole, Na was only a few shots off the lead on a difficult scoring day. His tee shot left him in an impossible tangle of Texas brush. He took an unplayable lie and a penalty, re-teed, and hit it right again into an impossible tangle of Texas brush and the really bad part began. His next shot struck him—another penalty.

"I hit a shot, felt like it hit me, and I called it on myself. I looked at my caddie and I said, 'I think that just hit me,' and he goes, 'How does it hit you and end up behind you?'"

Twelve shots later, including a whiff, Na putted out for what he thought was a 15. To be safe, he met with PGA Tour rules officials after the round and pored over the bruising videotape. "We went and checked the camera," said Na, who maintained his composure throughout. "I counted it myself. It was 16."

> KEVIN NA: **How are we going to count all the shots?**
> CADDIE: **I have no idea.**

Rory McIlroy
2011 Masters

It's rare that Augusta National hikes the kimono. The green curtain keeps many of her secrets far from public view. For instance, millions of viewers know about the cabins that dot the property, but until 2011 few viewers knew of the clapboard village that lurks deep in the woods along the 10th hole. The only reason we saw it was because the tournament leader took us there.

It's said the Masters doesn't begin until the second nine on Sunday. Never has that been more true than when twenty-one-year-old McIlroy, the hottest young talent in the game, came to the second nine with a one-shot lead. Expectations were dashed quickly, as early as the 10th tee, when the can't-miss kid missed.

"I felt comfortable on that tee shot all week," said McIlroy, "and for some reason I just started it a little left of where I wanted to, hit that tree, and I don't think anyone's been over there in those cabins before." The Ulsterman took the tour of homes and wrestled his way to a triple-bogey 7. The Masters was lost. McIlroy ended up in a tie for 15th but bounced back with a dominating win in that year's U.S. Open.

I.K. Kim
2012 Kraft Nabisco
Championship

"Golf is one of very few sports where the fans actually play the game," says Brandel Chamblee. That's why we can so easily identify when the unpredictable raises its head in championship competition. The International Archive of Short Putts Missed is housed in our collective unconscious. There are the thousands we've witnessed on weekends, not to mention the shockers we've seen missed by Scott Hoch, Doug Sanders, and even Hale Irwin, who whiffed a one-inch putt on 14 in the 1983 Open Championship.

At least I.K. Kim had youth on her side. The twenty-three-year-old South Korean came to the 18th green with a one-shot lead and a makeable birdie putt. She missed the putt but still had the lead. Simply make the one-foot come-backer, par the hole, and walk off with the hardware. Kim went through her routine and stroked the putt well, only to see it circumnavigate the cup and come defiantly to rest on the edge closest to Kim. The horror of her miss and the shock in her reaction underscored the moment. The young qualifier left the green in an obvious daze. She fell into a playoff with Sun Young Yoo and lost.

She'll mark and go through the routine. And wait for that final group to finish up to make it official. In all likelihoo... *Ooooh.* *Hang on!* *Oh my gosh.* I'm not sure I've ever seen a putt that short missed at a moment like this, Judy.... This was just a formality. And it's no longer that.

TERRY GANNON

2012 Masters

Bubba Watson

Playoff

Bubba Watson is an original. There is no professional golfer who swings like him or thinks like him. Notably he hits shots that only he can hit. Such was the stunner he played on Sunday afternoon to close out the 2012 Masters.

After hooking his ball into the trees on the right side of No. 10, the second hole of his playoff against Louis Oosthuizen, Watson had about 164 yards to the hole as the crow flies but much more than that as the ball would fly. The situation called for a low, then sweeping hook covering some forty yards from left to right. He hit his fifty-two-degree gap wedge that started low to clear the trees in front of him and then found altitude. The shot seemed impossible, but not for Watson, who has yet to find a shot he can't hit.

The first time Watson ever worked with his caddie, Ted Scott, he told him, "If I have a swing, I've got a shot." That Sunday afternoon, the duo was heading down the 10th fairway to find what challenge awaited them in the tree-filled right side of the fairway. Scott piped up, saying to his boss, "If you've got a swing, you've got a shot."

The ball came to rest less than ten feet from the hole. The rest is history.

OOPS

Adam Scott
2012 Open
Championship

Heavy lies the head that wears the label "Best Player Never to Win a Major." With four holes to go in The Open Championship at Lytham, Adam Scott finally seemed poised to win his first major championship and drop out of the bidding. Holding a four-shot lead with four holes to play, and boasting the most envied swing in the civilized world, Scott was a shoo-in to win. But nobody asked Golf.

Scott inexplicably bogeyed the last four holes. Each of his bogeys seemed to be answered by an Ernie Els birdie. Before we knew it, Els was rejoicing what was likely to be a second Open Championship title, while Scott was wallowing in difficulty. Still, Scott did eke out a chance to tie Els and force a playoff with his good friend, but the Aussie missed a ten-foot par putt at the 18th hole.

Els comforted his defeated friend, telling him not to beat himself up and convincing the young Australian that there were major championships in his future. Els' words would prove correct nine months later, when Scott would become the first Australian ever to win the Masters.

ADAM SCOTT VS. ERNIE ELS
2012 OPEN CHAMPIONSHIP

There are thousands of professional golf tournaments conducted around the world on an annual basis. That surfeit of competition typically allows the wayward, the losers, the embarrassed to find solace in the shadows. But for contenders in the major championships, the experience, played out in front of millions, can be searing. As one of the best players in the world who hadn't yet won a major title, Adam Scott was under intense scrutiny as The Open Championship returned to Royal Lytham. Scott, who had led all week, came into a windy Sunday with a four-shot lead. When he still led by 4 with four holes to play, it seemed clear that this was going to be Scott's long-awaited breakthrough.

But Scott imploded. He bogeyed the last four holes. "I know I've let a really great chance slip through my fingers today. But somehow I'll look back and take the positives from it," he said. "I don't think I've ever played this well in a major championship, so that's a good thing for me moving forward. All the stuff I'm doing is going in the right direction. Today is one of those days, and that's why they call it golf."

Ernie Els had backed into an Open Championship title, his second. But Scott was right. He was moving in the right direction, even if Sunday at Lytham was a small step backward. In 2013, Scott would break through with a major championship at the Masters. And in May 2014, he would displace Tiger Woods as the world's top-ranked player.

Ernie Els was typically gracious in his victory over Adam Scott at The Open Championship.

RORY McILROY
2012 PGA CHAMPIONSHIP

What were you doing on weekends when you were twenty-one? Odds are it was something slightly less productive than what Rory McIlroy was doing in April 2011 when, after the third round of the Masters, the baby-faced Ulsterman held a four-shot lead.

Of course, it all fell apart the next day as McIlroy proceeded to shoot the worst round ever turned in by a fifty-four-hole leader of the tournament. His back-nine 43 began with a drive so far left on No. 10 that the youngster was wandering like an uncredentialed patron amid Augusta National's private cabins.

The few who wrote McIlroy off after his embarrassing collapse were educated two months later when Rors won the U.S. Open in a cakewalk, beating perpetual major contender Jason Day by eight shots. McIlroy rewrote a healthy portion of the record books that day. His seventy-two-hole score of 268 beat the previous record of 272 held by, among others, Jack Nicklaus, and he became the youngest winner of the U.S. Open since Bobby Jones.

There were those who considered his Congressional romp a fluke. They, too, were proven wrong in 2012, when McIlroy won the 2012 PGA Championship by a record eight strokes, surpassing Nicklaus's thirty-two-year-old record margin of seven shots set in the 1980 edition. A few things set McIlroy apart that day. Aside from his dazzling swing and killer short game was the easy boyish pleasure he took in dismantling the devious Ocean Course at Kiawah, one of Pete Dye's most demanding tracks. He started Sunday with a three-shot lead and never so much as twitched. He shot a bogey-free 66 to leave the field stranded on the beach. The win, which made McIlroy the youngest multi-major champion since Seve Ballesteros, was so dominating that no one even remembers who came in second (David Lynn).

"To sit up here and see this trophy and call myself a multiple major champion, I know I've talked about it in the past, and not many people have done it," said McIlroy. "Yeah, I'm very privileged to join such an elite list of names."

Rory McIlroy watches his drive from the 8th tee during the final round at Kiawah Island.

PHIL MICKELSON

2013 OPEN
CHAMPIONSHIP

Phil Mickelson chips onto the
16th green at Muirfield.

In June 2013, Phil Mickelson finished second in the U.S. Open for the sixth time. To many observers this one was a senseless, needless, heartbreaking loss.

The next month, Mickelson took his game to Scotland for the Aberdeen Asset Management Scottish Open. Although Mickelson had fared adequately in previous pilgrimages to the U.K., the consensus was that for Mickelson, who hits a high, yawning ball, the most difficult of the four major championships would always be the browned-out, wind-ravaged rota of The Open Championship. Sure, he'd lost a playoff for the 2007 Scottish Open to Frenchman Gregory Havret, but that championship had been played on the American-style parkland course at Loch Lomond GC. So when he won the 2013 edition on the stunning Castle Stuart links, beating Branden Grace on the first hole of a sudden-death playoff, Mickelson proved his doubters wrong. Critics began to wonder if maybe he could actually win the Open, which was scheduled for the coming week at Muirfield. Mickelson, who also won the week before he captured the 2006 Masters, was asked if such a Scot-slam was possible.

"I certainly hope so," he said. "I don't think there's a better way to get ready for a major championship or an Open Championship than playing the week before, playing well the week before, and getting into contention. And coming out on top just gives me more confidence. But there's a lot that's involved in the British Open.

You need some luck; you need some luck with your tee times, and you need to play well and have some good bounces."

Mickelson had all of the above at Muirfield. He was lucky that Lee Westwood, who led the championship by two shots going into the final round, hobbled in with a final-round 75. Few of the other contenders made Sunday moves, while Mickelson may have had the finest single round of his life. His 66 included birdies on four of the last six holes and will go down in history as one of the finest final rounds in major championship history.

"[I played] probably the best round of my career and hit some of the best shots that I've ever hit and certainly putted better than I've ever putted," said Mickelson, as the pain of losing another U.S. Open weeks earlier seemed to slip away. "I was getting ready for today and I just thought, 'I need to bring my A-game today. I need to show up and play some of my best golf.' And I did. You have to be resilient in this game, because losing is such a big part of it. And after losing the U.S. Open, it could have easily gone south, where I was so deflated I had a hard time coming back. But I looked at it and thought I was playing really good golf. I didn't want it to stop me from potential victories this year, and some potential great play. And I'm glad I didn't, because I worked a little bit harder. And in a matter of a month I'm able to change entirely the way I feel."

ADAM SCOTT
2013 MASTERS

Considering the impact that Australia has had on the game of golf, it's hard to believe that as of Saturday, April 13, 2013, not a single Aussie had won the Masters. The next day, three Aussies—Jason Day, Marc Leishman, and Adam Scott—were all in contention. In the end, Down Under honors went to Adam Scott, who turned back Angel Cabrera, the Zelig of major championship final rounds, in a sudden-death playoff. For denizens of the northern hemisphere, it's hard to appreciate just what Scott's win—made all the more redemptive for his collapse at the 2012 Open Championship—meant for Aussies, New Zealanders, and probably even residents of Papua New Guinea. Augusta National member and native Kiwi Craig Heatley hosted the post-Masters press conferences.

In introducing the newly robed champion, Heatley said that after Scott holed out for the win, Heatley himself "heard about thirty million people in Australia and New Zealand all cheering as well." At that point, the lump in Heatley's throat took over. He turned to Scott and mumbled, "I can't talk much, can you?"

Adam Scott's tee shot on 17 during a practice round at the Masters.

BEST
OF THE
MAJORS

INBEE PARK
2013 U.S.
WOMEN'S OPEN

When Inbee Park won the 2008 U.S. Women's Open at Interlachen CC, she was nineteen years old. Calm, unaffected, and cheerful, the young South Korean embodied golf's rarest exacta: the studied skills of a veteran and the nerveless aplomb of youth. As the contenders that day ceded one by one to the weight of history, Park strolled in, seemingly unaware that each step brought her closer to history. By day's end, she had become the youngest-ever winner of the game's most demanding championship.

"I didn't know what was going on at that time," Park said. "I played very good golf then, but I didn't know what I was playing for."

Then Park went her next seventy-two starts without a win. Maybe she was maturing. By June 2012, the caterpillar had become the butterfly, and Park embarked on one of the most dominant runs the game has ever seen. In twelve months she won eight times, including back-to-back majors, a four-stroke win in the Kraft Nabisco Championship, and a playoff win over Catriona Matthew in the Wegman's LPGA Championship.

By the time she arrived at Sebonack GC, in Southampton, New York, the much-talked-about Tom Doak–Jack Nicklaus collaboration on the Peconic Bay, Park was as poised and proven as a twenty-four-year-old can be. The pre-tournament hype focused almost entirely on her pending bid to join Babe Zaharias in winning the first three major championships of the year.

In order to manage the pressure of expectations, Park leaned heavily on her Korea-based mental coach, Sookyung Cho. "She tried to let me focus on one thing on the golf course. You know, not to think about something else. If it's red, just think about red. That is just an example."

Red, as in red numbers. Thanks to flawless putting and hugely improved driving, her first three rounds at the par-72 course were all under par, affording Park a virtually prohibitive 4-shot lead heading into the final stanza. "What are you going to do when you go against someone that hot?" said awestruck contender Paula Creamer. "You've got to kind of match her and practice harder, work harder. She is one of the best putters I think I've ever seen. Right now, she's just literally making everything. It helps when you are a good ball striker, too." With breezy conditions and pin placements that baffled the field, Park carded a worry-free 74, good enough to win by 4 shots.

In twelve months she won eight times, including back-to-back majors, a four-stroke win in the Kraft Nabisco Championship, and a playoff win over Catriona Matthew in the Wegman's LPGA Championship.

Inbee Park's victory celebration after winning the U.S. Women's Open at Sebonack GC.

The Changing Game

*This isn't your grandfather's game.
Whether it's the demographics of the people playing the sport,
the equipment we're using, the technology we're embracing,
the turf we're treading, or even the rules under which we play,
the game has undergone a radical evolution.
Or has it?*

All the technology we have today is excellent as long as you have someone to filter it and dilute it for you. Otherwise, you should make standard operating procedure of having in your golf bag a very large bottle of Advil.

MARTIN HALL

An illustration of a fictional adjustable club hints at how far new technology has brought the game.

For most of its life, golf has been an experiment based on a simple query: "What if?"

What if I hit this rock with this staff? What if we make a hole and see who can make it to the hole in fewer strokes? What if we made implements specifically designed for the contest or fashioned a ball that was more obedient and predictable? What if we implemented grooves or dimples or steel shafts? What if we gripped it this way? Or maybe the way Harry Vardon grips it?

Golf is a passion augmented by science and technology, but like other, more serious pursuits, technological innovation is now pushing the enterprise. The most obvious example is video. Until golf appeared on TV (the first telecast of the game was the 1947 U.S. Open at St. Louis CC broadcast by KSD-TV, the NBC affiliate in St. Louis), very few golf swings were ever seen in moving images. Newsreels shared with the masses the swings of icons like Bobby Jones, and in 1931, just after completing the Grand Slam, Jones himself starred in a series of humorous instructional films produced by Warner Bros. But the mass distribution of cheap, accessible, instant video didn't begin until the 1980s, when handheld camcorders replaced the 8mm film cameras on which so many family movies were recorded. Today, with complete video capability in virtually every person's pocket, golfers and their instructors have the ability to see swing images on demand and separate "feel from real."

One product of that revolution is Golf Channel. "I think Golf Channel is one of the biggest, if not the biggest, reason that we see so many great young players making their way in professional golf right now. Golf Channel gave young players a very clear understanding of who professional golfers were," said Golf Channel analyst and longtime PGA Tour player Brandel Chamblee. "When I was growing up, we saw only the very best players in the world, playing their very best for about an hour on Saturday and Sunday. There was this mystique to professional golfers that took me a year or two or three to overcome when I got out on tour. I thought I was walking amongst gods. But at eight, ten, or twelve years old, today's kids are tuning in on a Thursday or a Friday, and they see Tiger and Phil and Rickie Fowler shooting 77 sometimes. That humanizes them. It shows every player from 360 degrees. So when kids come out on tour now, they know every course; they know every shot; they know every tour pro, and so there's not as much intimidation."

The more recent trend transforming how we engage with golf is social media. At last count there were 234 professional golfers on Twitter, ranging from Jimin Kang with 245 followers to Tiger Woods, with nearly four million. For the lesser-known player, Twitter has proven an effective way to grow a fan base and gain some awareness for a player and his or her sponsors. For the more heavily followed players, particularly Woods, the service provides a dedicated medium, alternative to or parallel to the mainstream press, for distributing announcements and scheduling information. As a fan-outreach tool, Twitter is unmatched, allowing players and fans instant dialogue at a seemingly safe remove. Followers of Ian Poulter and Lee Westwood have had a front-row seat for the British duo's tongue-in-cheek battle over each other's apparel choices.

Twitter has not always been the athlete's friend, however. Steve Elkington has earned his share of critics for his politically charged tweets. And in 2014, after breaking off his high-profile engagement with tennis star Caroline Wozniacki, Rory McIlroy, who had been a devotee of the 140-character service, swore off Twitter. It didn't last. (Stacy Lewis and Lee Westwood have also sworn off the tweets.)

As impactful as technology has been on the swing and on the fan experience, its most profound effect might be found far from the range or the ropes. The whole spectrum of technological innovation, from computer modeling to GPS, has added immeasurably to the business of designing and maintaining golf courses.

Today's courses are still designed by humans with sharp pencils and keen imaginations. And the detail work, the finish that goes into the greens of a place like Pinehurst No. 2, where the margin for error on an approach shot is inches or less, can only be done by a human being with old-school tools such as a level and a rod.

Still, technology and the overwhelming amount of data now available have taken much of the guesswork out of designing golf courses. It used to be a designer's hunch as to where the proper landing area for a hole should be placed. Not anymore. "With GPS we can track what golf balls are doing now," says golf course architect Bill Bergin. "We know how far people are hitting it better than we ever have, so we know where to put the landing area and where to put the green."

The technology is arguably more vital to the growing restoration segment of the golf course design market than original design. Older courses that are trying to create a record of their topography or trying to restore a course to its original design are benefiting from advanced laser-mapping technology (some of which is used by television networks to "read" putts for viewers). The National Golf Links of America recently mapped all of its greens with lasers. The club is also using GPS to assist in maintenance. "GPS technology has certainly made recording and irrigation planning much better," said Bill Salinetti, the superintendent at National. "Before GPS, valves and lines were lost all the time. GPS also enables rebuilding to be much more precise than ever before."

Twitter has proven an effective way to grow a fan base and gain some awareness for a player or his or her sponsors.

GPS, in smartphones and hand-held devices, has brought powerful data to every golfer.

So much of the current global economy is based on data, it would be naive to think that golf would be immune. What if all that data being transmitted via iPhones and GPS and yardage-measuring devices and tools such as ShotLink and Arccos cold be collected and put to work for game improvement? "I think that's the next big step," said David Feherty. "We have all this data going out and coming in, and someone is going to find a way to tie it all together and make players better."

One of the most fruitful areas for technology advancement has been television. The experience of viewing golf in 2015 is immeasurably different and better than it was in 1995. Tommy Roy, executive producer of golf for Golf Channel on NBC, has been working in golf television for twenty-three years. He was asked what he considers the three biggest advances in golf television over the past twenty years.

High Definition

"Golf is played on a three-dimensional field," explains Roy, "So you need to know the lie and the undulations, and because TV is a two-dimensional medium, it doesn't do that very well." As an example of traditional TV's shortcomings, Roy invokes the dynamic terrain of Augusta National. "Here's the first thing someone says when they visit the Masters for the first time: 'Wow, I never knew it was so hilly.' Having high definition really helps with that. It's not perfect—until we get holographic TV it's not going to be perfect—but it really helps the viewer at home know what players are dealing with."

Audio

A little-known fact: Audio feedback from well-hit (or poorly struck) shots is as instructive, if not more so, than the visual feedback of ball flight. No surprise that Roy ranks advances in audio technology among the most significant. "We're now able to listen in on conversations between players and caddies," he says. Because the microphones are so good and viewers can hear the ball strike so clearly at home, viewers can tell immediately if it's hit fat or thin, and if the ball is headed off line you can hear it bounce off a railroad tie or splash into a pond.

Wiring

Maybe the greatest advance in the coverage of golf is the advent of eighteen-hole coverage. This is a huge leap from the early days of golf TV, which typically featured one green. This bonanza would not have been available without advances in the technology that wires TV cameras. "When I first started in this business, the wires to cameras were about an inch and a half thick, and only one camera was served by one wire," says Roy. "Today we have fiber-optic cable. It's about the width of your little finger, and eighteen cameras and eighteen microphones go down that one line. That has made eighteen-hole coverage a reality."

The biggest advance in golf equipment over the past twenty years is also the most mundane. It has nothing to do with space-age technology or mind-bending fabrications or Internet wizardry (although all of them can play a part). It's the simple act of getting into golfers' hands clubs that actually fit them.

There was a time when custom-fitting was reserved for the elite, the finest players in the game. The great players of the past century often had their clubs custom made. For instance, Jack Wulkotte was the genius behind Jack Nicklaus' clubs for decades. But as custom-fitting technology became less of a trade and more a computerized function, it became far more widely available and far less

Brandel Chamblee's Best & Worst Things That Have Happened to Golf

I have this vision of golf in the near future: My kids are playing a three-hole course in fifteen minutes with their caps on backwards, YouTubing every swing, tweeting every thought, and partially paralyzed by swing-tip apps they just downloaded. Such is the nature of our over-caffeinated, increasingly distracted youth, as well as some of the proposals to counter the decay of the number of people who are playing golf today. Indeed, the governing bodies are desperate to grow the game. Well intentioned as they are, when I hear these "grow the game" proposals, I can't help but think that golf may not be for everyone. Perhaps it's just too expensive and hard, but other trends in the game have hurt its growth, too.

But I'm not totally pessimistic about golf's future. There have been other, more positive developments in the game that give me hope that my kids might one day break 80 playing eighteen holes in four hours, with their shirts tucked in while enjoying each other's company and savoring the opportunity to be outdoors.

I'm certain of one thing: that the good things that have happened in this game over the past fifty years far outweigh the bad.

THE WORST

1. Losing Tony Lema and Payne Stewart

The deaths of Lema in 1966 and Stewart in 1999, both as the result of aircraft accidents, robbed golf of two of its most engaging champions in the primes of their lives. Stewart made the putt of his life to win the 1999 U.S. Open, his third major title. But what he did afterward said more about who he was than that putt. Taking Phil Mickelson's face in both hands, Stewart tried to ease the pain of the loss by reminding him of the larger picture of impending parenthood. When Grantland Rice wrote, "For when the One Great Scorer comes to write against your name, He marks—not that you won or lost—but how you played the game," he was writing of men like Tony and Payne.

2. Slow play

It gets blamed for declining participation numbers more than the changing social dynamic of women working more and men playing less. Because of technology, players are longer and far less accurate, so they take more time to size up shots. Holes have reached absurd distances, which take longer to walk, and greens have reached insane speeds, which take longer to putt. There is no chance tour players will move appreciably faster in the future. Because what we see is what we do, the rest of us won't be speeding up, either.

3. The rule against anchored strokes

Golf is supposed to be a game for a lifetime, and the anchored putter was a port in the storm of fraying nerves caused by aging. The USGA and R&A, both of which have done so much good, stood silent on this issue for forty-plus years and then stood insolent to the petitions of many.

4. The Stimpmeter

It's a device used to measure the speed of greens, which seems harmless enough, but it has led to an addiction to slicker greens. Greens committees put pressure on golf course architects to stress the grasses by mowing them to whisker height so they can brag about their

I'm certain of one thing: that the good things that have happened in this game over the past fifty years far outweigh the bad.

THE BEST

1. Arnold Palmer and Jack Nicklaus
No sport has ever had two better examples of how to compete, how to win, and how to lose. The game is indebted to these two for the safekeeping of its traditions, as either could have used his immense power to avoid the obligations that come with enormous success.

3. Advances in equipment
Golf equipment intoxicates us. Much-maligned developments such as perimeter-weighted irons, investment-cast clubs, square grooves, metal-headed drivers, fairway clubs, hybrids, and two-piece balls have made this game more exciting and easier for everyone. Critics say the governing bodies have been remiss in their duties to protect the game. Hogwash.

course's green speeds, oblivious to the fact that putting on such slippery surfaces inevitably slows play to a glacial pace.

5. Overly complicated instruction
The Golfing Machine, a book written by Homer Kelley and published in 1969, breaks the swing down into numerous components, each of which has three to ten variables, resulting in an almost endless number of possible combinations. Kelley, who died in 1983, seems to have been a well-meaning and well-educated man, but his book achieved cult status and unfortunately spawned copycat books and teachers who want to make the game so complicated that they alone are the ones with the answers.

2. Tiger Woods
He possesses an aptitude for this game that we cannot explain. Such virtuosity, comparable to that of a Mozart, a Michelangelo, a Picasso, a da Vinci, a Rembrandt, makes us wonder how gifts so absolute come into being. We evaluate artists and athletes by how they are able to change history. Tiger has no rival for impact in his profession.

4. The Golden Age revival of golf course architecture over the past twenty years
It has given us Bandon Dunes, Cape Kidnappers, Ballyneal, Friars Head, and Sand Hills, to name a few. The popularity of these venues illustrates the lengths to which golfers will go to play a course uncorrupted by someone's contrived aesthetic appeal, both of commercialism and design.

You want to play golf in three hours with one ball and breathe inspiring air? Play Old Macdonald at Bandon Dunes.

5. Keeping it simple
Harvey Penick, with his direct way of communicating, avoiding all technicality, was the well-known teacher of Ben Crenshaw, Tom Kite, Mickey Wright, Kathy Whitworth, and countless others, famous and not. All of them came away better golfers and people for having been in his company. Penick, who died in 1995 shortly before Crenshaw's second Masters victory, was known to take a day to answer a student's question, so careful was he in choosing the right words, realizing their lasting impact. He took this complicated game and made it simple and charged $5 for a lesson.

"Everybody can see that my swing is homegrown. That means everybody has a chance to do it."
WATSON

"Without your downs, without the hardship, I don't think you appreciate the ups as much. I think the fact that I struggled so much, the fact that I went through a hard period of my life, the fact that this trophy is right next to me, it means so much more to me than it ever would have when I was fifteen."
WIE after winning the 2014 U.S. Open

BUBBA WATSON

Hubba Bubba, Watson's a two-time Masters champ.

Career wins: 6 on the PGA Tour

Major championships: 2 (2012, 2014 Masters)

▼ KARRIE WEBB

Caught in her Webb: Karrie dominates the LPGA Tour in a Major way.

Career wins: 57 (41 on the LPGA Tour, No. 10 all-time)

Major championships: 7 (2000, 2006 Kraft Nabisco Championship; 2001 LPGA; 2000, 2001 U.S. Women's Open; 1999 du Maurier Classic; 2002 Women's British Open)

"I still can't believe that I've achieved what I have. It's like I've lived a dream for about five years now."
WEBB

MICHELLE WIE

Wie-sy does it! Former teen star Wie becomes a major player at the 2014 U.S. Open.

Career wins: 4 on the LPGA Tour

Major championships: 1 (2014 U.S. Open)

TIGER WOODS

Wounded Tiger is tracking the Golden Bear's record.

Career wins: 79 on the PGA Tour (second all-time)

Major championships: 14 (1997, 2001, 2002, 2005 Masters; 2000, 2002, 2008 U.S. Open; 2000, 2005, 2006 Open Championship; 1999, 2000, 2006, 2007 PGA Championship)

"I still think he'll break my record. He's thirty-eight years old and he's probably got another ten years.... That's forty more majors to win five of them. It shouldn't be too difficult."
JACK NICKLAUS

expensive. Custom-fit clubs still cost more than off-the-rack models, and the fitting process alone can take well over an hour, but the results—clubs that fit your proportions and your unique swing—are worth it. While many golfers feel their 15-handicap doesn't warrant the expense or time, the fact is, they can benefit more from a fitting than the scratch player. Martin Hall, host of Golf Channel's *School of Golf*, calls proper fitting a huge leap forward. "In this particular regard," says Hall, "technology has been very, very helpful."

"Custom-fitting has allowed people to make a more dynamic motion," adds Golf Channel's Michael Breed. "Take a guy like George Archer. Six-foot-five or so, his golf swing was largely affected by the fact that everybody had the same-length golf clubs. That changed once custom-fit clubs came around. For the club player, club-head speed has increased significantly. There is a right club for each individual."

The Shaft

The shaft is the transmission of the swing, storing and transferring the power of the player's coil and uncoil into the ball. It's vital, but it's not sexy. Most casual players can tell you all about their clubheads but little about their shafts. Yet some of the most exciting and profound changes in how we play golf are happening there as advanced materials are infused into the game.

If the emergence of the steel shaft in the 1930s can be tagged as the beginning of the modern era of golf shafts, then the early 1970s can be regarded as the very dawn of the ultramodern age. It was then that companies such as Union Carbide, after years of experimentation with carbon fiber for other purposes, began to look at the use of such fibers in golf shafts. When Gay Brewer won the 1972 Taiheiyo Masters in Japan—then one of the highest-purse tournaments in golf—with black graphite shafts, the trend toward advanced materials in golf shafts accelerated. For a time in the 1980s, graphite seemed to threaten steel's hold, but in the years since, graphite has come to dominate only the driver segment, while steel remains the shaft of choice for most irons. In recent years, however, graphite has been gaining ground, particularly in 3-woods and some fairway woods and hybrids. We are even seeing graphite and steel combined in one shaft.

Today, graphite is much more consistent and is growing again in popularity, along with composites and mixes of materials, such as carbon fiber and steel. For all their material advancement, the biggest key to shaft evolution over the past twenty years has been the endless quest to shave weight from the shaft while maintaining or enhancing power. "Lighter shafts create higher clubhead speeds, particularly later in a round when the player might be getting a little bit fatigued. They can make shafts that weigh half what they did just a few years ago," says Breed.

The Ball

The golf ball is one of the most abused and among the most misunderstood pieces of equipment in all of sports. It also happens to be among the most sophisticated.

It all started hundreds of years ago. Scots first started playing with "featheries," golf balls painstakingly constructed of animal skins stuffed with feathers. When golfers then progressed to the more mass-producible rubbery molded ball known as the "gutty," the Scots quickly realized that older, pockmarked gutties were flying farther than their newer, smoother ones. The rough edges were producing a turbulence near the surface of the spinning, flying ball that actually reduced drag. Dimpling was born and has been part of the game ever since.

Golf ball fabrication has undergone significant change and advancement in the past twenty years. Well into the 1990s, three-piece wound balata balls (a liquid core, surrounded by wound elastic band and covered with dimpled balata) were the preference of the better player who was willing to sacrifice distance, durability, and cost for greater spin on his or her approach shots. Higher handicappers preferred two-piece balls for their durability, their length, and their relative inexpensiveness.

"When I was younger," says Breed, "I had to choose between a spin ball and a distance ball."

What if one ball could offer all of the benefits of these two?

In the late 1990s, golf ball manufacturers informed the USGA that they were on the verge of just such a development. The new balls could provide significantly more distance to balata players, while granting "rock" players improved playability. "The distance ball doesn't go any farther than it already did," says Breed. "It's just that the other ball caught up to it." The new ball technology blossomed. In October 2000, Titleist's ProV1 made its debut on the PGA Tour. In his very first tournament using the new ball, Billy Andrade captured his fourth Tour title, the 2001 Invensys Classic.

The Putter

For much of its life, the putter was the fourteenth club out of fourteen clubs, an implement found in the garage or hand-me-downed by an uncle or a brother who'd lost faith. Now, it's one of the most exciting pieces of equipment in your bag.

Putter technology has always lagged behind that of the other clubs, but since the 1990s, the focus on putters and putting has intensified. According to Breed, putting has benefited most from:

Face technology. "It's become vital in furthering our understanding of how to get a ball rolling better, more efficiently."

Moment of inertia. "Today's awareness of MOI [moment of inertia], the club's resistance to twisting at impact, is helping people who have a hard time swinging the putter head through the ball."

Face balancing. "This is really important and can help an awful lot of people putt better."

Fitting. "Yes, even for putters."

But there is a much bigger story in recent putter history: the rise and fall of the long putter. It was a long time coming. The long putter has been around for decades. Way before today's current crop of tour professionals reached for the crutch, Johnny Miller used it to salve some putting demons. For almost as long, traditionalists have been bemoaning its use. Some see it as a perversion, maybe even a circumvention of the putting stroke. Others see it as just plain unsightly. The debate reached a crescendo in 2011 when Keegan Bradley became the first person to win a major championship with a long putter.

Not long after Bradley's win, golf's ruling bodies, the USGA and R&A, proposed a ban on anchored putting. Long putters could still be used, but players would be forbidden from "anchoring" the club to either the belly or the chest.

The Tour, defending its players' rights, protested, as did the PGA of America, on grounds that the ban would limit the capabilities of everyday golfers who had

Historic golf balls (above) stand in quaint contrast to the interior technologies of today's balls (right), as documented by photographer Jim Friedman.

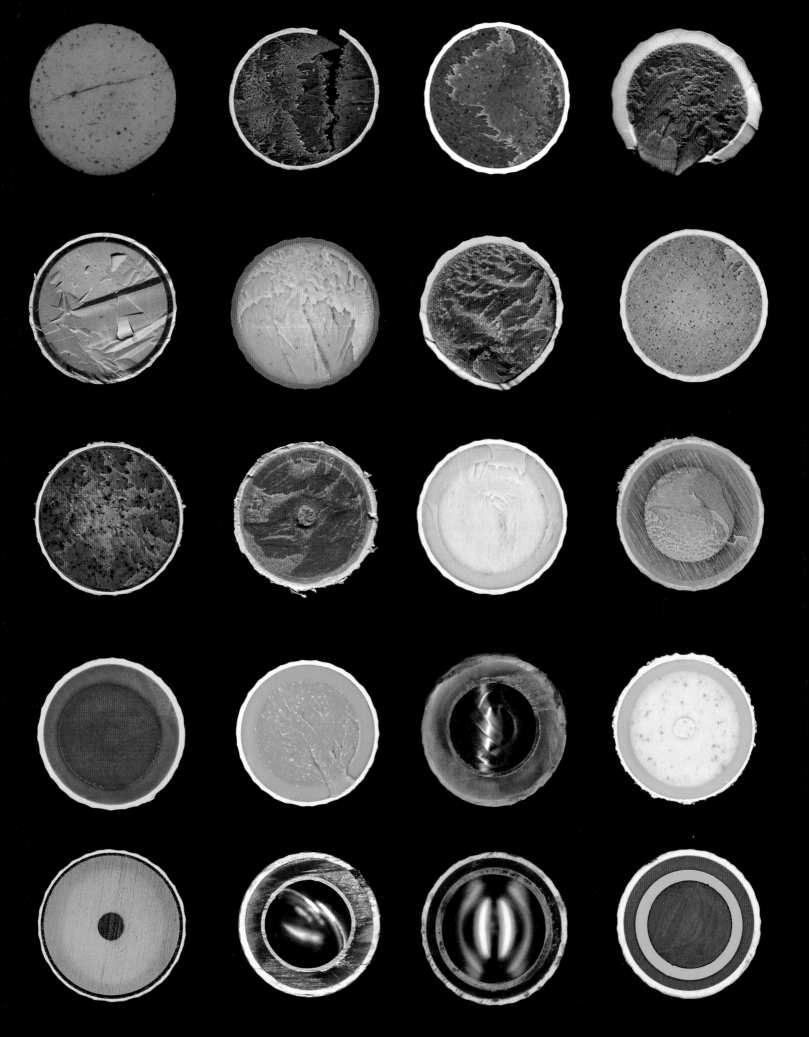

come to rely on the long stick. But in May 2013, the ban was enacted with an effective date of January 1, 2016. Golf Channel's Hall supports the ban. "If the putter is anchored, then you have a mechanical advantage over another putter that isn't anchored," he says. "I think that controlling your nerves is part of performance, and I would not be in favor of anything that takes that away."

Interestingly, the regulatory heat on the long putter spurred a countertrend: counterbalancing. Players have been adding weight to the grip end of clubs for decades, but since the stable sensation that comes with using a counterbalanced putter is similar to the sensation derived from a long putter, the countertrend is providing hounded long-putter users with a refuge.

Most Important Clubs of 1995–2015

Hello, Hybrid. Goodbye, Long Irons

It comes down to which you like more: romance or accuracy. So far romance is getting crushed. There was something mystical about watching Jack Nicklaus command a 1-iron into the 17th green at Pebble Beach. If in 1950 at Merion, photographer Hy Peskin had snapped an image of Ben Hogan posing with a 1-hybrid, it might not have become the iconic image of mid-twentieth-century golf. That's because irons connect players of all eras. Sure, shafts and balls and turf are different, but the heft and unforgiving look of a 1- or 2- or 3-iron make all golfers kin. Hard to hit? Yup. But when you did it right, there was a feel unmatched in golf, a feeling that fewer and fewer players know.

The long putter has been a point of controversy from its first arrival on professional tours. Adam Scott adopted the putter style in 2011.

2003 PGA Championship
Shaun Micheel
Final Round

Until August 2003, the best shot Shaun Micheel had ever hit was holing a 6-iron to make the cut in a Hooter's Tour event. Consider what he did at Oak Hill in the final round of the 2003 PGA Championship an upgrade. His nearly perfect 174-yard 7-iron approach rocked the world when it came to rest only two inches from the hole. The shot not only fended off challenger Chad Campbell, but it won Micheel's first PGA Tour title of any kind, and a major championship to boot.

The good news is that hybrid clubs—a design mix of an iron and a fairway wood—largely do what they promise: that is, they offer the average player more options and better results. They not only make it easier to get the ball aloft from all kinds of lies but also easier to hold the green. Hall puts it succinctly: "Hybrids are as close to cheating as you can get without breaking the rules." In fact, hybrids have become so entrenched in the game that many PGA Tour players are dropping their long irons from their bags. Of course some can't break the habit. At the 2013 PGA Championship at Oak Hill, Jason Day was looking for an option to his driver, something he could use off the tee but that would offer greater accuracy. Day, who has been a serial contender in major championships, yanked his 4-wood and replaced it with a 2-iron that was bent and lengthened into what was essentially a 1-iron. He finished tied for eighth.

Adjustability

As children we all had our outlandish visions of what life would be like in forty or fifty years. And while we're still waiting on flying cars and self-making beds and radio-controlled golf balls, the adjustable club is here to stay.

The last decade has witnessed the advent of genuine adjustability: high-end clubs with adjustable options for lie, loft, and face angle in order to promote or combat a draw or a fade. The adjustments can be made with the twist of a small wrench or the simple slide of a weight. The primary benefit of adjustable drivers is that they offer the player who struggles to get the ball off the ground greater loft. And for the player who manages to improve his swing and thus his control of the golf ball, he can adjust his club rather than buy a new one. The one caveat

They not only make it easier to get the ball aloft from all kinds of lies but also easier to hold the green.

The primary benefit of adjustable drivers is that they offer the player who struggles to get the ball off the ground greater loft.

regarding adjustables: USGA rules still forbid adjustment of the club during a round.

Michael Breed believes we are only at the very infancy of the adjustability revolution. "I think the future of the game is adjustability," says Breed, who adds that adjustability will change not only the clubs in our bags but also how we buy them. "In ten years you'll order entire sets of clubs directly from a manufacturer. You won't go through a PGA pro. You'll have a thirty-day money-back guarantee. Manufacturers will have two fully adjustable clubheads, one that goes from two degrees upright to two degrees flat; the other, standard lie to four degrees upright. Everybody will fit somewhere in the spectrum, and then adjustability will allow you to tweak it from there. That's where it's going to go."

Groovy, Baby, Yeah

Grooves have been among the most contentious topics over the past twenty years. "Grooves have absolutely changed the game in the last twenty years," says Breed. "The question is: For better or worse?"

The debate goes back to the 1940s, when the USGA and R&A adopted a rule requiring that the grooves on the face of a club be in a "V" shape, and that the space between the grooves be at least three times the width of the groove.

In 1984, the USGA and R&A adopted a new rule permitting clubs with U-shaped grooves but did not specify how to measure the width. Karsten began producing and selling Ping EYE2 irons with U-shaped grooves. These irons were enormously popular.

In 1987, the USGA announced a new method for measuring groove width, the "30-degree method," under which the Ping EYE2 was deemed nonconforming and barred from all championships. Karsten sued for $100 million. The case was settled in January 1990, and EYE2s were allowed again.

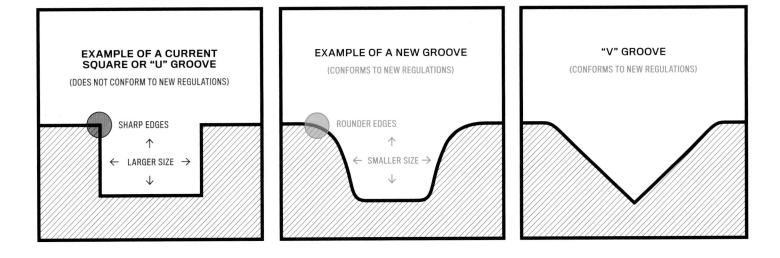

EXAMPLE OF A CURRENT SQUARE OR "U" GROOVE

(DOES NOT CONFORM TO NEW REGULATIONS)

SHARP EDGES
↑
← LARGER SIZE →
↓

EXAMPLE OF A NEW GROOVE

(CONFORMS TO NEW REGULATIONS)

ROUNDER EDGES
↑
← SMALLER SIZE →
↓

"V" GROOVE

(CONFORMS TO NEW REGULATIONS)

The PGA Tour got into the act, too, banning the Ping EYE2 from Tour play in 1989. Karsten leveled another $100 million suit against the Tour, and three years later that suit was also settled.

In 2010, taking note of the fact that greens in regulation were decreasingly correlated to fairways hit, the USGA began a rollback to smaller and less sharp grooves. As of January 2014, all USGA and R&A championships require the new grooves. In January 2020, the USGA will review the grooves legislation and its effect on the game.

"Grooves obviously create spin," says Breed. "It can be argued that one of the reasons why the ball goes so far is that modern grooves have taken the spin out of the shot. At the same time, it can be argued that by lessening the impact of grooves, you'll make it harder for the average player—who hits two to three greens per round—to spin the ball."

Turf

The Tiger Woods era has brought with it all kinds of comparisons. We compare Tiger with Jack, Woods with Jones, the persimmon era with the metalwood era, hickory with steel with graphite, and the merits of wound balata or modern balls. These are fun arguments, but any fair comparison between the golf of our era and its preceding sepia-toned decades typically misses an obvious element. It's right under our toes. Grass.

Technology has made massive leaps in the four hundred years of golf history, but it's not all in our clubs and balls. Advances in agronomy have had a massive impact on the game and how it's played. New varieties of turfgrass that can thrive on less water and at lower cut-heights add to rollout on drives and make putting surfaces more severe.

"Turf conditions have absolutely improved. It's not only that fairways and greens are firmer," says Breed, "it's that the grass itself has become more uniform. I remember hearing Billy Casper and Byron Nelson talk about all this stuff, and they said that when they would hit a ball into the fairway, it didn't necessarily mean they had a great lie. Back when they cut the grass with gang mowers, you'd get huge tufts of grass behind the ball. You could get a flier lie from the middle of

With less resistance from the grass, Stimpmeter speed increases, and as speed increases, the movement inherent in the putting surface itself is exaggerated. Putting has become measurably faster and more difficult.

the fairway. The turf has gotten better, and the equipment used to cut the turf has gotten better."

New strains that can lengthen a course's playing season add more enjoyment. Bill Salinetti is the superintendent at the famed National Golf Links of America on Long Island. He's seen enormous advances in turf maintenance in his twenty years in the business.

First on his list are growth regulators. "I can remember running trials using the first version of Primo [MAXX, a turfgrass regulator] back when I was an intern student at Winged Foot," says Salinetti. "It enabled you to safely regulate plant growth to increase green speeds and reduce clipping yield. This was the first product that was really safe to use on greens.

"Another advancement is the quality and variety of liquid fertilizers that are available now to turf managers. We can apply exactly what the turf needs in amounts that will be used efficiently. These products were just starting to get going when I was at Winged Foot and have advanced to the point where 75 percent of our fertility is done with liquids in small amounts."

The technology that has gone into the mundane task of cutting grass may be the most overlooked facet of agronomy's impact on the game. "We now have electrically driven and controlled mowers and reels," adds Salinetti. "This has eliminated the necessity for most of the hydraulic lines and can increase clip frequency, giving you a much better cut in one pass."

With better care and cutting, golf courses are enjoying turf that remains healthy at previously unimaginable heights. In the 1950s, putting surfaces at the best private golf courses would have measured about a quarter of an inch. Today they're less than half that, about one-tenth of an inch. Shorter, healthier grass and firmer putting surfaces have played a key role in the defense of par in the age of 350-yard drives. With less resistance from the grass, Stimpmeter speed increases, and as speed increases, the movement inherent in the putting surface itself is exaggerated. Putting has become measurably faster and more difficult.

Today's fairways are often cut to a height of a half-inch, much shorter than in the past.

The effect is notable on fairways as well. Decades ago, the grass on a well-maintained course would have measured roughly three-quarters of an inch. Technology has cut that back to half an inch. Less grass, less resistance. Less resistance, more roll. One of the most overlooked contributors to the length of today's drives is more roll.

Finally, there are spikes. The clackety-clack of steel spikes on a cement walkway was as much a rite of the game as formulating the bet on the first tee or shaking hands with your caddie. That was true until the early 1990s, when a group of golfers in the Pacific Northwest dropped the hobnailed shoes in order to protect fragile dormant fairways. From that point on, the soft spike or "spikeless" revolution caught fire and became the single largest and fastest equipment change in the modern game. Only twenty years later, the vast majority of golf courses—public and private—forbid metal spikes. The consumer is well ahead of them, as virtually every player has made the move to either soft-spiked shoes or the rapidly growing spikeless sneaker-style models. The benefits—lower impact on putting surfaces, less tracking of turf disease, less damage to clubhouse floors, and easier walking—have proven to far outweigh the presumed drawback of less traction.

"I think the change away from spikes is one of the reasons why green speeds have been able to get so much faster," says Breed, who sees that particular development as something of a double-edged sword. As nice as it might be to have a virtually perfect putting surface, Breed sees the downside as well. "In my candid opinion, green speed is the major reason why rounds of golf take so long. I think the advent of the soft spike has allowed our greens to get a lot faster. The overall effect has been very positive for putting surfaces but negative for pace of play. The faster the greens, the more putts are played. The more putts are played, the more thought, planning, reading goes into each putt. As greens get faster, breaks increase, and as breaks increase, it's harder and harder to putt."

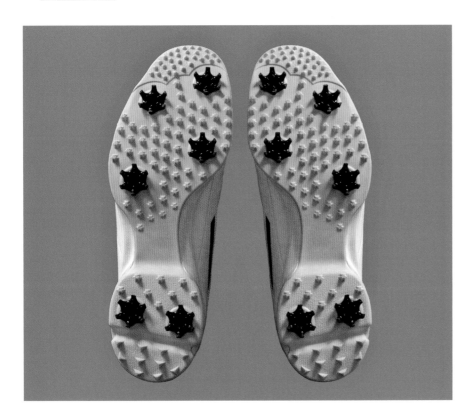

The death of metal spikes—and their replacement with innovative rubber and plastic cleats—was a change that happened in just a few years.

2004 Ford Championship
Craig Parry
Playoff

Craig Parry's brother was on the bag when he faced Scott Verplank in a playoff for the Ford Championship. "My brother said to me when we're going down 18, 'I feel a Shaun Micheel from the PGA coming on.' I just thought I would be happy to knock it on the green and have an opportunity for birdie," Parry said. "Sure enough, knocked it on line and it went in the hole." His 176-yard 6-iron brought an abrupt end to the playoff festivities. The same jury-rigged golf swing that Johnny Miller had earlier said would "make Ben Hogan puke" had won the day.

Asked about his self-styled move, Parry said looks are overrated. "It's a matter of getting the job done, I think," said Parry. "There are too many players that get up there and swing it really good and miss the cut. What would you rather do? Get up there and know where it's going or swing it really pretty? I think that's the lesson to be learned for a lot of young kids coming through. Don't just work on swing. Work on actually getting the ball around the golf course."

2004 Women's British Open
Karen Stupples
Final Round

If you're born and raised in England and you're going to win one major championship in your life, make it the Women's British Open. Even better: Win it at Sunningdale. And do it in historic fashion.

The Dover native had enjoyed a promising junior and collegiate career only to fall short of funds and return to her restaurant job in England after a short stint as a professional. When a customer at the restaurant offered to fund a three-year mulligan on the professional circuit, Stupples jumped at the opportunity. She earned her limited status on the 1999 LPGA Tour, returned to Q School, and earned exempt status onto the 2000 LPGA Tour. For the next three seasons she was a stalwart competitor, but it was in 2004 where her career took off. She set the record for lowest 72-hole score in LPGA history at the 2004 ANZ Ladies Masters.

It was on the Old Course at Sunningdale, in the shadow of her childhood home in Kent, where Stupples not only won the only major championship of her career but did so in jaw-dropping fashion. En route to a final round eight-under 64, which tied the record-low score in women's major championships, Stupples did something that will almost certainly never happen again: She started the round eagle-albatross. It started with her fifteen-foot eagle putt at the 485-yard par-5 first hole. Then Stupples topped herself at the next, holing out a 5-iron from 205 yards for a double-eagle two. She was 5-under par after two holes. It was the start to a historic day.

"I was really anticipating just birdie. Something like that would have done quite nicely," said Stupples, who retired in 2014. "But then when I hit a good shot in at the first, I thought, 'Well, let's see if we can make this and get off to a good start,' and, of course, the putt went in. On the second it just was a nice yardage for me to hit, and it was just right on line all the way. Unfortunately I didn't see it go in the hole, but the cheer from the crowd was absolutely unbelievable and really could not have come at a better time. When it went in, you think, 'Well, today could be my day.'"

Rules Are Rules

The Rules of Golf have always had sort of an Old Testament view of justice: "It's stroke and distance, Samson. Says so right here on the stone tablet."

But the rules of the game, which were first written in the mid-1700s and codified throughout Scotland more than a century later, are highly evolved documents that undergo continual review by the USGA and the R&A, the ruling bodies of the game. Every four years the organizations revisit the rules, while every two years they consider the Decisions on the Rules of Golf, which are simply examples of how a particular rule can be interpreted or applied. (During the most recent USGA-R&A conclave in 2013, some eighty-seven changes or additions were made to the decisions.) In the course of this endless editing of the game's manual, some of the harsher rules, such as the stymie or the restriction on cleaning one's golf ball, have gone by the wayside. In recent years, the rules have continued to evolve with an eye toward fairness, equity, and even speed of play.

"Gone with the Wind"

The kinder, gentler approach of the current-day rulesmakers is most apparent in their new exception to Rule 18-2b. The rule used to hold that if a player had grounded his club (usually a putter) behind the ball and a gust of wind or gravity then moved the ball, the player was deemed to have made the ball move and was assessed a stroke. This seemed especially harsh given the speed of today's putting surfaces. Among the many victims of the so-called windblown ball rule (Freddie Jacobson at the 2008 Open Championship, Padraig Harrington at the 2009 Masters, and Rory McIlroy at the 2011 Open Championship) was Webb Simpson. In 2011, on the 15th green in the final round of the Zurich Classic, Simpson, then looking for his first PGA Tour title, was enjoying a one-stroke lead over Bubba Watson and facing a five-inch putt. Simpson had grounded his putter well behind the ball, by his own estimate about four inches, when a gust of wind blew the ball about a quarter-inch from its resting place. Simpson called the penalty on himself, was assessed a 1-stroke penalty, and lost his lead. He eventually lost the tournament to Watson in a playoff. "When wind or other natural things affect the golf ball, the player shouldn't be penalized," said Simpson at the time.

Fittingly, Simpson was among the first Tour players to benefit from the rule change. In the final round of the 2013 RBC Heritage, as Simpson was getting ready to putt on the 6th hole, the wind off Calibogue Sound caused his ball to move. He was not penalized.

Bunker Mentality

In the third round of the 2008 Zurich Classic, Stewart Cink's drive at the 15th came close to a bunker. As part of his preparation for his second shot, Cink walked through the bunker. He played his second shot into a greenside bunker. In keeping with golf etiquette and tradition, Cink's caddie raked the fairway bunker before he addressed the third shot. Uh-oh. Cink's caddie had unwittingly violated Rule 13-4a of golf's Abrahamic code, which prohibits testing the condition of a hazard when the player's ball lies in a hazard. Of course, neither Cink nor his caddie were aware of the violation. So...he failed to add the requisite 2-shot penalty to his score, which meant that he had submitted an incorrect scorecard for the round, which meant he was DQ'd from the tournament.

Subsequently, common sense won again. Now, when the player's ball lies in a bunker: "it would not be a breach of the Rules if the player were to smooth the sand in another bunker, provided (a) the smoothing is for the sole purpose of caring for the course, (b) the smoothing does not breach Rule 13-2 (Improving Lie, Area of Intended Stance or Swing, or Line of Play) with respect to his next stroke."

I'm Late, I'm Late...

Maybe you overslept, maybe you were overserved, maybe the traffic really was that bad. Either way, golf never really cared. The official rule on tardiness to the tee box used to hold that a player had a five-minute grace period from his appointed tee time to arrive and commence a match. After five minutes, the miscreant was disqualified. In a rare acknowledgement that stuff happens, the USGA and R&A reduced the penalty to loss of the first hole in match play or 2 strokes at the 1st hole in stroke play.

Extreme Measures

Never mind that knowing exact yardage was never a part of the ancient game. Forget that most of us would do better if we had more feel in our games and fewer figures in our heads. Put that aside and remember the endless slogs to find a yardage marker. Or maybe you called over to your buddy to ask his yardage. Only after you came up forty yards short did you learn he'd flunked math. Those Dark Ages were cast away in 2014, when the USGA allowed the use of distance-measuring devices in all of its amateur championships. While the PGA Tour does not allow the devices during play, they have become a staple of practice rounds.

Couch Potato's Lament

Golf has distinguished itself as the only sport where the players call the penalties on themselves—and if they don't, an angry viewer from the heartland might do it for them. In the past few decades, numerous players have been undone by an armchair official at home.

In March 2013, LPGA star Stacy Lewis was assessed a two-stroke penalty after a caller spotted her caddie testing the surface of a bunker.

At the 2013 Wells Fargo Championship, Sergio Garcia was accused by a caller of improperly marking his ball on the 17th green at Quail Hollow. He was cleared.

In 2011 at Kapalua, Camilo Villegas idly moved a divot as his anemic chip rolled back down the hill fronting the 15th green. What seemed harmless was noticed by several call-in viewers. Villegas, who had long since signed his card, was DQ'd.

At the 2013 BMW Championship, Tiger Woods was cited for accidentally moving his golf ball. Woods disputed the assertion, but the infraction was caught on video. Later that year, the USGA changed the governing rule. Starting in January 2014, a ball will only be deemed to have moved if that movement was reasonably discernable to the naked eye at the time. While that possibly would have spared Woods his 2-shot penalty at the BMW, it would have done nothing to resolve the granddaddy of all over-the-shoulder rulings.

No Closer to the Hole

The 2005 LPGA Samsung World Championship was wunderkind Michelle Wie's debut as a professional. The hype accompanying the nineteen-year-old's debut was as monumental as it was warranted. Wie was the most impressive young talent to grace the women's game since Annika Sorenstam in the early 1990s.

Every four years the organizations revisit the rules, while every two years they consider the Decisions on the Rules of Golf, which are simply examples of how a particular rule can be interpreted or applied.

What should have been a joyous occasion for Wie, her parents, coaches, and caddies ended in ignominy after the 7th hole in round three. It was there that Wie hooked her approach into a bush and opted for an unplayable lie and the accompanying 1-stroke penalty. But when Wie took her drop, a nearby sportswriter, Michael Bamberger of *Sports Illustrated*, noted that the drop violated Rule 20-7, which mandates that such a drop be "no closer to the hole." Bamberger approached Wie, who expressed her confidence in the drop, but the next day he studied videotape of the incident and determined that, indeed, she had inadvertently broken the rule. When Bamberger alerted rules officials to his concern, the facts came out, and Wie was disqualified for signing an incorrect scorecard the previous day. A massive debate ensued. The game had been inured to anonymous callers phoning in, but did a writer overreach his role as an objective observer? Does the ethical responsibility of protecting the field trump the journalistic requirement of distance? The Rules of Golf don't answer that question.

How We Learn the Game

One of the myths of the game of golf is that through eons of instruction, centuries of practice, and endless advancements in equipment, players have not improved. It's a convenient belief for those who see the sport as a massive Sisyphean

Michelle Wie examines her unplayable lie at the 2005 LPGA Samsung World Championship. Her subsequent drop became controversial.

struggle. These critics often point to the stagnation of the average handicap, or USGA Index. It's true, the average handicap has hovered at about 16 or 17 for decades, but in that time golf courses haven't remained static. Golf courses spent most of the past century getting longer, faster, and much tougher. If courses are getting tougher and handicaps are holding steady, then players are getting better. Further, if you look only at committed players, not the nomads who enter and leave the game, and track them over a ten-year period, they do improve. Golf Channel's Martin Hall concurs. "Over the last twenty years, the people I've taught—because of information and sharing of knowledge—hit the ball way better in 2014 than they did in 1994," he says.

The single largest leap in golf instruction is the blossoming of accessible video. Until the late 1970s, only two kinds of people enjoyed easy access to moving images of their swings: tour players who caught a glimpse of a tape-delayed broadcast, and players committed enough and patient enough to develop Super 8 film of their swings.

"That technology was available, but it was so limited, because it was so expensive," says Breed. "I remember the first camera that I bought back in 1988, it cost me $1,000, and now the camera that I have on my phone is a better camera."

Video technology has indeed become a huge part of modern instruction, but, warns Hall, video analysis is only as good as the analyst. "It's just like a doctor reading an MRI or an X-ray; you need an expert to read it," says Hall, who envisions a not-too-distant era in which 10,000-frame-per-second cameras will be widely available for consumer use. "Unless you know what you're looking at, you can get a lot worse."

A Uniform Swing

If you are old enough to remember players such as Miller Barber and Don January, even Lee Trevino or Raymond Floyd, you know that the PGA Tour was once a bastion of originality, a place where self-styled swings were welcomed, even cherished.

That's a far cry from today's professional golf scene, where, aside from the occasional Jim Furyk or Paula Creamer, the swing has largely been homogenized. Is there really much difference between the swings of Adam Scott, Tiger Woods, Charl Schwartzel, and Louis Oosthuizen, and so on?

The trend toward a uniform swing is fueled by several elements. First, the ubiquity of golf instruction TV, videos, and online video has given up-and-coming players far more reference points on good swings. Second, in the wake of Tiger Woods' historic success, youngsters are getting instruction at earlier ages and learning the proper fundamentals.

More important than either of those is a related influence: swing plane. "The heightened awareness of swing plane has been a huge advancement in the game," says Breed. The concept of swinging the club along an invisible plane running roughly parallel to the line of flight and up through the shoulders has existed for some time. Many credit Ben Hogan's influential book *Five Lessons: The Modern Fundamentals of Golf* with popularizing the image of the swing plane, even though Seymour Dunn ran a very similar image in his 1920 book, *Golf Fundamentals*.

Hogan described an imaginary pane of glass, along which the club would track. This was sketched in memorable detail by his illustrator, Anthony Ravielli. Dunn took the illustration of swing plane a step further by actually placing a wooden plane around his shoulders, swinging, and having a photograph taken.

The single largest leap in golf instruction is the blossoming of accessible video.

Most Influential Instructors of the Past Twenty Years

John Jacobs

"He's influenced everybody who's had any influence at all," says Michael Breed, who calls Jacobs the grandfather of modern instruction. Virtually every instructor living today is aware of what John Jacobs did and taught. In a sense, Jacobs was the Isaac Newton of golf swing theory. It was Jacobs who moved the emphasis for teachers from their students' body movements to the ball's movements. His theory in a nutshell: Ball flight doesn't lie. Jacobs was far less interested in positions than he was in results. His simple, direct teaching is evident in the first two sentences of his book *Practical Golf*: "The only purpose of the golf swing is to move the club through the ball square to the target at maximum speed," he wrote. "How this is done is of no significance at all, so long as the method employed enables it to be done repetitively." Jacobs, who was also a skilled player and played a critical role in the late-twentieth-century rise of the European Tour, was inducted into the World Golf Hall of Fame in 2000.

The Harmon Family

The Harmons are America's first family of golf instruction. It started with the patriarch, Claude Harmon, the legendary pro at Winged Foot GC, who in 1948 won the Masters. No full-time teacher has won a major championship since. He and his wife, Alice, left behind an incredible family legacy of golf instruction. Butch, the best known of their four boys, gained worldwide fame after taking on young Tiger Woods as a student in 1993. Woods won eight of his fourteen major championship titles with Harmon at his side. Past and current clients include Phil Mickelson, Ernie Els, Rickie Fowler, Stewart Cink, Greg Norman, Davis Love III, Fred Couples, and Adam Scott, to name a few.

Brother Craig had a major championship winner in his stable in Jeff Sluman, and Bill helped tutor Bill Haas to the 2011 FedEx Cup. A fourth brother, Dick, who died in 2006, worked at times with Couples, Craig Stadler, Lanny Wadkins, Steve Elkington, and 2009 U.S. Open winner Lucas Glover.

David Leadbetter

There was a time when David Leadbetter was not very good at what he did. As a player on both the European and South African tours, he struggled. But in 1984, a fellow Englishman asked Leadbetter to look at his swing. The Englishman in question was Nick Faldo.

Despite winning the European Tour Order of Merit in 1983, Faldo was unsure whether his swing was capable of delivering the Open Championship he craved. Leadbetter set out to remake Faldo's swing, but ended up changing the face of modern golf instruction.

Although Faldo and Leadbetter would split in the late 1990s, Leadbetter had gained a reputation as a master instructor, which he has leveraged into an instructional empire spanning academies in ten countries and best-selling instructional books and a stable of world-class players. Most recently his longtime student, Michelle Wie, won the 2014 U.S. Women's Open.

"David was really the one who took video analysis to the next level," says Breed.

Homer Kelley

Odds are you've never heard of Homer Kelley. But your golf teacher has. In May 2005, *Sports Illustrated* asked a cross section of top teachers to vote on the top ten most influential golf swing coaches ever. Homer Kelley, who died in 1983, was ranked No. 6 on that list. He got there by publishing a book in 1969 titled *The Golfing Machine*. It may be the most compelling and confounding instructional tome ever written. A painfully difficult read, the book is loaded with science and fact as opposed to theory. For those brave enough to take the book on, there are genuine nuggets to be found, particularly in Kelley's thoughts on the importance of lag. As Kelley wrote, lag "is simple, elusive, indispensable, without substitute…"

"That book has had a huge effect on what people teach today," says Breed.

MICHELLE WIE
2014 U.S.
WOMEN'S OPEN

Wie's win was built largely on her self-styled "table top" putting technique. It was remarkably effective all week.

She was only twenty-four, but by 2014, Michelle Wie was at risk of falling into that odd cultural chasm in which people are famous simply for being famous. She arrived in most golf fans' consciousness in 2003, when at the tender age of thirteen she won the U.S. Women's Amateur Public Links Championship, making her the youngest person ever to win a USGA title against adult competition. But rather than progress through the typical junior golf channels, Wie's advisers, chiefly her parents, chose a unique path. The youngster, who had awed none other than Fred Couples with her power ("It's just the scariest thing you've ever seen," said the long-hitting Couples after seeing the phenom play), began playing in LPGA Tour events at age twelve and PGA Tour events at fourteen. The hype was considerable, and for most of her young adulthood, Wie was unable to match it with on-course success. Increasingly, she was simply an attraction, a circus act. Her father came under heavy scrutiny for controlling her scheduling.

In 2007, Wie got the normalcy she needed when she enrolled at Stanford University. It wasn't complete normalcy, because Wie was a professional and therefore unable to play for the Cardinal women's team, but it was at Stanford that she gained some of the maturity she would need to handle the fame she'd already gained. During college and after graduating from Stanford in 2013, Wie enjoyed success on the LPGA Tour, but her four wins were nothing near the Tiger-like projections laid out for her. Her handful of leads in major championships before her seventeenth birthday was both promising and confining.

Wie's win in the 2014 U.S. Women's Open, her first on the U.S. mainland, was built largely on her self-styled "table top" putting technique, in which she bends forward at about ninety degrees, her back virtually parallel to the putting surface. It was remarkably effective all week, particularly on the biggest putt of Wie's career. She faced a twenty-foot birdie bid on Sunday on the 71st hole. The birdie would give her a two-shot cushion over world No. 1 Stacy Lewis, who had the clubhouse lead. Wie drained it center cut. After a par at 18, Wie had won a major, and her often bizarre, always complicated past faded into the background.

"If I hadn't made mistakes, if I hadn't done what I did, I wouldn't be the person I am right now," said Wie, who it's worth noting was the only player under par for the week.

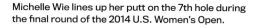

Michelle Wie lines up her putt on the 7th hole during the final round of the 2014 U.S. Women's Open.

Instructor Crazes

Stack and Tilt

It was a genuine craze. It wasn't necessarily new—in fact, Homer Kelley's 1969 book, *The Golfing Machine*, touched on the idea. But in the late 1990s, when little-known professionals Michael Bennett and Andy Plummer dropped competitive golf for careers in instruction, their calling card was the Stack and Tilt swing. The idea behind the swing was fairly simple. The traditional golf swing requires shifting one's weight toward the back foot on the backswing and toward the front foot on the through swing. For many players, this delicate bit of timing and coordination was simply too much. Stack and Tilt essentially gave these players another option, a swing in which the weight never really leaves the front foot. The swing attracted several well-known PGA Tour players, including Steve Elkington, Mike Weir, and Aaron Baddeley, and quickly became the talk of practice ranges everywhere. *Golf Digest* put the trend on the cover of its June 2007 issue. Baddeley won twice using the concept, but when he, along with Weir and Elkington and other Stack-and-Tilters, entered a slump, the craze began to die out. In 2009, Baddeley returned to his longtime coach, Dale Lynch, and in February 2011 he won the Northern Trust Open, his first PGA Tour win in four years.

"Toward the end, I was sort of struggling with the same things in my swing, and I felt like it was a lot of hard work. Also, I felt like I was thinking too much. I remember as a kid growing up, I was very much—if I wanted to fade it, I'd fade it; if I wanted to draw it, I'd draw it. I wanted to hit all sorts of shots without thinking too much, and that's the sort of golf I wanted to get back to playing. That's why I made the switch back to Dale," said Baddeley.

There are still some proponents of Stack and Tilt on tour, both among players and coaches, but the craze has long since passed.

Ready, AimPoint, Fire

It may just be a coincidence that when both Adam Scott and Stacy Lewis attained the world No. 1 ranking, it was shortly after they each adopted what is becoming the next craze in game improvement, the AimPoint putt-reading technique.

AimPoint uses the same technology Golf Channel uses on the air to show viewers the break of an upcoming putt. Mark Sweeney developed the technology and is now using the science behind it to teach players how to best read greens. Sweeney's first iteration was a chart-based system, which, though effective, was complicated to use. Today, he preaches a much more feel-based model, one focused primarily on the slope of the putting surface. Simply put, the player uses his feet (notice how Scott now straddles his ball before he putts) and eyes to rate the slope of the green from one to ten. If the slope is a two and the break of the putt appears to be going left, the player holds up two fingers in front of his or her face and "positions" them on the right edge of the hole. This is what you see Scott doing when he holds up his fingers in front of his face.

Scott learned about the technique from his coach/brother-in-law Brad Malone, who in turn learned it at a class in Hawaii in January 2014. As for results: The world No. 1 ranking is pretty compelling, but Scott's stat for Strokes Gained Putting tells the tale. For 2013, he was ranked 102nd in the category. As of late June 2014, he was ranked 17th.

It may just be a coincidence that when both Adam Scott and Stacy Lewis attained the world No. 1 ranking, it was shortly after they each adopted what is becoming the next craze in game improvement, the AimPoint putt-reading technique.

One major evolution of pro golf is the uniformity of swing styles, seen here with Rory McIlroy (left) and Martin Kaymer (right).

While it's likely that Hogan was influenced by Dunn, the concept has been communicated in books and instructional magazines for nearly a century. But proper plane is hard to teach, and even harder to feel. The easy access we now have to video with line-drawing capability and even 3-D analysis has made swing plane easier to teach and to practice.

Specialization

Arnold Palmer had his dad, Deacon. He was the touchstone for the King's game. Whether it was the long game, chipping, or putting, Arnold got his help from his father. For Nicklaus, it was largely Jack Grout. For most of Grout's life, he was Nicklaus' ringman. Nicklaus would return from the road with questions about his swing, and Grout would talk it out with him.

Contrast that with Phil Mickelson, who in recent years has used a full-swing coach, a chipping coach, and a putting coach. The field of instruction is becoming a specialized field. That doesn't surprise Breed. "Our entire world has turned toward specialization," he says. "Look at what's happened with baseball. In the 1960s Mickey Lolich and Bob Gibson were pitching and winning twenty games a season, and the relief pitcher was an afterthought. Nowadays, if you can get your starter through six innings, you automatically turn it over to the bullpen. Same with football. We have third-down specialists, pass-defense specialists. Specialization in golf instruction doesn't really surprise me."

Such specialization is out of reach for most players, although Breed shares a meaningful statistic. The average player, he says, takes a putting lesson once every four years. Meanwhile, in that four-year period, they'll buy four putters.

The Ryder Cup

It was there all along. Even during the decades of American dominance, the passion and pride was palpable. But at Kiawah, something clicked. Forever. In the past twenty years, the Ryder Cup has served as the game's most exhilarating and excruciating stage.

With the players here, they have a very simple goal. They are itching to get out on the golf course and get out and play. That's how I was in my day.
NICK FALDO

Sergio Garcia, at left, is sprayed with champagne after his European team won the 2006 Ryder Cup.

The Ryder Cup wasn't always the Ryder Cup, which in part is what made the Ryder Cup what the Ryder Cup is today. Put another way, if you, like millions of other golf fans, didn't really tune in to the Ryder Cup until the early 1990s, you didn't miss much. Sure, you missed a couple dozen transatlantic trips as the U.S. contingent did biennial battle with the Brits (until 1971) and the Brits and Irish (through 1977). There was lots of haggis and double-breasted blazers, but the result was almost uniformly the same: From the first match in 1927 through the twenty-second match in 1977, the United States won nineteen times. The U.S. won thirteen in a row between 1959 and 1983. It was ugly. It was pointless.

"I wrote a history of the Ryder Cup several years ago in a drunken stupor," says Golf Channel's David Feherty, "and it occurred to me about eight or nine Ryder Cups in that I was going to have to make a lot of stuff up because there are only so many ways you can describe the ass-kicking that Great Britain and Ireland [GB&I] underwent for the first fifty years."

It got so bad that after the 1977 matches, Jack Nicklaus insisted that the GB&I team be expanded to include all of Europe. When, just a few years later in 1985, Europe won its first Ryder Cup since 1957, that was news. But when they retained the cup by beating the United States on American soil at Nicklaus' own Muirfield Village GC two years later, the Ryder Cup began to gain traction. The 1991 version at the Ocean Course at Kiawah, the infamous "War by the Shore," was an essay in human drama. The United States narrowly avoided yet another loss to the European team. Even though the U.S. won 14½ to 13½, the competition was so close, so tense, so gripping, that the Ryder Cup was reborn. A once amiable get-together had evolved into an epic intercontinental battle. Not for a purse, but for pride and a four-pound trophy.

The Ryder Cup Should Give Us

What's a given is that the Europeans will outdress the Americans. They always do. What's a given is that Colin Montgomerie will outtalk Corey Pavin. Monty in the mood can really talk. What's a given is that Wales won't feel like San Diego. Wales in October can be damp and dark. Those are givens. Here's what else we'd like the Ryder Cup to give us:

Give us the Brothers Bash, Bubba Watson and Dustin Johnson, against the brothers Molinari.

Give us a smiling Matt Kuchar against a snarling Ian Poulter in a match that means something.

Give us even a minor American altercation with vice captain Sergio Garcia, just to spice it up.

Give us Rickie Fowler and Bubba against Rory McIlroy and Miguel Angel Jimenez in a better-ball hair pair.

Give us Dustin, Phil Mickelson, and their coach, Butch Harmon, against Graeme McDowell, Lee Westwood, and their underrated coach, Pete Cowen. Or Tiger Woods, Hunter Mahan, and their coach, Sean Foley, against Pete and his boys.

Give us California cool against Irish mettle, Mahan and Fowler against McIlroy and McDowell.

Give us Fowler and Poulter in a Sunday swinging singles fashion showdown.

Give us Tiger and Steve Stricker against Westwood and Martin Kaymer in a powerhouse four-ball.

Give us Euro fans chanting "Olé, olé, olé, olé" and the United States making some putts to silence the song.

Give us Tiger and Rickie against Rory and Padraig Harrington in a television bonanza.

Give us a Monty moment or two, just to spice it up.

Give us Tiger and Rory in Sunday singles with everything riding.

Is that too much to ask?

RICH LERNER, SEPTEMBER 2010

From any vantage point—press coverage, buzz, TV ratings, attendance—the modern Ryder Cup is unrecognizable from its predecessors.

Feherty is in the unique position of having been a European Ryder Cup team player (1991) and, as a result of his 2010 American citizenship, an American Ryder Cup team supporter (now). His study of the competition revealed two ingredients vital to its survival. The first was pride.

"It was always incredibly important to make the team," says Feherty. "And when I say that, I mean for both sides. Nicklaus and Palmer and Snead and Hogan, they really, really wanted to make that team. It was their only chance to play for the United States of America, and they were all immensely proud of that."

The second was Europe. "The British and Irish teams were so sadly beaten for all those years, but that new vanguard that started in the late 1970s with Seve Ballesteros gave it a shot in the arm," says Feherty. "It was around the same time that Sandy Lyle and Nick Faldo began to win the Masters. I think all of that gave the following generation of European players tremendous inspiration, that they could do this and compete with the Americans. Obviously, they have done so very successfully ever since."

Faldo summarizes the evolution of the matches in more guttural terms. His sense is that the Ballesteros group fed off Europe's underdog image and found motivation in the disrespect Europe had earned through the 1970s. "There was a genuine bit of hate there," says Faldo, who played on ten Ryder Cup teams, eight of them alongside Ballesteros. "He brought passion to it, that element of 'you have to win.'"

From any vantage point—press coverage, buzz, TV ratings, attendance, barroom banter—the modern Ryder Cup is unrecognizable from its predecessors. But the most obvious difference is in results. Whereas the U.S. dominated play for the first fifty years, Europe has been dominant for the past twenty-plus years. Since 1993, when the American team won at The Belfry, the Europeans have won seven of the last nine competitions. Faldo notes the irony of today's Ryder Cup. "It's in a dangerous state right now," says Faldo. "America almost needs to win now."

The home-country crowd at Valhalla Golf Club in Louisville, Kentucky, cheered on the U.S. team—which did break Europe's winning streak.

1995	
OAK HILL CC	
ROCHESTER, NY	
EUROPE	**U.S.**
14½	**13½**
CAPTAIN **BERNARD GALLACHER**	CAPTAIN **LANNY WADKINS**

Europe trailed by two heading into the final day's singles matches. Sparked by early wins by Britain's Howard Clark, who defeated Peter Jacobsen 1-up, and his countryman Mark James, who crushed Jeff Maggert 4 and 3, the Europeans staged a comeback.

While Fred Couples and Davis Love were able to stop the bleeding, the middle of the American lineup couldn't withstand the European onslaught and lost four straight matches to David Gilford, Colin Montgomerie, Nick Faldo, and Sam Torrance. Faldo's win over Curtis Strange was especially damaging to U.S. hopes, as Strange finished bogey-bogey-bogey despite three excellent drives on those closing holes. Philip Walton sealed the deal with a win over Jay Haas, who'd holed out on 16 and eked out a win on 17 but hit a pop-up to left field off the 18th tee and struggled in. From the insult-to-injury department: Walton's cup-clinching putt was for bogey.

Golf Channel contributor Ken Schofield, who was then the executive director of the European Tour, knew soon afterward that this was the beginning of a sea change, not only for the Ryder Cup but for the course of European golf. Later that year, Schofield was playing golf at Desert Mountain in Scottsdale when the young American golfer he was playing with said, "Ken, I won money from my buddies on Europe winning the Ryder Cup at Oak Hill." When Schofield inquired as to how, the young man said, "I watch the Euro Tour on Golf Channel and I knew how good the David Gilfords and the Philip Waltons were—my buddies didn't!"

"Until the arrival of Golf Channel, *only* Europe's major champions, Seve, Nick, Bernhard, etc., were known to U.S. audiences—and similarly *only* courses on the British Open were viewed in the U.S.," says Schofield. "Suddenly, hundreds of thousands of golf fans were seeing an entirely new angle on the game."

Philip Walton and Bernard Gallacher embrace after clinching the Ryder Cup on the final day.

1997	
VALDERRAMA GC	
SOTOGRANDE, SPAIN	
EUROPE	U.S.
14½	**13½**
CAPTAIN **SEVE BALLESTEROS**	CAPTAIN **TOM KITE**

If you ever doubt the influence that Seve Ballesteros had on European golf and global golf, consider this: Between 1927 and 1995, one of the most tradition-bound competitions in arguably the most tradition-bound of sports had never been contested outside of the United States or Great Britain. In 1997, as tribute and testament to the leadership of Spain's most beloved player, the Ryder Cup made its first appearance on the Continent. That year, too, the tenure of Bernard Gallacher, who captained the Europeans from 1991 to 1995, came to an end when the reins were handed to Ballesteros. Building a new and inspired crop of European players such as Lee Westwood, Darren Clarke, and Thomas Bjørn, the host team built a 10½ to 5½ lead after team play. The Americans would need to dominate Sunday's singles and did, winning the day 8-4 but still falling one point short. When Europe's Colin Montgomerie halved his match with Scott Hoch, the run was over. The Europeans had retained the cup.

Costantino Rocca celebrates the European team's victory in Spain.

The Americans would need to dominate Sunday's singles and did, winning the day 8-4 but still falling one point short.

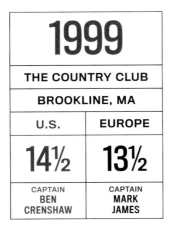

1999

THE COUNTRY CLUB	
BROOKLINE, MA	
U.S.	EUROPE
14½	13½
CAPTAIN BEN CRENSHAW	CAPTAIN MARK JAMES

"I'm gonna leave y'all with one thought and then I'm gonna leave: I'm a big believer in fate. I have a good feeling about this."

Good thing someone did. Those were the ridiculously optimistic words of 1999 U.S. Ryder Cup captain Ben Crenshaw. They were spoken, finger-pointing and wink thrown in for effect, at the completion of a Saturday in which the European team had shredded a powerful American lineup. To put Crenshaw's remarks into context, this was after the Euros had won the last two Ryder Cups in a row. Out of a possible sixteen points available in the first two days, the Americans had claimed six. Tiger Woods, who should have been the Americans' nuclear weapon, had captured only one of a possible four points. The U.S. box score had more zeros than a lottery billboard. Crenshaw looked foolish.

What people may not have known when Crenshaw made those comments is that his appreciation for fate is largely built on his study of golf history and on the tangible experience of his own life. Among the two most powerful lessons: Francis Ouimet's miracle win as an underdog amateur on this same golf course in 1913, and Crenshaw's own "arrival" as a player when he made it to the quarterfinals of the 1968 U.S. Junior Amateur there as a sixteen-year-old. Crenshaw knew that this was a place where amazing things happened. Why should Sunday's singles be any different?

Saturday evening was a motivational casserole. The players offered match-up ideas. Crenshaw showed a funny and inspiring motivational film. Texas governor George W. Bush entered the room and read William Barret Travis' stirring call to arms written during the siege of the Alamo, which ends with the famous words "victory or death." The players then offered reflections, often very emotional, on the week they'd had. The overall effect was therapeutic as well as motivating.

The next morning the U.S. team donned the ugliest shirts ever worn in Ryder Cup competition and initiated a charge that would have made Travis blush. The Americans won the first seven singles matches in a row. It was devastation. And these were not 1-up wins. The Americans had swallowed up the biggest deficit ever and taken a 3-point lead late into Sunday. The match tightened as Padraig Harrington and Sergio Garcia stoked European hopes, but the biggest comeback in Ryder Cup history would be punctuated by Justin Leonard. The slight Texan had trailed José María Olazábal by four holes with seven to play but clawed back, winning four straight. But it was Leonard's indescribable putt, perhaps the single most celebrated putt in American golf history—a snaking forty-five-footer for birdie on the 17th green—that put the Americans in the driver's seat. Not lost on Crenshaw was the fact that it was the same green where Ouimet had sealed his Open title eighty-six years earlier. Olazábal would birdie 18 to halve the match, but the United States had won the cup 14½ to 13½ in what may have been the greatest day the game had ever known.

The United States' Hal Sutton heads back to the clubhouse after winning his final-round match.

2001	
EUROPE	**U.S.**
0	0

9/11/2001 Whither the Ryder Cup?

On that sunny Tuesday morning when the United States was attacked by Al Qaeda terrorists, everything changed, including golf. In the wake of thousands of innocent lives stolen and a great nation rocked, the game rightly seemed superfluous. Pointless.

The top players were due in St. Louis for the WGC-American Express Championship. When the World Trade Center was attacked, Commissioner Tim Finchem drove to the golf course to inform Tiger Woods and Mike Weir, who were engaged in an early-morning practice round, of what had happened.

It quickly became apparent that with the unprecedented grounding of all airplanes in the country, a large number of players would not be able to make it to St. Louis. And even if they could, what sense would a golf tournament make? Finchem canceled the event and the entire slate of tour-related competitions for two weeks. The players scrambled for rides, Woods driving all the way from St. Louis to Florida. Some players caravanned in courtesy cars. International players were stranded in St. Louis until a chartered 757 took them overseas.

Even an event as commanding as the Ryder Cup was abandoned. Just a few days after the attacks, the PGA of America, in consultation with the European PGA and the PGA Tour, postponed the event until 2002. When it was again contested, the team uniforms and signage would still include "2001" as a reminder of what it was that forced the change. The players already selected for 2001 also remained the same.

As Paul Hayward wrote in *The Telegraph* after the postponement was announced, "The Ryder Cup had become unthinkable. The sorrow of the last six days was not the end of our turmoil but the beginning. Funerals—thousands of them—will be autumn's grim convoy.... How, in this context, could golf have encouraged even playful antagonism between Europe and the U.S.?"

<table>
<tr><td colspan="2" align="center">2002</td></tr>
<tr><td colspan="2" align="center">THE BELFRY</td></tr>
<tr><td colspan="2" align="center">SUTTON COLDFIELD, ENGLAND</td></tr>
<tr><td align="center">EUROPE</td><td align="center">U.S.</td></tr>
<tr><td align="center">15½</td><td align="center">12½</td></tr>
<tr><td align="center">CAPTAIN
SAM TORRANCE</td><td align="center">CAPTAIN
CURTIS STRANGE</td></tr>
</table>

The first two days were a standstill, with the Euros earning a 1-point edge after Day One and the United States taking a 1-point edge on Day Two. Tied heading into Sunday's singles, European captain Sam Torrance seriously frontloaded his lineup, sending his stalwarts out early. Colin Montgomerie, Sergio Garcia, Darren Clarke, Bernhard Langer, Padraig Harrington, and Thomas Bjørn were sent out to earn the European team an early lead, and they succeeded, taking 4½ of a possible 6 points. Trailing 12½ to 8½, the Americans needed wins in the second half of the Sunday lineup but could manage only halves. Of the six Americans who went out in the second half of the lineup— Verplank, Azinger, Furyk, Love, Mickelson, and Woods—only Verplank earned a full point. The haplessness of the U.S. squad was exemplified by Mickelson. Then the No. 2-ranked player in the world, Mickelson lost 3 and 2 to No. 119-ranked Phillip Price. Among the lowlights was Mickelson missing an eighteen-inch putt in the early going. Even Tiger Woods could manage only a half against Jesper Parnevik. The stalwart for Europe, as was so often the case, was Montgomerie, who went 4-0-1 for the week.

Europe's Paul McGinley and his caddie victory-leap after McGinley's winning putt in his Sunday singles match at The Belfry.

2004	
OAKLAND HILLS CC	
BLOOMFIELD TOWNSHIP, MI	
EUROPE	U.S.
18½	9½
CAPTAIN BERNHARD LANGER	CAPTAIN HAL SUTTON

Front-loading a lineup was a fairly common practice among Ryder Cup captains. It had worked flawlessly for Sam Torrance during the singles matches at The Belfry two years earlier, so why wouldn't it work in 2004 for Hal Sutton and the United States? Because Sutton tried it on Friday morning in the far more complicated four-ball matches, and his front-loaded pair was Mickelson and Woods. It was the worst pairing since stripes and plaids. The American duo, whose body language alone reeked of surrender, drew Colin Montgomerie, arguably the greatest European Ryder Cup player of all time, and the fiery Padraig Harrington.

It would be easy and cynical to say that this one was over with the first match on Friday morning. It would also be true. When Mickelson and Woods walked off the course without so much as a half point, the American side was seemingly stripped of its confidence. Of the five sessions, the United States won one, the Saturday morning four-ball, by a point. The 9-point loss was the worst-ever defeat for the American side.

Tiger Woods and Phil Mickelson wait to hit their approach shots during the first-round four-ball match. The pairing did not win a point.

The 9-point loss was the worst-ever defeat for the American side.

2006
THE K CLUB
COUNTY KILDARE, IRELAND

EUROPE	U.S.
18½	**9½**
CAPTAIN IAN WOOSNAM	CAPTAIN TOM LEHMAN

The good news for the Americans heading into Ireland was that it couldn't get any worse. The previous Ryder Cup had seen the most complete thrashing of a United States team ever. The only problem: The team the U.S. was bringing to the K Club was one of the least experienced Ryder Cup teams assembled in recent decades. Certainly U.S. captain Tom Lehman had some cagey veterans such as Woods, Mickelson, and Furyk, then the top three players in the world. But at the other end of the spectrum, four rookies—Vaughn Taylor, J.J. Henry, Zach Johnson, and Brett Wetterich—had earned their way onto the team. Ian Woosnam's European side had only two newcomers.

Woosnam, fully aware that this was the first Ryder Cup ever staged in Ireland, played to the home crowd and put out Padraig Harrington first, pairing him with his compatriot from Oakland Hills, Colin Montgomerie. Lehman responded with Woods, but rather than handcuff the World No. 1 as Hal Sutton had done in Michigan, Lehman paired Woods with Furyk, a good fit for both players. In a match that the Americans badly needed to win, Woods and Furyk prevailed 1-up. While in another era the win against the indomitable

Monty might have spurred the Americans on, it didn't happen here. Woods and Furyk posted the Stars and Stripes in the opening match, but it wouldn't be until eleven matches later, in Saturday morning's four-ball, that the United States would post another win. At the end of the day Saturday, the U.S. trailed, again by four, 10-6. Fueled in large part by Darren Clarke's emotional return to play after the death of his wife from cancer and the passion engendered among the local fans, the Europeans ran away with Sunday's singles.

Europe's Darren Clarke after sinking a long putt in a singles match against Zach Johnson.

2008

VALHALLA GC

LOUISVILLE, KY

U.S.	EUROPE
16½	11½
CAPTAIN PAUL AZINGER	CAPTAIN NICK FALDO

Something had to change. The United States had now lost five of the last six Ryder Cups. The PGA of America tapped Paul Azinger, who would bring new ideas to the task. First, he forced the PGA to rethink the way it comprised the Ryder Cup team. Out was the two-year period during which players earned points from top-ten finishes. Azinger insisted on having the hottest players on his team, and the only way to do that was to emphasize more recent play. The second condition for Azinger was an increase in captains' picks from two to four. Again, for his picks he would focus on a player's recent performance, particularly in the three-week period leading up to and including the 2008 PGA Championship. "My desire," said Azinger, "was to find the four players who were playing the best, who were the most confident after the PGA Championship."

But that was just the beginning of Azinger's revolutionary approach to captaining. He made a point of pumping up the home-team crowd, referring to players engaging with the fans as "the 13th man." The biggest difference between the 2008 U.S. team and the other, less successful predecessors was Azinger's creative approach. He was far less a captain or a coach than he was a manager. With the assistance of Dr. Ron Braund, a consultant, Azinger studied the training methods of the Navy SEALS and found that one of the keys to getting highly trained and highly regarded military superstars to perform at their best is to create small teams, or "pods," within the larger group. In a move that would likely have been blasted as psychobabble if it had failed, Azinger took the twelve-man team and divided it into three three-man pods and allowed each pod to pick its own fourth. "We just decided to come together in small groups," said Azinger. "We put four guys together in practice rounds, and they played together every day, and they were the four guys that stayed together the whole week, and they were never going to come out of their little group. That's the way I did it."

The United States broke out to an early lead, winning both Friday sessions for a 5½-to-2½

lead. By Saturday afternoon, the gap had been closed to 9-7, setting the stage for what could have been the most competitive Sunday singles in more than a decade, but the Americans held fast. After losing two of the first four matches, they won six of the last eight to win comfortably, 16½ to 11½. The final point came when Miguel Angel Jimenez conceded Furyk's two-footer on the 17th hole.

"You dream of winning the Ryder Cup, knocking in the ten-footer for your team and having the place go bananas," said Furyk. "Mine was a two-foot conceded putt, but I'll take it."

U.S. captain Paul Azinger is surrounded by the media after his team's victory.

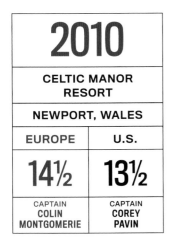

2010

CELTIC MANOR RESORT

NEWPORT, WALES

EUROPE	U.S.
14½	13½
CAPTAIN COLIN MONTGOMERIE	CAPTAIN COREY PAVIN

The Ryder Cup's inaugural trip to Wales will be remembered almost as much for the dismal Friday weather as for the thrilling finish. The first day's play was halted twice and ultimately moved Day One into Day Two and Day Three into Monday.

The messy start did not bode well for the Americans. The red, white, and blue led by a point after the four-ball session and expanded that lead to two points after the Saturday foursomes. But the Europeans drastically turned the tables in late Saturday and early Sunday play, drubbing the United States 5½ to ½. U.S. captain Corey Pavin tried to put a brave face on the collapse. "I watched twelve men out there that fought hard and held their heads high, played every shot hard, and we got a couple of matches to 18," said Pavin. "I saw guys fighting and not getting quite the result that we were looking for.... I'm sure tomorrow... they are going to come out firing."

Some did. Starting the day down three points, Steve Stricker got an American flag on the board right off the bat with a 2 and 1 win over Lee Westwood. Teams essentially traded matches through midday. Tiger Woods' win over Francesco Molinari kept U.S. hopes alive. Then came Mickelson, who one day earlier had broken a dubious record for most career lost matches in the Ryder Cup, and his commanding win over Peter Hanson. Next up was Rickie Fowler, a Ryder Cup rookie and captain's pick no less. His gutsy half with Edoardo Molinari brought the United States to within a point. When Zach Johnson beat Padraig Harrington, the matches were all square. It would come down to the Graeme McDowell vs. Hunter Mahan match, which McDowell would take, 3 and 1. Europe reclaimed the Cup.

Graeme McDowell plays to the crowd after his birdie putt on 16 in a singles match against the United States' Hunter Mahan.

The Presidents Cup

Nowhere is it written that Europe and the United States get to have all the fun. For the better part of a century, the Ryder Cup had a pretty easy job: promote the game of golf in Great Britain and Ireland, and then all of Europe, and the United States. That was enough until the 1991 Ryder Cup. After the famed matches at Kiawah, the cup had a reputation and a television audience to live up to. Soon the PGA of America, which organizes the matches along with the European PGA, had a towering event on its hands and a huge financial windfall.

None of this was lost on the PGA Tour, which in 1994 introduced its own international match play competition, the Presidents Cup. Whereas the Ryder Cup was open only to European and American competitors, the Presidents Cup gave golf-rich nations such as Australia, South Africa, and Japan an opportunity to experience the thrill of international match play competition. The inaugural Presidents Cup was played at Robert Trent Jones GC in Gainesville, Virginia, and the International team was composed of players from South Africa, Japan, Australia, New Zealand, Zimbabwe, and Fiji. Since then, players from Canada, South Korea, Paraguay, Argentina, and Colombia have competed.

The high-water mark of the Presidents Cup's brief history is undoubtedly "The Tie." In 2003, the U.S. team was captained by Jack Nicklaus, and the International team was captained by

Nicklaus' old friend Gary Player. The match was contested on the Links Course at Fancourt Hotel and Country Club, one of Player's finest designs. The early going was tight. After Thursday's matches, the United States trailed by a point, but by the end of Saturday's play, the Americans trailed by three. Thus began a furious Sunday charge by the U.S., which won five of the first Sunday singles matches en route to tying the overall match at 17. In the Ryder Cup, a tie goes to the incumbent, who retains the cup (the 2000 Presidents Cup had been won by the United States). But the Presidents Cup rules were designed to obviate ties. In the event of a tie, each captain had placed one of his charge's names in an envelope. Those two players would enter a sudden-death playoff. Nicklaus had selected Tiger Woods. Player had selected Ernie Els. A head-to-head sudden-death match between two of the greatest players in the world would decide the Presidents Cup. Both players parred the first three holes. But as darkness descended, Nicklaus and Player were forced to improvise. Nicklaus and Player agreed that it was too dark to continue. Nicklaus suggested, with backing of PGA Tour Commissioner Tim Finchem (who was connected by cell phone to the scene on the dusk-covered putting surface), that the U.S. retain the cup. But Els and the International team objected, arguing to play on. At one point, a fired-up Gary Player told his pal Nicklaus, "On we go."

The teams then huddled with their captains. "I went over and said, 'Guys, why don't we share the cup? These guys take it half the time and pass it around the world, and we'll keep it half the time? I think that's what the spirit of the matches were about,'" said Nicklaus, who'd made headlines in 1969 when he conceded a Ryder Cup tying putt to Tony Jacklin. Had Jacklin missed, the United States would have won the cup outright. With the concession, Great Britain managed a tie, and the U.S. merely retained the cup.

The Internationals wanted to either win outright or at least share the cup, but not concede it entirely to the Americans via a tie. With the wisdom of Solomon, Nicklaus and Player and their teams agreed to call it a tie and award each team the cup for six months of the coming year. The deal was blessed by Finchem and the 17-17 tie went into the record books.

"We ended up having twenty-four winners rather than twelve winners," said Nicklaus. "I thought it was the right thing, and I still think it's the right thing."

2012	
MEDINAH CC	
MEDINAH, IL	
EUROPE	U.S.
14½	13½
CAPTAIN JOSÉ MARÍA OLAZÁBAL	CAPTAIN DAVIS LOVE III

The European dominance of the Ryder Cup over the past twenty years was punctuated at Medinah. Not on Friday or Saturday, during which the United States built a commanding four-point lead on stirring play throughout the first two days, particularly from the seemingly unbeatable pairing of Phil Mickelson and Keegan Bradley. The duo rattled off three huge wins in a row, beating Luke Donald and Sergio Garcia in the Friday foursomes, Rory McIlroy and Graeme McDowell in the Friday-afternoon four-ball, and Lee Westwood and Luke Donald in the Saturday-morning foursomes. It seemed as though under Captain Davis Love III, the United States was loose and excited. That became clear when Bubba Watson actually incited the home crowd to scream throughout his preshot routine as well as his swing on the first hole of his first match Friday afternoon.

At the end of Saturday, the United States was in complete control. Sunday morning, as if cued by recent history, they collapsed under the ceaseless forward-leaning attack of European captain José María Olazábal's squad. One by one, the U.S. players went out, and one by one they came back, defeated. Watson lost. Brandt Snedeker was crushed. Bradley lost. When Webb Simpson lost to Ian Poulter, perhaps the most dogged Ryder Cup player ever, the overall score was tied. Dustin Johnson pulled the United States ahead with a 3–2 win over Nicolas Colsaerts. Then Mickelson, who along with Love created some controversy when he opted to sit out Saturday afternoon's play, lost to Justin Rose, who won both the 17th and 18th holes. Zach Johnson's gutsy win over McDowell gave the United States a one-point lead again, but they just couldn't hold on. Once Matt Kuchar lost to Lee Westwood and Sergio Garcia beat Jim Furyk, the Euro momentum was building. Jason Dufner beat Peter Hanson to tie the overall match, but the pivotal match was Martin Kaymer against the U.S. captain's pick, Steve Stricker. The match came down to the 18th hole, and Stricker had long ago realized that the outcome might turn on his performance. "I had a pretty good idea

it was going to be important pretty early in the round," said Stricker. "When I went past the board at No. 10 tee, saw a lot of blue [flags] up on the board, started doing the math. Kind of figured that it was going to come down to Tiger or I in the last two groups."

When Stricker lost his match on a nerveless putt by Kaymer, the Europeans had retained the cup. Woods, who was still on the course and had a chance to craft a tie for the United States, in which case the Europeans would still claim the Cup, conceded a par putt to Francesco Molinari to give Europe the outright win.

"It was already over," said a downcast Woods, whose lackluster performance was a microcosm of his team's (he earned ½ point out of a possible four). "The Cup was already retained by Europe, so it was already over."

Martin Kaymer's putt on 17 on Sunday won the match and the tournament for Europe.

The Next Twenty

*Two decades ago, no one could have foreseen the totality
of Tiger's dominance, the emergence of the long putter, the return of golf to
the Olympic Games, or even the extinction of the metal spike.
What does 2035 have in store for the sport?*

What does the future hold for golf? Twenty years ago, people probably scoffed at the notion someone might soon challenge Jack Nicklaus' record for career majors. What's next? Cars that park themselves? Or the ability to turn off the lights in your kitchen from the other side of the globe? The future has a way of sneaking up on you. The possibilities for golf are unimaginable.

JIMMY ROBERTS

PGA Tour pro Berry Henson leads a clinic for young golfers at the 2012 Hong Kong Open.

The greatest advances in this ancient game took place more than a hundred years ago in six leaps that made the sport modern.

Toilsome featherie golf balls gave way to mass-producible gutta-percha balls. The St. Andrean model of eighteen holes was ratified as the game's standard unit. Most of the clubs throughout Scotland and Great Britain agreed on a uniform rulebook. In 1895, the newly formed USGA adopted a rulebook based on the Scottish/British tradition. Charles Blair Macdonald transplanted the great holes of U.K. golf to the United States at his National Golf Links of America. Finally, in 1913, Francis Ouimet alerted large numbers of Americans to the glories of the game by winning the U.S. Open as an underdog amateur.

These events, especially the last, put the game on a trajectory that has since been supported by stars such as Jones, Hogan, Palmer, Nicklaus, and Woods, lifted by advances in equipment technology, and broadcast to the world as communications evolved from newspapers to radio to television to the Internet.

So where does it go from here? If the three biggest stories of the past twenty years are the emergence of Tiger Woods, the eastward movement of golf's center of gravity, and a new, media-centric environment fostered by Golf Channel, what can we expect of the game in the next twenty?

Here are a few sneak peeks of golf's future—though we make no guarantees.

Go East, Young Woman

It seems only appropriate that a game born on the linksland of Scotland and raised in the suburbs of the United States would in full adulthood return to its roots. But the rise of the European golfer is only the beginning of what may be an all-out migration of the game fully across Europe and well into Asia. "In the

A new generation of great golfers has emerged from Asia. From left: Se Ri Pak of South Korea, K.J. Choi of South Korea, Ryo Ishikawa of Japan, and Guan Tianlang of China.

next twenty years, golf is going to be bigger in South America and Asia. It will be a much more international game," predicts Golf Channel's David Feherty. "We're already seeing great players from all over the world, especially Asia. Golf is erupting over there."

We've seen in South Korea what can happen when an Asian nation embraces the game. The influx of über-talented Korean women onto the LPGA Tour over the past decade is a hint of what the broader game may look like in 2020 or 2030. Consider that the seeds for Koreans' interest in golf were planted in 1988, when Seoul hosted the Summer Olympic Games. Although golf was not featured in those games, the host Korean culture was steeped in the glory that sport can reflect on a nation. South Korea quickly saw sports in general as the doorway to a twenty-first-century Western lifestyle. Golf, which is extremely expensive throughout much of Asia and highly reflective of socioeconomic status, became a national passion.

The appetite only increased when Se Ri Pak left Korea to join the LPGA Tour at age twenty-one in 1998. She won four times in her rookie year, including two major championships. Golf in Asia has never been the same. Korean women have won well over a hundred titles on the LPGA Tour in the past fifteen years, and

The trend transcends Korea, of course. The entire continent of Asia is cultivating champions.

they're not alone. In 2009, Pak's countryman Y.E. Yang turned back Tiger Woods to win the PGA Championship, becoming the first Asian ever to win a men's major championship. K.J. Choi, a native of Wando, South Korea, has been a stalwart of the PGA Tour since 2000 and ranks seventeenth on the Tour's all-time money list.

The trend transcends Korea, of course. The entire continent is cultivating champions. The 2013 Masters saw the fruits of a budding grow-the-game effort in China. That year, fourteen-year-old amateur Guan Tianlang, who gained entry to the elite Masters field by winning the Asia-Pacific Amateur Championship, won low amateur honors at Augusta. Ryo Ishikawa, the reluctant prince of Japanese golf, is a familiar name in American golfing households and a household name in his native Japan; and in 2014, Hideki Matsuyama, another Japanese player, won the Memorial Tournament. The migration is also showing signs of taking hold in populous India and other regions of Southeast Asia. As the economies of these nations grow and build a reliable middle class with greater disposable income for recreation, sheer numbers alone will dictate the rise of the Asian superstar. "I think we'll see some phenomenal Chinese players coming through," says Feherty. "It's in their culture to excel. Look at music. I'm not sure I agree with their entire system, but they're churning out musicians unlike any other country, and golf is just another form of art."

The 2016 Olympics

The explosion of golf across the Far East was inevitable long before 2009, when the International Olympic Committee announced that for the first time since 1904, the sport of golf would again be included in the Olympic Games. The return of the sport to the grandest stage in international competition likely means an acceleration of that trend through a combination of unprecedented visibility and new avenues of financial support.

The Olympics is the largest TV franchise of all time. The top ten most-watched television events in U.S. history are all Olympics, with the 2012 London Games coming in first. That's just the U.S. audience. Nielsen Media Research says that 4.7 billion people—an astonishing two out of three people worldwide—watched at least some of the Beijing Games in 2008. For golf, and for players from countries as diverse as the games themselves, to be put on that stage means greater awareness of the game.

Although the United States does not provide federal funding for Olympic hopefuls, many other nations do. In those countries—China and Korea to name two—Olympic sports, whether table tennis or tae kwon do, receive massive government support for facilities, coaching, athlete development, nutrition, even

> # "Golf's inclusion in the 2016 and 2020 Olympics can be a catalyst for government support of the game."
> GREG NATHAN

LEFT: Dustin Johnson and Sergio Garcia during the 2012 Olympics in London, driving balls in a preview of golf's return to the Olympic Games in 2016. ABOVE: Gil Hanse's sketch of the 2016 Olympic course in Rio de Janeiro.

housing for athletes and coaches. With golf being added to the Olympic slate in 2016, these nations will be funding golf development programs in the pursuit of national pride though medals.

"When I first heard that the golf industry was actively pursuing golf in the Olympics, my first thought was that the last thing golf needs is another professional championship," says Greg Nathan of the National Golf Foundation. "But Joe Beditz [foundation president and CEO] was very quick to correct me and say, 'No, you're missing the point. There are ministries of sport around the world who will only fund facility and player development for sports that are in the Olympics.' And that's what this is all about. It's about development of golf around the world. Golf's inclusion in the 2016 and 2020 Olympics can be a catalyst for government support of the game."

Brown Is Beautiful

The real estate collapse late last decade put the brakes on golf course development for some time. Adding to the inertia for developers is an increase in the regulatory hurdles confronting traditional golf course development. Whether it's wetlands mitigation, chemical usage, or zoning, federal, state, and local governments are increasingly tying developers' hands. In Arizona, the Department of Water Resources already limits how much water golf courses in the Phoenix area may use. Several years ago, Canadian authorities cut back on the list of chemicals golf courses could utilize. Expect these trends to continue. Golf courses will use less land, fewer chemicals, and less water.

If you don't believe that water is the next frontier in golf, look at Pinehurst. The biggest story of the 2014 U.S. Open and Women's Open wasn't the excellence of Martin Kaymer or the resurgence of Michelle Wie. It was the new, brown Pinehurst No. 2. Sure, the goal of the Coore & Crenshaw redesign was to bring Donald Ross' baby back to its Golden Age self, but that could only be done by letting the place dry out. The soft, lush, verdant Pinehurst of just a few years ago was replaced by a drier, browner, dustier, and far more clever golf course, one that Ross himself would actually recognize. By replacing the ever-expanding rough with

One sure thing about golf's future is less water-intensive courses, as at Tobacco Road (above) and Pinehurst No. 2 (right).

For golf course design legend Tom Fazio, it's about matching expectations and reality. "Are we going to change our expectations?"

native sand and vegetation, Coore & Crenshaw not only restored Ross' vision, they reduced the total number of irrigated acres on No. 2 by thirty-six. That meant the removal of five hundred sprinkler heads, which produced water savings of forty million gallons a year. This redesign was done by choice, but in the years to come, look for regulatory trends to move courses in this direction.

The brown course is coming, says golf course architect Mike Young. "I think a lot of people in my generation are already ready for it. But for the fifty- to seventy-year-old group, everything's always been green. In my opinion, we're too green unless you play in the prairies." Reduction in irrigated acreage, something Tom Doak has been doing for years on his golf courses, will certainly be part of the solution, as will new grasses. We may be seeing more velvet bent, which ironically is a really old grass. With velvet, the worse you treat it—the less fertilizer, the less water—the better it performs.

For golf course design legend Tom Fazio, it's about matching expectations and reality. "Are we going to change our expectations?" asks Fazio. "We may be economically forced to. We've had the greening of America. Maybe golf has to see the browning of America from the standpoint of not as lush, less water, smarter uses of resources. We will get to that point of expecting less when we find we can't afford it anymore."

Let Me Entertain You

There is a long-running debate about the extent to which a sport is entertainment. One school of thought says the debate itself trivializes sport, that it reduces the noble pursuit of athletic excellence to the equivalent of popcorn and a movie. The other, more pragmatic view says that if the popcorn and movie are competing with a sport for the same dollars, then that sport is, by definition, entertainment.

Regardless of where you stand on this issue, it's safe to say that over the next twenty years, the lines between golf and entertainment are going to blur even more. They'd better.

This will happen in two distinct ways. First is the in-game experience, the elements and play of the game. Slow play, a cancer on the sport, will be reduced. While the PGA Tour seems reluctant to take the lead on the issue by forcing its players to pick up the pace, a PGA of America task force has implemented a pilot program in the Midwest utilizing time clocks and a fee structure that charges golfers by the minute rather than by the hole. The idea of playing nine holes may also become far more acceptable, and for most people, shorter courses will be the order of the day. In a recent column in *Golf World*, historian David Normoyle suggested that the USGA stage a national nine-hole championship to spur interest in the format.

In the meantime, if architect Bill Bergin's experience is any indication, efforts such as the USGA and PGA of America's Tee it Forward initiative are paying off. Bergin has been doing a lot of renovation work in recent years and is seeing demand for forward tees grow. "For every back tee we add, we're adding two forward tees," says Bergin. "What does that tell you? The first thing it says is our golfers are getting older, which is normal. The second thing is that those golfers

> # Regardless of where you stand on this issue, it's safe to say that over the next twenty years, the lines between golf and entertainment are going to blur even more. They'd better.

LEFT: Mobile devices with GPS and range finding have changed how many amateurs play the game. ABOVE: Many efforts are being developed (such as stand-up personal carts) to make golf more accessible and more "entertaining."

are finally catching on that golf is more fun on a golf course where you can occasionally putt for birdie. It has taken forever for people to accept it, but I would say there's a groundswell now."

Finally, the game will grow between now and 2035 if it bends over backwards to appeal to young people. People under thirty years old are inundated with entertainment options never imagined by previous generations. Most of them have never known life without the Internet or Skype or cell phones that double as pocket entertainment systems. They're wired for speed at all times, and the game needs to catch up.

Greg Nathan of the National Golf Foundation writes a blog under the pen name Mayor of Crazy Town. Although the views expressed on the blog are not those of the NGF, he writes with authority and humor about how the game might look twenty years from now. Or two years. "You want golfers (of all ages) on your course on a college football Saturday or NFL Sunday?" Nathan asks. "Encourage players to stay connected while enjoying their golf. Make it easy for an iPhone video of a shanked 8-iron into a McMansion window to go viral from the course. Enable your players to challenge a golfer in Argentina to a skins match. Make sure the Twitter-verse is feeding the world to your golfers nonstop over eighteen holes."

Nathan believes that if this new atmosphere is embraced, older golfers, the generation in its forties and fifties, will enjoy the connectivity and entertainment just as much.

Credits & Acknowledgments

Produced by

 **MELCHER MEDIA**

melcher.com

Publisher: Charles Melcher
VP, Operations: Bonnie Eldon
Senior Editor: David E. Brown
Production Manager:
Susan Lynch

Design by Pure+Applied

We would like to offer our gratitude to Arnold Palmer and Joe Gibbs, who graciously provided their time for this project.

At Golf Channel, thanks to Mike McCarley, President; Chris Murvin, SVP, Business Affairs; Geoff Russell, SVP & Executive Editor; Regina O'Brien, SVP, Marketing; David Schaefer, VP, Communications; David Piccolo, VP, Creative Services; Dan Higgins, Senior Director, Communications; and Gil Capps, Managing Editor.

Additional thanks to Golf Channel/NBC personalities Michael Breed, Brandel Chamblee, Sir Nick Faldo, David Feherty, Matt Ginella, Martin Hall, Rich Lerner, Roger Maltbie, Frank Nobilo, Jimmy Roberts, Tommy Roy, Ken Schofield, Geoff Shackelford, and Kelly Tilghman; staff members Reed Burton, Kelly Cuddihy, Jessica Forte, Matt Hegarty, Courtney Holt, and Kris Lanman; as well as Cori Britt, Donald "Doc" Giffin, Bill Bergin, Tom Biersdorfer, Richard Hurley, Richard Morris, Greg Nathan and the National Golf Foundation, Bill Salinetti and Troy Vincent. Finally, the author would like to thank David Brown at Melcher Media, who lent invaluable creative vision and guidance to the project.

Melcher Media thanks Eva Bochem-Shur, Paul Carlos, Cheryl Della Pietra, Max Dickstein, Paige Doscher, Tom Eykemans, Barbara Gogan, Heather Hughes, Luke Jarvis, Ji Sub Jeong, Andrew Kennedy, Rit Limphongpand, Mike Matvey, Naomi Misuzaki, Lauren Nathan, Kate Osba, Marta Schooler, William van Roden, and Megan Worman.

Image Credits

Front of case. Illustrations: Pure+Applied; back case photo: Robert Beck. **Frontmatter.** 1: Richard Heathcote/R&A/R&A via Getty Images; 2-3: Robert Beck; 4: Brian G. Oar; 5: Richard Heathcote/R&A/R&A via Getty Images; 6: Robert Beck/*Sports Illustrated*/Getty Images; 7: Mike Ehrmann/Getty Images; 8-9: Mike Ehrmann/Getty Images; 10 (Foreword): AP Images; (Introduction): Mike Ehrmann/Getty Images; (The Channel): Golf Channel (The Pro Game): David Cannon/Getty Images; 11 (Tiger): Phil Sheldon/Popperfoto/Getty Images; (The Course): Russell Kirk; (The Pro Game): Tannen Maury/epa/Corbis; (The Changing Game): James Friedman; (The Ryder Cup): Robert Beck/*Sports Illustrated*/Getty Images; (The Next Twenty): Gareth Gay/Getty Images; 12-13: AP Images. **The Channel.** 16, 19, 20, 21, 22, 23: Golf Channel; 25, 26, 28: Phil Sheldon/Popperfoto/Getty Images; 29: Jacqueline Duvoisin/*Sports Illustrated*/Getty Images; 30-31: David Cannon/Getty Images; 32: Golf Channel; 33: Craig Jones/Getty Images; 34: Golf Channel; 35: Andy Lyons/Getty Images; 36: Doug Pensinger/Getty Images; 39: Neil Leifer/*Sports Illustrated*/Getty Images; 41: Tami Chappell/Corbis; 42: Mike Ehrmann/Getty Images. **The Pro Game (1995-2004).** 44-45: Tom Able-Green/Allsport/Getty Images; 47: Phil Sheldon/Popperfoto/Getty Images; 48: Jacqueline Duvoisin/*Sports Illustrated*/Getty Images; 49 (Ballesteros) Phil

Credits & Acknowledgments

Sheldon/Popperfoto/Getty Images; (Couples) Mounce/Corbis; (Daly) Tony Roberts/Corbis; (Els) Scott Miller/Icon SMI/Corbis; 50: J.D. Cuban/Getty Images; 51: Charles Rex Arbogast/AP Images; 52: Elise Amendola/AP Images; 54: Michael Caulfield/AP Images; 55: (Garcia) M. Spencer Green/AP Images; (Love) Carlos Osorio/AP Images; (McIlroy) Jeff Roberson/AP Images; (Mickelson) Leo Mason/Corbis; 56, 58 (top) Al Tielemans/*Sports Illustrated*/Getty Images; 58 (bottom) Bob Martin/*Sports Illustrated*/Getty Images; 59: Montana Pritchard/PGA of America via Getty Images; 60: Ross Kinnaird/Getty Images; 62: Roberto Schmidt/AFP/Getty Images; 64: Robert Beck/*Sports Illustrated*/Getty Images; 65: Jacques Demarthon/AFP/Getty Images; 66 (Montgomerie) Laurent Rebours/AP Images; (Norman) Dear/AP Images; (Pak) Charles Baus/Icon Sports Media/Corbis; (Scott) Darren Carroll/Corbis; 67: Robert Beck/*Sports Illustrated*/Getty Images; 68: Simon Bruty/*Sports Illustrated*/Getty Images; 69: Phil Sheldon/Popperfoto/Getty Images; 70: David Cannon/Getty Images. **Tiger.** 72: Philippe Lopez/AFP/Getty Images; 75: Augusta National/Getty Images; 76: Fred Vuich/*Sports Illustrated*/Getty Images; 78: Per-Anders Pettersson/Corbis; 81: Golf Channel; 82: Lennox McLendon/AP Images; 83: Mark Perlstein/The LIFE Images Collection/Getty Images; 84: John Iacono/*Sports Illustrated*/Getty Images; 86: Timothy A. Clary/AFP/Getty Images; 89: Golf Channel; 90: Lenny Ignelzi/AP Images; 91: Alastair Grant/AP Images; 92: Amy Sancetta/AP Images; 93: Donald Miralle/Allsport/Getty Images; 94: Stephen Munday/Allsport/Getty Images; 95: Stan Badz/PGA/Getty Images; 96: Harry How/Getty Images; 98: Getty Images; 100: J.D. Cuban/Getty Images; 102: Morry Gash/AP Images; 104: Fred Vuich/*Sports Illustrated*/Getty Images; 106: Golf Channel; 107: Thomas Lovelock/*Sports Illustrated*/Getty Images. **The Course.** 108: Peter Wong; 111: Nicklaus Companies; 112: Laurence Lambrecht; 114: Laurence Lambrecht; 116: The Henebrys; 118: Tom Breazeale/Corbis; 119: Streamsong Golf Resort; 120: Aidan Bradley; 122: Gene J. Puskar/AP Images; 123: Chip Henderson; 124: Kevin Murray; 125: Hanse Golf Design; 125, 126: Laurence Lambrecht; 128: Streeter Lecka/Getty Images; 129: Kevin Murray; 130: Brian G. Oar; 132: Russell Kirk; 134: Aidan Bradley; 136: Laurence Lambrecht; 138: Chad Wadsworth; 139: SeaPines; 140: Joann Dost; 142 (Coore & Crenshaw) Coore & Crenshaw; (Doak) Renaissance; 143 (Nicklaus) Nicklaus Companies; (Dye) Dye Designs; (Fazio) Corbis; 144 (Hanse) Corbis; (Jones) AP Images; 145 (Phillips) Kyle Phillips Golf Course Design; (Kidd) DMK; (Schmidt and Curley) Schmidt-Curley. **The Pro Game (2005-2014).** 146: Doug Miles/The New York Times/Redux; 149: Robert Beck; 150: Paul Mounce/Corbis; 151 (Singh) Dave Martin/AP Images; (Sorenstam) Mark J. Terrill/AP Images; (Stewart) Mike King/Corbis; (Van de Velde) AP Images; 152: Jeff Chiu/AP Images; 154: Jerome Davis/Icon SMI/Corbis; 156: Eric Risberg/AP Images; 158: Robert Beck/*Sports Illustrated*/Getty Images; 159: Don Emmert/AFP/Getty Images; 160: Scott Halleran/Getty Images; 161: Robert Beck/*Sports Illustrated*/Getty Images; 162: David Cannon/Getty Images; 164 Isaac Brekken/AP Images; 165: Eric Gay/AP Images; 166 (top) Dave Martin/AP Images (bottom) Chris Carlson/AP Images; 167: Streeter Lecka/Getty Images; 168: Ross Kinnaird/Getty Images; 169: Nick Potts/AP Images; 170: Evan Vucci/AP/Corbis; 171: Jon Super/AP Images; 172: Gerry Melendez/The State/MCT via Getty Images; 174: Carlos M. Saavedra/*Sports Illustrated*/Getty Images. **The Changing Game.** 176: Eric Gay/AP Images; 179: Eddie Guy; 180: Courtesy GolfLogix; 182: John M. Burgess/Time Life Pictures/Getty Images; 183 (stimpometer) Darren Carroll/Corbis; (Palmer and Nicklaus) AP Images; 184 (Watson) Scott A. Miller/AP Images; (Webb) Marco Garcia/AP Images; (Wie) Nam Y. Huh/AP Images; (Woods) Matt York/AP Images; 186: Chris Gallow; 187: James Friedman; 188: Dom Furore/Golf Digest; 189: Richard Mackson/*Sports Illustrated*/Getty Images; 190: Callaway; 193: Shutterstock/Alex Staroseltsev; 194: CanStock; 196: Martyn Hayhow/AFP/Getty Images; 195: David Adame/AP Images; 199: Darren Carroll/*Sports Illustrated*/Getty Images; 201: (Jacobs) Peter Dazeley/Getty Images; (Harmon) Chris Trotman/Getty Images; (Leadbetter) AP Images; 202: Bob Leverone/AP Images; 205 (all) Stuart Franklin/Getty Images. **The Ryder Cup.** 206: Bob Martin/*Sports Illustrated*/Getty Images; 209: Peter Morrison/AP Images; 210: David Cannon/Getty Images; 212: Stephen Munday/Allsport/Getty Images; 213, 214: Elise Amendola/AP Images; 216: Fred Vuich/*Sports Illustrated*/Getty Images; 218: Mike Blake/Reuters/Corbis; 219: Adrian Dennis/AFP/Getty Images; 220: Ross Kinnaird/Getty Images; 222: Robert Beck/*Sports Illustrated*/Getty Images; 223: Stuart Franklin/Getty Images; 224: Robert Beck/*Sports Illustrated*/Getty Images. **The Next Twenty.** 226: Jed Jacobsohn/Getty Images; 229: Gareth Gay/Getty Images; 230 (Pak) AP Images/Claude Paris; (Choi) Robert Cianflone/Getty Images; 231 (Ishikawa) Stuart Franklin/Getty Images; (Guan) Don Emmert/AFP/Getty Images; 232: Mike Ehrmann/Getty Images; 233: Hanse Golf Design; 234: Brian G. Oar; 235: Kevin Murray; 236: Koji Sasahara/AP Images; 237: Robyn Beck/AFP/Getty Images

HarperCollins books may be purchased for
educational, business, or sales promotional
use. For information, please e-mail the
Special Markets Department at SPsales@
harpercollins.com.

Published in 2014 by
Harper Design
An Imprint of HarperCollins*Publishers*
195 Broadway
New York, NY 10007
(212) 207-7000
harperdesign@harpercollins.com
www.hc.com

Distributed throughout the world by
HarperCollins Publishers
195 Broadway
New York, NY 10007

First Edition

Library of Congress Cataloging-in-Publication
Data is available upon request.

ISBN 978-0-06-236456-2

15 16 17 18   10 9 8 7 6 5 4 3 2